cite two other b[c]
this same foot[i]
[S17], page 263, note #2
pages
263-266

# Frames
# of
# Remembrance

Mearsheimer - Back to the Future
Waltz - forgetting as the
current generation
dies off? - in which
reference?
role of museums in preserving Anderson?
past/present/future

# Frames of Remembrance

The Dynamics of Collective Memory

## Iwona Irwin-Zarecka

**Transaction Publishers**

New Brunswick (U.S.A.) and London (U.K.)

Library of Congress Catalog Number: 93-8802
ISBN: 978-1-4128-0683-1
Printed in the United States of America

Library of Congress Cataloging-in-Publication Data

Irwin-Zarecka, Iwona.
    Frames of rememberance : the dynamics of collective memory / Iwona Irwin-Zarecka.
        p. cm.
    Includes bibliographical references and index.
    ISBN 978-1-4128-0683-1
        1. Memory—Social aspects.    2.    History—Psychological aspects.
    I. Title.

BF378.S65178    1993
153.1'2—dc20                                                    93-8802

To Mama

# Contents

# Preface

"June 12, 1992. Another long talk into the night about Poland's current predicaments. One more government fell, this time amidst vicious rumors and accusations ignited by a new law that would make all public officials open to charges of collaborating with the Communist regime. Mom is flying back to Warsaw the day after tomorrow, fearful of what this last round of battle has done to the already ugly climate on the streets. Her stories help me to fill in the emotional detail behind the often dry words of printed debates. Just how is one to define what "collaboration" should mean in a country that after all had functioned rather normally for the forty-five years of the Communist rule?

August 12, 1992. It is cold and rainy again; this holiday has been really good for reading. Took along the two thick volumes from the Smithsonian; in both *Exhibiting Cultures* and *Museums and Communities*, I hear many echoes of my own troubled accommodation to the "last Jews of Poland" put on photographic display back in 1986. Rationally, I have to accept being a remnant of a once vibrant culture, but this does not take away the unease I feel at serving as a specimen, prepared by and for non-Jews. But then, at the time, it could be argued that for Poles actually to see that "real Jews" still lived in the country was beneficial in itself. Should my Native Canadian student be equally relieved at the sight of tribal artifacts in our university library?

Another set of echoes, these in the now daily newspaper reports about the carnage in Yugoslavia. "Cattle trains," "Dachau," "officially unconfirmed" ... Israel issues a statement, appealing to Jews worldwide to forget *who* were the victims and the perpetrators in the Balkans of the 1940s, and to remember *what* they learned about the complicity in atrocities; this breaks a long silence about the situation. Could the Serbs themselves be made to forget?

October 12, 1992. An interesting conference in Philadelphia. On Sunday, the city hosts America's largest Columbus Day parade. My seven-year-old son and his Dad readily agree to this bit of "data collection." Watchers are sparse, but the parade does take nearly four hours to move through. There are many Italian community groups, Luciano Pavarotti as a grand master, lots of music, plus historically costumed marchers. Columbus is there, of course, so are (twice) the Spanish royals, and then, the colonials. Among the different characters from the past, a lonely girl, dressed in what to me resembles a Halloween get-up, walks as an Indian. The theme being "500 years of transportation, exploration and travel," we see monocycles, old-fashioned cars and wagons, and next, a big contingent of bikers, at their familial best. The parade ends with a very long string of military vehicles, including two tanks playfully rotating together. Was not the *New York Times* proclaiming this morning that Americans are rethinking their history? My analytical self is sharply reminded of the distance from the ground ... or is it my Canadian self that looks in amazement at a celebration so totally impossible this year anywhere up North?"

As I think back, most of the ideas I have worked with when questioning societies' engagement with the past came from just such a diverse storehouse of mental notes, notes taken over a period of now close to ten years, beginning with my first forays as a graduate student into the historical gaps and silences. In the essays that comprise this book, the reader will be occasionally made proxy to the process; much of the time, though, it is only the end product that is being shared. To trace the exact itineraries of my reflecting on the dynamics of collective memory might, in any event, prove impossible. What is possible, and what I would like to do here as a way of introducing *Frames of Remembrance*, is to reconstruct the key concerns orienting this inquiry.

First, the practical ones. As I set out to write, I kept thinking about my own predicaments as a doctoral student in the early 1980s, embarking on a project that I could not well define and realizing quite late that I was indeed studying the dynamics of collective memory. I wanted this book to be of some help to others facing the challenge of working in a field that does not properly belong to any one discipline, yet one in which (now) a great deal of empirical research as well as theorizing is actually getting done. And I felt that the best way to accomplish this would be to take on a small set of analytical problems and delve into them as areas for investigation, with all the conceptual toolmaking this would imply. The essays here were thus made to function as relatively self-contained units, as diverse "entry points" defined by questions rather than the lines separating disciplines or empirical territories.

The strategy, I believe, worked. But it also produced a greater need for explaining why it should. Thus the opening chapter of the book, "Setting the Analytical Parameters," is the place to start, while all the others invite the reader to sample according to individual interests.

The impetus for writing was thus rather pragmatic; I wished for the book to offer ideas that could be worked with. And this very much reflected the central question I worked with—how can we better understand the dynamics of collective memory? The question, once examined, led in a number of directions with three broad themes soon emerging, themes that would run through all of the essays, each with different emphases.

First, there was my concern with the role experience itself plays in the subsequent construction of memories, both individual and collective. Critical of analytical strategies that treat discourse about the past as totally disconnected from that past, I was aiming to inject it back. Second, I was interested in shifting the attention away from purely textual "readings" of the contents of collective memory, interested in questions about cultural sensibilities and norms that inform both the structure and the texture of remembrance. Here, the goal was to move beyond the predominantly political interpretations of the uses of the past. The third theme, or agenda, was the integration of heuristically separate domains, all the while accounting for their differences. A better understanding of the dynamics of collective memory could only emerge, I was consistently to argue, once we develop customized tools for studying museums alongside Disney's theme parks, history books alongside novels, television movies alongside monuments. At issue here is also the formulation of critical standards that would take into account the diversity of our engagements with the past, intellectually, emotionally, morally.

Just how difficult this last task may be is the focus of chapter 2, "Ultimate Challenge." I have placed it next to the broad outline of the inquiry to serve as a modesty-producing reminder of our limitations. For readers who prefer a more optimistic stance while on the analytical job, this chapter may best be encountered as the conclusion.

While inviting individualized sequencing of the book, I have grouped the remaining essays into two "problem clusters." Part II consists of reflections on how the past comes to be relevant to people, in smaller as well as larger communities. The discussion here centers around the roles that a past can play, is made to play, does play.

In Part III, the emphasis shifts to a closer look at how this is actually done. Now, the focus is on memory work itself, on the practices and the practitioners. It is here that questions are raised about the construction of meaning at its most basic. Included in Part III is an essay on "Absences" that deserves a separate mention. As much as it addresses the work that produces social forgetting, it belongs with those dealing with the more tangible accomplishments. But it is also closely paralleling themes in Part I, problematizing the analytical strategy itself.

At the end of the book, the reader will find a select, critically annotated bibliography—this too reflects my overall objective of proffering useful research tools. As the range of works listed suggests perhaps better than any argument, the study of the dynamics of collective memory is rapidly gaining momentum. I hope that these reflections contribute further to its becoming an analytical field of its own.

# Acknowledgments

I have been very fortunate when writing this book. The support and encouragement I received made all the difference. For this has been a special challenge, to reflect on the dynamics of collective memory when the topic, rather suddenly, moves into the spotlight. Not only have the world events supplied more than ample material here, academic studies poured out as well. Gratifying developments, both, yet intellectually daunting nevertheless. That I was able to stay on course, I owe to many.

First, I would like to thank Irving Louis Horowitz for having confidence in this project from its inception, and Mary Curtis for her always helpful advice. One cannot ask for more supportive publishers.

I am also very grateful to my home institution, Wilfrid Laurier University, for both the financial assistance with research and writing as well as the less tangible, but no less important, rewarding of my endeavors. The editorial work by Kathryn Wardropper and the invaluable technical help from Dorothy Lim made preparing this manuscript a great deal easier.

Some mentors are simply happy to see their charges graduate; mine are different. For comments and suggestions on several parts of the draft, I thank Bennett M. Berger, Ioan Davies, Kurt Jonassohn, and Michael Schudson. For my frequent stubbornness, I apologize.

Recent conferences on social theory, politics and the arts served as especially hospitable forums for trying out my ideas; I would like to thank Judith Balfe, Jeffrey Shandler, and Suzanne Vromen in particular for their input. As the most valuable of follow-ups, I very much appreciated Vera L. Zolberg's close readings of many of the chapters.

When nearing completion, the text underwent a critique from somewhat more unusual quarters; I thank Paul Viminitz, an analytic philosopher, for his insightful comments.

In the course of writing, I also received helpful comments on specific chapters from Alan L. Berger, Terry Copp, Modris Eksteins, Ron Grimes, H. David Kirk, Bruce Lincoln, Richard D. Madsen, and Robert Payne. Here, I need to extend a special thanks to Alice L. Eckardt, not only for her detailed reading of "Ultimate Challenge" but also for the many years of encouragement.

It is with deep sadness that I extend another special thanks to a friend; Maria Elster, who died last year, a Holocaust survivor and a historian, had been a source of both inspiration and much practical assistance since we met in Paris in 1983. I miss her.

Finally, a note of appreciation to my family. Without the emotional sustenance from my husband, Hugh Smyth, and our son Joshua, this book simply could not have been written. I owe the most, though, to my mother, Jadwiga Irwin-Zarecka, who lives in Warsaw. For over ten years now, she has worked hard to make my work possible, searching for books, clipping out articles, and generally acting as an excellent research assistant would. Deserving recognition for my first book, she had to forgo it; it was better that way. Now that the Communist regime is gone, I can finally repair the situation. This book is dedicated to her.

# PART I
# The Inquiry

# 1

# Setting the Analytical Parameters

Why be interested in studying the dynamics of collective memory? And, moreover, why insist that the subject matter define the terms of its analysis, to the effect of virtually erasing interdisciplinary boundaries?

Let me begin with the second question; it is the easier one. For a person of my generation—I was born in Poland in 1955—the world in which we were growing up would have been quite incomprehensible without reference to World War II and its aftermath. I could not directly remember the war, of course. I learned about it in school, listened to stories told by my parents and their friends, read books, watched movies and, later, television programs, recited poems at various commemorative occasions. Most of all, perhaps, as I walked through the streets of Warsaw, a city rebuilt on the ruins, I would be surrounded by reminders of the war—buildings with bullet holes still there, memorial plaques, the very newness of the "Old Town." At first, as a child, I tended to see that past in terms of high drama and adventure; even my Jewish father's accounts of the fate of the family fitted the pattern—he and his sister both survived by "passing" on the Aryan side. Later, the picture acquired a far more sombre tone, and, as I was trying to understand my Jewish heritage, I would rapidly become aware of the pieces that had been missing, missing in my city, my books, and the lessons at school. Making sense of the past became a struggle, not to be resolved until much later when I embarked on an academic study of Polish-Jewish relations. By that time, I lived in North America and my quest was very much a private endeavor. Had I so chosen, I could have separated myself completely from memory of the war. On the other hand, although there were no bullet holes in buildings around me, the libraries were of help. I gathered the missing pieces.

3

My relationship with "collective memory" may be an especially close one, partly of necessity, partly by choice. But it is not unique, in that we all make sense of the past with the help of a whole variety of resources, that this making sense is motivated by our personal experience but facilitated (or impeded) by public offerings, and that such public offerings are a mixture of presences and absences. A "collective memory"—as a set of ideas, images, feelings about the past—is best located not in the minds of individuals, but in the resources they share.[1] There is no reason to privilege one form of resource over another—for example, to see history books as important but popular movies as not. For some people, in a given place, at a specific time—the East Germans in 1992—it is the raw contents of the Stasi archives that inform, wound, stir debate. For others, elsewhere—the American voters in the same year—the echoes of Vietnam may still resound in political speeches and commentary. And it is through an empirical investigation, rather than theoretical fiat, that we assess which resources matter to whom.[2]

It is also empirically that we need to establish the relationships between publicly articulated and privately held views of the past; an abundance of resources does not guarantee that people actually use them, nor is persuasiveness of an account a predetermined constant. As we look at a collective memory, at what it offers and at how its offerings change, we ought to remain modest in our claims. Individuals are perfectly capable of ignoring even the best told stories, of injecting their own, subversive meanings into even the most rhetorically accomplished "texts"—and of attending to only those ways of making sense of the past that fit their own.

Allowing for highly idiosyncratic reactions to what is publicly available does not mean that we abandon cultural analysis altogether. It means that the analytical tools we use need to be capable of illuminating, if not accounting for, the dialectic between public and private. The notion of "framing" serves this purpose, I believe, very well. Generously borrowed from Erving Goffman's approach to social situations as well as "texts,"[3] questions about framing direct our attention to the powers inherent in public articulation of collective memory to influence the private makings of sense. Questions about framing are essentially about limits to the scope of possible interpretations. Their aim is not to freeze one particular "reading" as *the* correct one, rather, it is to establish the likely range of meanings. Following Goffman, I too treat our interpretive practices as patterned by the ways we define the situation at hand. And how we define the situation at hand is largely, but not totally, dependent on socially shared framing strategies and devices.

Framing can be an explicit procedure; to be on the safe side with strangers, we often introduce a potentially problematic story with the "it's a good joke" tag, for example. More often than not, though, framing devices are more subtle, relying on our common sense of the world for effectiveness. Newspaper editorials do not ordinarily restate the principle that they are expressions of opinion, their special positioning within the newspaper does that, on the assumption of the readers' tacit knowledge. Framing cues can also be mixed and confusing. In a classroom situation, when a male student comments on a female professor's "nice new haircut," it is not clear what is going on. In Oliver Stone's film *JFK*, the seamless combination of documentary footage with fictional accounts works against the concluding description of the movie as a "*search* for truth."

But what exactly do framing devices do? Rather than approach the question in general terms, let us now focus on the realm of collective memory. Frames that can be found here are put to a great variety of uses; indeed, it is that elasticity of the concept that accounts for most of its heuristic value.

First, there are frames that define the status of a particular "text," the kind of reading it is to receive. History books presenting themselves as "true accounts" to be incorporated into "basic knowledge" differ from a television docudrama aiming to entertain and only secondarily to teach. Considering the tremendous variety of symbolic means securing some presence of the past, it is not surprising that the framing devices operating at this level are also tremendously variable. Most, though, establish a particular claim to historical truth together with a particular claim on our attention. In some cases—commemoration ceremonies, for example— we are being asked actively to remember. In other cases—a magazine article about Columbus—we may be asked to reflect and to inform ourselves. And if there are certain patterns to be observed here, related to the differences among cultural forms themselves, there is also room for surprises and contradictions. The already mentioned *JFK*, for example, represents an unabashedly didactic exercise, rarely to be encountered in commercial cinema. The Vietnam War Memorial in New York, covered with writings but made up mostly of glass, does not allow for much contemplative reading.[4] Thus when inquiring into how different "texts" work, we may be equipped with several general rules but still need to attend to their individual qualities.

We also must attend to the qualities of the authorial voice itself. While many of the frames here *are* genre-related, how a "text" functions can rarely be separated from *who* produced it. Within a specific genre, such as history books, the authority granted to individual authors varies; differences in scholarly reputation, political perspective, sponsorship and also the personal connection to the events being described may all come into play.

The two commercial films, both made by Oliver Stone—*JFK* and *Born on the Fourth of July*—and both making strong claims to historical truth, are actually very different. Stone served in Vietnam and he was an observer, albeit a concerned one, of the Kennedy assassination aftermath. A conservative in France may trust a story in *Le Figaro*, but not in the Communist *L'Humanité*. The factors responsible for these differences in authority are context-specific; what matters to Canadians is not the same as what matters to Cambodians. Once again, if there are some general rules likely to apply—such as the importance of being a witness—there is also the need for case-by-case specificity.

This principle—that while one can posit certain patterns of how framing of the past operates, we must resort to empirical, context-sensitive inquiries for a fuller understanding of the dynamics of collective memory—informs this book as a whole. The analytical tools developed here are exactly that, tools. They are to be used, and some have already been used by others, and myself, to illuminate the subject at hand. When it is possible to formulate a general proposition, such is always meant to be tested against case studies, those now available and those still to be done. In other words, what is being offered is a heuristic approach, a "way of seeing" but especially a way of asking questions.

The preceding paragraph is in itself an example of framing, of course. I am calling on you to read my book in a particular way, although I know that some of you will not. I am also, rather deliberately, making my case through the use of examples instead of theoretically sophisticated rationales. This too is a framing device, in that it helps define the "ideal reader" as someone who may come from any number of disciplinary backgrounds or indeed be a novice in the field. Finally, my use of language, favoring common usage terms even when proposing new concepts, also contributes to framing this work as a tool-kit open to many. My own intentions notwithstanding, how this book is read—if at all—very much depends on the subsequent "editorial" input from other people. Critics, reviewers, teachers, the reader's colleagues or friends, all may have a say in the matter. And this too is an example of how framing works. The process is not static, nor to be located solely with the "text" and its "reader." A whole chain of intermediaries could be involved, opening for multiple possibilities of reinterpretation. Collective memory is a terrain especially prone to such overlaying of different frames, I would argue, because it is filled with reused and reusable material. What is one day an heirloom stored in your attic can tomorrow become a precious part of a museum exhibit. American textbooks describing the history of the "evil empire" are already becoming testimony to their age. And the novels written by minority writers increasingly gain status as part of mainstream heritage.

Some of these shifts in meaning are a result of deliberate effort and much public discussion, others may be occurring more naturally within complex social and cultural changes. Whatever the source, the appearance of new frames is an opportune moment for the analyst, as it allows one better to expose the *dynamics* of collective memory. At issue here, however, is a great deal more than our continuous "rewriting of history." Just as any given "text" implicates certain claims to truth together with demands on our attention, public discourse about the past when seen as a whole does more than telling us what happened. Framing devices employed at this meta-level, as it were, provide the structure to *both* the contents of the past and the forms of remembrance. The debates about the meaning of 1492, for example, introduced both the conflicting versions of historical facts and figures as well as serious questions about the propriety of commemoration itself. The fiftieth anniversary of the attack on Pearl Harbor was an occasion to retell different stories, but also to ponder the virtues of forgetting.

To understand how collective memory works, we cannot restrict our inquiries to tracing the vicissitudes of historical knowledge or narratives. We must also, and I believe foremost, attend to the construction of our emotional and moral engagement with the past. When looking at public discourse, this translates into questions about how the past is made to matter.[5] Framing events, heroes, places as worthy of remembrance and honor is quite different from defining whole historical chapters as a burden to be mastered. Marketing European castles as a tourist attraction is not the same as making it compulsory for schoolchildren to visit a local museum. Speaking of the need to understand the legacy of the Communist system in the name of success for economic and political reform may be a lot more appealing and effective than evoking the moral principles of punishing those responsible for its crimes.

Here, once again, some of the framing devices may be visible to all while others require patient unearthing. Advocates of constructing the Holocaust Memorial Museum in Washington, D.C. were explicit[6] about Americans' obligation to this chapter of—now defined as universal—history; a few years earlier, producers of the television drama *Holocaust* implied something similar. But when looking at the fate of the same memory during the preceding decade, we would need a whole combination of clues, from those found in textbooks to the responses to Holocaust literature, in order to reconstruct the dominant frame that had then assigned that remembrance to the Jews.

Considering the now high level of analysis, it is not surprising that questions about framing become more complex. To trace how—and which—past is made to matter, we also need to ask: by whom, to whom, when, where, and why. If we stay close to the empirical ground, as I do here, we immediately recognize that rarely are these issues settled within public discourse, on however limited a scale. Even within the relatively small community of Vietnam veterans, for example, we would find great dissonance in publicly voiced views about their experience and its "proper place" in Americans' memory; all this before we would begin to inquire about their private accounts and actions. Disagreements, however, often make our analysis manageable. The otherwise dormant framing strategies then become articulated and open to our inspection. Collective memory becomes activated, as it were, allowing for more direct access to its construction. This also happens when people engage in what I call "memory projects"—concerted efforts to secure presence for certain elements of the past, efforts often coupled with self-justifying rationales.

Disputes, discussions, introduction of altogether new frames—these are all heuristically invaluable opportunities for students of the dynamics of collective memory. They also remind us, and in North America such reminders may indeed be quite necessary, that our subject matter matters. Different people, at different times, care about their past in different ways. Some kill because of memory obligations. Some demand political change. And some are content to look to the future, even if entertained by stories of past adventures.

How—and how much—people care is, as we observed before, strongly influenced by idiosyncratic factors. But equally strongly, it is informed by the socially shared "frames of remembrance." If the roles assigned to the past are by no means constant, even within a given community, there are at least two reasons why collective memory is a factor in human affairs we must reckon with. First, collective memory is intricately related, though in variable ways, to the sense of collective identity individuals come to acquire. And second, it is imbued with moral imperatives—the obligations to one's kin, notions of justice, indeed, the lessons of right and wrong—that form the basic parts of the normative order. On both counts, collective memory is then a significant orienting force, or, something we need to understand better in order to account for why people do what they do.

It may well be that seeing collective memory in this light is the result of my being European; I know that when first introduced to the subject, my students in southwestern Ontario look interested but also puzzled. And yet, if they start out with the notion that the past is at best a pleasant diversion, after a little coaching they too have no trouble recognizing how much their family bonds rely on shared reminiscing—or how inadequate their knowledge of Canadian history is for dealing with the country's constitutional (and identity) crisis. They also become quick to point out how their high school training had not prepared them to understand current world events, with the bloody conflict between Serbs and Croats being perhaps the most baffling. Here, it is not simply that they lack the background information, but more importantly, they have few means of empathizing with the peoples for whom the past so clearly matters. The issue is not academic, either. There are many Serbs and Croats living in our area and while not yet violent, mutual hostility has been high.

Students in Ontario are only required to take one Grade 9 Canadian history course to graduate, I should add. And I suspect that even with a more structured curriculum, they would still be ill prepared to understand the feelings of their Croatian friend. If the interest in collective memory has increased dramatically in recent years, we are still very far from mainstream status as explainers of social dynamics. This book is written with the hope that some day in the future, after a great deal more work is done, an appreciation of the dynamics of collective memory might indeed belong in the classroom.

Such an appreciation can only come about through a combined effort of scholars from a variety of disciplines; indeed, as the listings of our annotated bibliography suggest, both the interest and the research can already be found in many analytical corners. My own perspective, being that of a cultural sociologist, is not exclusionary; it might, in effect, predispose me to be academically democratic, as it were, to welcome insights and inquiries from history and media criticism, anthropology and political science, psychology and literary studies. To render justice to the phenomenon itself, to the varied manifestations of collective memory and remembrance, we must, I believe, rely on varied interpretive strategies. At the same time, though, we do need to establish more linkages between them, more of an analytically shared vocabulary. Present reflections are a step in this direction.

Two facets of academic life impede much of this needed bridge building. There is the common affliction of rigid disciplinary boundaries, strongly affecting our graduate training in particular. If some of the barriers have come down, many more are still there, preventing an effective use of each other's knowledge. More serious, though, for it is more difficult to overcome, is the natural division of labor along temporal and cultural lines. Someone who is interested in contemporary America may readily step out of the sociology department to talk to colleagues in film studies; chances are, however, that a colloquium on Nazi Germany, further down the hall, would be passed unnoticed, as would a talk by a visiting Lithuanian scholar. Ordinarily, this is not a problem. But for a student of the uses of the past, it may represent a serious loss of analytical opportunities for testing one's questions on another empirical terrain.

Working towards a better understanding of the dynamics of collective memory means that we cannot afford such lost opportunities. This book was conceived, in part, as a "meeting place" allowing for an exchange of ideas, concerns, and findings. The annotated bibliography is of necessity selective and aims at presenting just how wide the range of the potential participants here is. As a host to this gathering, I wanted for the occasion to be interesting enough to attend, thus the analytical offerings. Ideally, the reader would come to take part in this exchange by thinking through the issues raised with the help of materials on his or her shelves.

Admittedly not a perfect strategy for academic communication, this is as close as we can approximate a dialogue.

As the host, I have both the responsibility and the opportunity to facilitate the flow of conversation, to provide the opening lines. Understandably, I feel more comfortable with topics I know something about. Thus the reader is advised to expect illustrations and examples originating in the areas of my own research, or more broadly, my interest. These do cover a large territory, still, it is highly unlikely I would be connecting to all the equally idiosyncratic points of interest among the readers. This is why the book calls on your input for our "meeting" to succeed.

A note of caution is in order. As those readers with the useful habit of scanning references and the index first would have undoubtedly noticed, I devote considerable space and attention to issues concerning memory of the Holocaust. In part, this is simply a reflection of my particular research itinerary; to make sense of contemporary Polish-Jewish relations, I had to make sense of both what had happened to the Jews and its subsequent tellings. To do this properly, in turn, demanded a comparative perspective. Indeed, that challenge of making sense—of the past, of its memory—was what prompted my venturing into the larger terrain of the cultural analysis of "frames of remembrance." And many of the questions, concerns, ideas reflected here originate in that work. I fully recognize, though, that what to me is a logical extension of prior analytical efforts can appear to others as a jarring presence, a forced confrontation with material they would rather avoid. Deciding not to tone down my voice, as it were, might prove problematic for these readers. I am convinced, though, that the intellectual returns of this strategy far outweigh the emotional risks. There is a great deal to be learned, for any student of the dynamics of collective memory, from the extensive research on ways of remembering (and forgetting) the Holocaust. As an area of scholarship, it is one where interdisciplinary lines have long been crossed, thus providing a valuable model for the type of analysis advocated here. Most importantly, perhaps, delving into the problematics of Holocaust memory forces us to ask some rather disquieting questions about our own critical efforts. The continuous search for the "right" ways to remember, with all the voices of doubt and dissent that accompany it, is not only a testimony to the unique challenges the Holocaust poses but it is also a powerful corrective on our valued certainties, all those tacit principles we ordinarily apply when critically assessing others' memory work. It is a reminder that as we study what people do, both they and we would be involved in establishing standards for what "ought to be done." And even if ours are more sophisticated, perhaps, theirs are equally important to consider. At the same time, since the evaluative criteria *we* use have a tremendous impact on the analytical process, we should at least make an effort at self-reflection.

What is the value we place on "telling the truth" and why? What do we see as legitimate and illegitimate uses of the past? When do we become angry at trespassing the lines of good taste? How do we decide that something/someone ought to be remembered?

Bringing such questions into clear focus serves a dual purpose, even if we cannot come up with clear answers. It makes for a more intellectually and morally honest inquiry. And it sensitizes us to the importance of these issues in the social practices of framing remembrance.

Just yesterday (January 20, 1992), the Berlin Regional Court convicted two former East German border guards of killing a man they saw fleeing to the West; in rendering the verdict, the judge invoked the injustice of the Nazi system to show how some laws should never be obeyed. The case sparked wide debate and understandably so. It is not at all clear that punishing those (and so far only those) at the end point in a whole chain of command is morally right. And it is also problematic, clearly good intentions notwithstanding, for a German judge to equate Communism with Nazism. Since it is precedent setting, the verdict would likely be appealed, thus also allowing us to gain further insight into the negotiating of rules remembrance is to obey.

In this case, and in many others of this nature,[7] our position as analytical observers cannot be separated from our ethical stance. Nor should it be. To pretend moral neutrality on morally troubling issues would be exactly that, pretence. At the same time, as we work to *understand* the dynamics of collective memory, we need to tune in to all the different voices, those we agree with as well as those we find reprehensible. And sometimes, we may have to say that we too do not know the "right" answers. Our task, in any case, is not to provide them. Rather, it is to trace the social practices that give particular frames of remembrance shape and stability, those used in repair work and those with demolition potential.

The imagery of "industrial production" applied here is not accidental. Heuristically, it is helpful to think of collective memory in very concrete

terms indeed. First, to secure a presence for the past demands work—
"memory work"—whether it is writing a book, filming a documentary
or erecting a monument. Produced, in effect, is what I call here the
"infrastructure" of collective memory, all the different spaces, objects,
"texts" that make an engagement with the past possible.[8] The tasks are
as varied as the forms such an infrastructure can take; as mentioned
before, several people could be involved, each doing different things,
before the "final product" emerges. At times, efforts on many smaller
construction jobs combine, in their desired effect, into a "memory
project"; the work of feminists for the inclusion of women in our sense
of history would be a good example here. At times, the work is done not
to build but to destroy; the bringing down of monuments to Communist
heroes in many parts of the collapsed Soviet empire comes to mind.

To recognize the concreteness of memory work is also to be usefully
reminded of its mundane, yet analytically important qualities. That work
takes time, energy, and money, and resources are often in short supply
and carefully allocated. The very process of production is thus frequently
a site for articulating priorities, obligations, goals, and intended audiences. As such, it is a valuable source of data for students of framing
remembrance; looking at the construction of the Vietnam War Memorial,
with all the subsequent modifications, is but one example of just how
rich this material can be. Even when not much public discussion takes
place, the very presence of community involvement—or government
sponsorship or commercial interests—provides us with valuable clues as
to what is going on.[9] Who deems the past important and why cannot
always be completely derived from such clues, but it is a good start. In
other words, people's actions, as well as their declarations, matter. When
the municipal authorities in Berlin decided (in 1991) yet again to
postpone the building of a Jewish museum due to budget considerations,
they were indeed making a statement.

If observing what memory work gets done offers us suggestive
material on the vicissitudes of remembrance, it becomes indispensable
when trying to assess the degree of social forgetting. A community
can—and often would—preserve memories of its past primarily through
private tellings; it is rare, though, not to encounter some physical markers
aiding the process. When even the minimal signs of memory work are
missing, when graves are left invisible and unattended, for example, or
stories remain untold, these are strong indications indeed of a past

confined to oblivion. And they are analytically irreplaceable, because we cannot simply ask people what they have been forgetting.

Investigating the dynamics of collective memory by focusing on the work that gets done (or not) is only a step, though an important one, towards better understanding of the subject. The production of symbolic resources makes certain forms of engagement with the past possible, sometimes even necessary, but it does not predetermine the uses to which such resources would be put. And indeed, if we were to take a snapshot of a particular collective memory, we would find a great deal of traces of the past that are dormant, as it were, left unattended. Books or buildings, exhibits or movies, these may all just be there, with only a few individuals giving them a thought. Just as in our private lives, cherished mementoes of the trips we took need not engage our attention—but we keep them around for comfort—the day-to-day social practices need not involve drawing from the storehouse of collective memory. When they do, when our sense of the past becomes "activated," memory becomes remembrance. At those times we do pay attention; whether through a commemorative gesture, a heated discussion or simply a moment of reflection, we are engaged with the past. Assuming such an active stance may translate into creative memory work, resulting in new ways of making sense. But it does not have to; we may be equally content with using the material already at hand. Most likely, we would encounter mixtures of the two modes; a yearly celebration of Passover, for example, with its core story of the Jews' exodus from Egypt, might include varied references to contemporary struggles for freedom, calling for new forms of ritual observance.

Working towards a better understanding of the *dynamics* of collective memory does mean that the attention here is directed primarily towards the more active aspects of our engagement with the past. Inquiring into what people say, do or make, whether when producing new resources or using/adapting the old ones is analytically rather different from the content-oriented studies of "texts." One is still required to interpret a given set of materials, be it schoolbooks or a television series. But this is now only a component in a larger heuristic task, where "texts" are never separated from social practices surrounding them. Textual analysis becomes a valuable companion to other context-specific interpretive strategies.[10]

Situating "texts" in their cultural and sociopolitical contexts is always a challenge; deciding which information counts and which does not is part and parcel of the inquiry itself, unless one adopts a theoretically derived single vision approach, that is. My own preference, lying with the empirically grounded, inductive strategies, does mean that before a final account takes shape, there is a certain "messy" complexity to sort through. Part of that complexity—and a challenge unique to students of collective memory—is "the past" itself. What we are investigating, after all, are the different ways of constructing a "reality of the past," be it by participants, artists, or scholars.[11] In the process, we often become acutely aware of just how tentative is the status of particular "historical truths." At the very least, we would be confronted with differences of interpretation of given events. It is not rare, though, to encounter disagreements about the most basic facts and figures. Yet as sensitive as we become to biases, distortions, gaps, and contradictions in the presentations of "the past," our very ability to detect them rests on *us* constructing a baseline historical reality, as it were. And just as much as we ought to reflect on our ethical principles, our convictions about what it is that actually happened also demand some self-scrutiny.

At times, deciding on a base line does not pose any great problems; when we trust particular historians and their professional expertise, we might still study their rhetorical strategies but remain confident in their findings. At other times, and this was very much my experience, it takes considerable effort to develop and justify trust in some accounts versus others; with writings on Polish-Jewish history filled with doubt-engendering statements, unwarranted generalizations and mutual invectives, I had to rely on an all-out critical and comparative reading to come up with the most rudimentary reality. Most of the time, I think, a student of collective memory operates in the multishaded grey zone between those two extremes. And however much we trust (or distrust) the historians, we cannot do without their help. Indeed, our own efforts are not unlike theirs, which ought to limit any self-righteous indictments on our part. In other words, as we proceed to question how the different "historical truths" are being established, we must recognize we too are doing it.

How people make sense of the past—intellectually, emotionally, morally—is not reducible, though, to the "truth" of their accounts. The stories of soldiers' camaraderie, emerging from the trenches of Verdun or the jungle of Vietnam are not "false"; rather, they testify to the human ability to find inspiration in the midst of the harshest of realities. Our knowledge of what happened, and especially the empathetic understanding of the actors' experience, is now indispensable for making sense of how such memories are constructed. It is not that we can simply deduce, from the "raw" reality at hand, the forms of future remembrance. We cannot. But appreciating that not all pasts are created equal, that traumas, for example, pose demands quite unlike the appeal of victories, gives us the essential tools for critical assessment of memory work.

Arriving at an historical base line thus serves two purposes. It allows us to evaluate different tellings about the past, most notably, to see what has been included—and excluded—within the various "texts." And, when dealing with the construction of memories still grounded in lived experience, it greatly enriches our ability to interpret the work being done.

Yet whether we study the efforts to secure a presence for the immediate past, or debates about Columbus and his legacy, we cannot do without another kind of historical base line—the context of memory work itself. Once again, deciding which among the social, political, cultural, or psychological factors of potential relevance should be given priority is no easy task. Whenever possible, comparative analysis is now of great value. When I studied memories of the Holocaust, for example, it was only after considerable research on France, North America, and both Germanies that I could make distinctions between the effects of psychological trauma, moral indifference, and political motivation on the texture of Holocaust remembrance I found in Poland.[12]

Factoring in of the mundane demands of time and money complicates the picture even further. That in Japan, commemorating the tragedy of Hiroshima has very much overshadowed remembering Nagasaki is at least partly a result of the early morning ceremonies in Hiroshima fitting conveniently within the live news broadcasts in a way that those later, in Nagasaki, do not.[13] While this might be a rather extreme example of the power of the media, there is no question that students of the dynamics of collective memory in the age of television face different issues than those analyzing earlier times. As a medium, television may indeed be a supreme recording device, yet in its varied actual uses, it can just as easily promote forgetting—when it chases after the next "big story," or inundates us with images of little personal relevance. And, once again, context specificity is a must. What may be crucial in a commercial television-saturated environment of North America is of secondary importance in a country such as France, where public discourse still privileges print.[14]

In trying to account for the memory work being done, we often privilege circumstances of the moment. Especially when the "reality of the past" under construction is of events far distant in time—or when dealing with mythic inventions—we would justifiably focus on the immediate context of the present efforts. Deep immersion in the experience of Columbus and his fellow explorers—or empathy with the aboriginal populations of the Americas—is not going to help us much in disentangling the lines of the current debates. But if there are indeed sectors of our analytical territory that require only scant knowledge of the past itself, these are exceptions, not the rule. For the most part, understanding the dynamics of collective memory demands from us keeping both the past and the work done on it in the foreground. Striking the proper balance between the two "data bases" is not an easy task. Indeed, it may be the most difficult aspect of the efforts to contextualize specific "texts."

The challenge is to recognize that as much as "realities of the past" are indeed socially constructed, the process is not a discursive free-for-all.[15] We have by now become so familiar with accounts of how history can be rewritten, manipulated for political ends, forgotten, or embellished, that we may be at risk of losing from view the experiential bases on which collective memory rests. In the most direct terms, as people first articulate and share the sense they make of *their* past, it is their experience, in all its emotional complexity, that serves as the key reference point. If their interpretive strategies are indeed products of culture, the plausibility of resulting accounts depends on the fit with the individuals' emotional reality. Someone who suffered great physical pain is not likely to define what happened as a pleasant diversion. A soldier who killed civilians may accept that it was all part of his duties, or adopt the more morally challenging position that it should have been up to him to decide; that soldier, though, could not as easily be convinced that nothing happened at all, even as he tries to forget. The sense that others are making of one's experience, in short, can only fall within a certain range.

In the less direct terms, when the past we attend to is not ours, the experiential base principle translates into the common sense idea that "memory" has a referent, a reality it connects us to. In ordinary usage, which as students of social life we are well advised to appreciate, all the terms connected to remembering follow this intuitive rule. Collective memory, by virtue of it representing mostly the pasts we have no experiential access to, cannot be subject to the same reality checks as discussed above. But it is subject to similar expectations, indeed, it draws its plausibility claims from the commonly perceived connection to lived human experience. Even, or perhaps especially, stories with no base in reality would frequently present themselves as accounts of actual events.[16]

This close connection to experience, whether real or imaginary, bounds collective memory in a number of ways. Certain stories are judged as plausible, others as not. And certain ways of remembering (and forgetting) are seen as appropriate and others as not. A narrative of victimization can serve to bolster group identity or to support political claims, it cannot be the basis for joyous celebration. Yes, we do use the past to various ends, and yes, we often liberally mix facts and fiction, if not inventing altogether. But no, collective memory is not a terrain where anything goes.[17] And indeed, part of our analytical task is to uncover the rules, the normative orders of remembrance.

These too are socially constructed; attitudes to death and rituals of mourning, for example, vary across time and cultures. But they are not arbitrary, in the sense of not bearing any relationship to the perceived qualities of the experience to be remembered. As I discovered when studying Poland's treatment of the Holocaust, it is possible for a people to define a trauma away; it certainly was possible to hear some Poles commenting on the destruction of the Jews as a job well done. And once this definition was in place, it would take hard work indeed to create an obligation to grieve. When a loss is not recognized as a loss, grieving is not natural. That the death of three million Polish Jews had not been a traumatic event for the majority of Poles could not be explained, how-ever, by the powers of persuasion of the postwar rhetoric. Rather, it had its sources in the long history of seeing the Jew as outside of the Polish family of moral obligation, and the acute traumatization the Poles them-selves suffered during the Second World War. The vicissitudes of their collective memory could not be detached from those of their subjective experience.

The stress here should be on the term "subjective," for however certain we may be, based on historical knowledge, that something actually happened, it is the definition shared by people we study which matters. In my case, there was a rather radical difference between the observer's and the participants' realities. It need not be so, of course. But whether the past as we understand it and the past as understood by our subjects are closer or further apart, we ought to consider both in our analysis. Our base line is a needed standard for critical judgment, their base line is what informs remembrance.

How such a subjective version of history comes to be is an important empirical question. As I have suggested here, individual memories of directly lived experience matter a great deal. But beyond this realm of immediate reality, as it were, lies a much larger territory of *mediated* past, the territory we have in focus when looking at the collective memory. And if we can posit that what people find there helps them to form their own views, to establish emotional and moral links with the past, the "how?" is very much open to further investigation. We know, for example, that the "official" version of history carries different weight in different political systems—and for different groups within a society; those who identify with it are likely to be people with power. What about the marginal groups, though? Theoretical arguments abound here;[18] I believe it is best, once again, to stay close to the empirical ground. It is entirely possible that when more research returns are in, we would be able to refine many a general rule, to allow for the "it depends." And the same holds for virtually all of the specific areas we study—the role of particular history textbooks, monuments, architectural landmarks, movies, family tales, museums, parades, or magazine articles needs to be established, not assumed.

The context-sensitive approach advocated here does not readily translate into theoretical labels. The best approximation may be the image of an intellectual "*bricoleur*," someone ready to try out various tools and strategies borrowed from many academic quarters in order to piece together a complex puzzle. The resulting picture has to make sense, but it could easily contradict established disciplinary certainties. And throughout, one remains sceptical of universal claims and explanations, reflective towards one's own tacit assumptions, open to empirical surprises.

The work of a *bricoleur* is not easy to describe; the few procedural suggestions outlined here spell out only the basic directions for context-specificity, the detail is by definition dependent on the research area itself. The thrust of the work is unabashedly antireductionist. Using insights of psychoanalysis, to take but one example, is acceptable as long as other ideas are also invited to play a part in the interpretive process.

In and of itself, the empirical orientation of our *bricoleur's* inquiries does not set limits on topics to be considered. In actual research practice, though, it tends to privilege subjects of greater social relevance over those with purely theoretical interest. Considering how the future of what once was the Soviet empire may very well depend on the rules established there for dealing with the Communist past, the fact that the whole region becomes a "laboratory" for students of collective memory is an added bonus, not the reason to get on with the work.

The following essays aim to accommodate this—in my view laudable—preoccupation with matters of social significance. Broadly speaking, concerns with identity formation, legitimacy, and moral order are what frequently bring scholars to the field in the first place. At the same time, though, I think it is important, at this, still early stage of our analytical endeavors also to look into other, less "lofty" areas where theoretical gains may be equally high. The diversity of means we use to construct "realities of the past" alone necessitates a warm welcome to students of various ways of telling, whatever their particular subject. And our understanding of the roles played by collective memory can only be enriched by inquiries that illuminate the obscure, the unnoticed, the seemingly trivial. Staying close to the empirical grounds, in contemporary North America, for example, may demand that just as much attention be paid to Disney's theme parks as to disputes about Columbus.

To put it in somewhat different terms, the study of the dynamics of collective memory can be approached as both a "pure" and an "applied science." My own predispositions notwithstanding, the development of sound analytical strategies in this area depends on insights generated on many empirical and theoretical grounds, on inquiries informed by social, ethical, as well as sociological concerns. The questions addressed in this book reflect such heterogeneity of the analysis itself, ranging from the rather formal investigation of the "division of labor" on memory construction jobs to the very pragmatic demand for a better grasp of the potential for violence inherent in memory conflicts. Reflecting on the challenges of remembering the Holocaust is in turn a means to question our questions—and certainties. It is a reminder that as students of collective memory, we, together with ordinary people, are now facing the limits to our long taken-for-granted ability to know how to remember. To render problematic what may otherwise be taken for granted, by both our subjects and ourselves, could indeed be said to define this book as a whole. The readers are welcome, no, encouraged, to disagree with me. All that I ask for is that they join me in reflection, open to the ideas that confirm as well as unsettle theirs.

## Notes

1. Pioneered in France (for the classic formulation, see Maurice Halbwachs, *La mémoire collective* [Paris: Presses Universitaires de France, 1968]), this approach has only recently gained ground among the English-speaking scholars. *Collective Remembering*, ed. David Middleton and Derek Edwards (London: Sage, 1990) is a good example of the still strong legacies of psychological views. *Memory and Counter-Memory*, ed. Natalie Zemon Davis and Randolph Starn, special issue of *Representations* 26 (Spring 1989) helps to place the interest in collective memory within the wider shifts in the studies of culture.
2. For the best illustration of how empirical materials enrich our theoretical understanding, see Michael Schudson, *Watergate in American Memory: How We Remember, Forget and Reconstruct the Past* (New York: Basic Books, 1992).
3. See, especially Erving Goffman, *Forms of Talk* (Philadelphia: University of Pennsylvania Press, 1981) and Erving Goffman, *Frame Analysis. An Essay on the Organization of Experience* (Boston: Northeastern University Press, 1986).
4. I am grateful to Judith Balfe for bringing this memorial to my attention.
5. For the most extensive treatment of this issue, see David Lowenthal, *The Past is a Foreign Country* (Cambridge: Cambridge University Press, 1985).
6. During a presentation to the Annual Scholars' Conference on Church Struggle and the Holocaust, Washington, March 1989.
7. By 1993, after several attempts at rendering justice at the highest levels of the officialdom in post-Communist countries, it is becoming more evident just how difficult the process is. For an insightful discussion of the situation in Germany, see Amos Elon, "East Germany: Crime and Punishment," *The New York Review* (May 14, 1992):6–11.
8. The idea parallels that of Pierre Nora and his collaborators studying "les lieux de mémoire" in France (in a multivolume work, beginning in 1982, Paris: Gallimard).
9. On this issue, Michael Kammen, *Mystic Chords of Memory: The Transformation of Tradition in American Culture* (New York: Alfred Knopf, 1991), is an especially rich analysis.
10. For one of the best examples of the high returns when pursuing this strategy, see Karal Ann Marling and John Wetenhall, *Iwo Jima: Monuments, Memories, and the American Hero* (Cambridge, Mass.: Harvard University Press, 1991).
11. An alternative approach, with stress on the habitual, bodily memories is presented in Paul Connerton, *How Societies Remember* (Cambridge: Cambridge University

Press, 1989). While I find it useful for understanding social practices, most of the work on the dynamics of collective memory demands that we pay attention to the "what happened" questions.

12. See Iwona Irwin-Zarecka, *Neutralizing Memory: The Jew in Contemporary Poland* (New Brunswick, N.J.: Transaction Books, 1989). [Unless otherwise indicated, further references to my work are to this book.]

13. Norma Field, *In the Realm of a Dying Emperor: A Portrait of Japan at Century's End* (New York: Pantheon Books, 1991), 179.

14. The relation between television and print media is not of simple opposition, of course. But the fact that for years, one of the most popular prime time shows in France was "Apostrophes"—an hour and a half discussion on current books—gives my Canadian students a pause.

15. See also Michael Schudson, "The Present in the Past versus the Past in the Present," *Communication* 11 (1989):105–113.

16. For a strong challenge to the 'fact vs fiction' perspective, offering an intricate analysis of the narrative genres instead, see James Fentress and Chris Wickham, *Social Memory* (Oxford and Cambridge, Mass.: Blackwell, 1992).

17. On this point, I clearly hope to counter the influence of Eric Hobsbawm and Terence Ranger, eds., *The Invention of Tradition* (Cambridge: Cambridge University Press, 1983).

18. For a useful introduction, see Barbara Kruger and Phil Mariani, eds., *Remaking History*. Dia Art Foundation Discussions in Contemporary Culture no. 4 (Seattle: Bay Press, 1989).

# 2

# Ultimate Challenge

Much of the time, when we attend to the past, we rather safely assume that we can find proper ways of remembering. Equipped with cultural traditions, moral guidelines, and the wide variety of symbolic systems, we have little reason to doubt our capability to do a decent job. Allowing for the fact that our knowledge of the past can never be fully adequate, we proceed with the telling of stories, commemoration rituals, building of monuments. We often disagree about what should be done and how, of course, but during such disputes the idea that it is indeed possible to *know* is, if anything, strengthened. The standards for judging memory work vary, but their very presence is again something we ordinarily take for granted. As analysts, we may employ the more sophisticated criteria than those explicated in public debates—and we do revise them from time to time—but we can hardly afford disposing with standards al-together. The notion that "anything goes" on the construction of collec-tive memory is too intellectually and morally unsettling. Even accepting that our answers are provisional, we need to believe there is a "right" way to remember.

Corollary to this is our need to trust in the communicative power of the basic tools we use—language, visuals, sounds, actions, gestures. Here too, there are many shifts of style, disputes over meaning, with tech-nological developments having their own profound effects. But here too, the very availability of such tools is mostly taken for granted; to question it would, after all, imply questioning our human abilities as producers of symbols.

Usually, those two layers of certainty need barely be acknowledged as one proceeds with the analytical task at hand. That people are capable of constructing a collective memory is so basic a premise it can hardly

23

carry much explanatory weight. What interests us is the process and the results, all within that complex web we define as social context. If there are limits to what is being remembered, such can surely be traced along the political or cultural paths. In short, delving into the preconditions for memory work seems superfluous, a theoretical or philosophical exercise at best.

Most of the time we *are* right to pursue such strategies. If we tune in our inquiries to the significant experiences out there in the world—as I have tried to do here—engaging in elaborate theorizing on the possibility of remembrance would not appear a priority. And yet, precisely because one has adopted an empirically driven approach, questions about ways and tools of memory construction must enter the analytical agenda. For such questions have been asked and continue to be asked, most centrally when reflecting on memory of the Holocaust.[1]

In Warsaw, the Jewish ghetto created by the Nazis occupied many blocks in the center of the city; of some 400,000 of its inhabitants, few survived; the buildings themselves were methodically razed to the ground after the 1943 uprising. After the war, Polish authorities decided to build on top of the ruins, literally covering up the remnants of human habitation, including the bodies buried there. Within a few years, only some street names and a monument to the ghetto fighters were left to speak of the past. Should something else have been done?

In Berlin, now again the capital of Germany, the buildings once housing the Nazi headquarters remained virtually intact. During the 1970s, and then the 1980s, the city governments (Western side) attempted, unsuccessfully, to gain a consensus as to what should be done with the abandoned site; proposals ranged from museums to a gaping hole in the landscape.[2] The question remains open.

At the other extreme of those problematics of memory space, there is the challenge of grieving without graves. Most of the six million Jews who perished were not accorded the dignity of proper burial. With whole communities destroyed, in Central and Eastern Europe, the old cemeteries too were often abandoned or worse, destroyed by the locals. In the Jewish tradition, funeral rites have great and sacred significance. What becomes of mourning when there is no place?

What becomes of remembrance when there are so few spaces left? The Jewish presence in communities throughout Eastern Europe left hardly any physical traces; buildings were either deliberately destroyed by the Nazis, ravaged by war or abandoned to decay later. When left standing, synagogues, for example, would serve as warehouses. The destruction of markers of Jewish life, if not as total as in Warsaw, proceeded beyond repair. Could it have been otherwise when the community was no more?

The questions raised here are both about the relationship between memory and space and about the obligations to remember. It was and still is not at all clear who ought to act as a memory keeper for Jews in Poland in particular, those Polish Jews who had once lived there and those European Jews who were killed in the camps.

Survivors implicitly answered that question when they severed their connection to Poland; memory keeping would be very much their task and responsibility, but without any support from the spaces left behind. Over the last few years, with a marked shift of attitudes on the part of Polish authorities, the question has been reopened, as Jews now participate in efforts to restore some memory markers. It is recognized by both sides that the physical presence of Jews, both in life and in death, on the Polish soil ought to be remembered. It is as if, after considerable delay, the places' haunting voice would be listened to. But, just as in Berlin, this willingness to listen does not translate into any clear sense of direction. What we should allow the spaces to tell us, we do not know.

The issue is not theoretical; the work involved is of practical nature indeed—restoring a building, cleaning up a cemetery, placing memorial plaques, rewriting guidebooks for tourists, or leaving things as they were, all involve bureaucratic decisions and financial considerations. If the results so far appear haphazard, it is because they are, owing much to local circumstances and individual involvement. There is no "grand plan," perhaps there cannot be, since to designate priorities would mean to *know* how to remember something that had never happened before.

The Holocaust was an unique event, and people were totally unprepared to accept it at the time; today, we may still be unprepared. But it is not the only event challenging our ability to remember. Mass atrocities, on a scale previously unknown, have marked this century. Millions of civilians died in wars or at the hands of their own governments. The kinds of questions raised in reflecting on the Holocaust are unfortunately becoming central to our understanding of the human condition in many parts of the world. Owing much to my own experience as a child of a Holocaust survivor, but also to the richness of literature in this area, the following discussion focuses on the vicissitudes of remembrance "after Auschwitz." What it is set to illuminate, though, is the universal dilemma of confronting the ultimate evil.

To secure remembrance, one must first be able to tell what happened. Experience must be named, words found to describe it in detail, metaphors perhaps added for further depth. With memory of the Holocaust, this is where the problem begins. The very term "Holocaust," introduced in the late 1960s as shorthand for the near total destruction of European Jews, is problematic.[3] Etymologically referring to burnt offerings, it invites a theological interpretation to deaths so difficult to reconcile with a presence of God. To speak of the "Final Solution" is historically correct, but it also gives the Nazi worldview the kind of prominence one would rather avoid. Recently, the Hebrew word *Shoah* has been widely adopted, both in English and in French, its neutral meaning of destruction recognized as most appropriate. Yet in popular parlance, "Holocaust" is still the term of choice; few are aware of its symbolic resonance. Now, the problem lies in its very popularity, as more and more crisis situations are being described as holocausts. A name that was to secure the sense of uniqueness thus begins to fail.

Language itself fails us, and yet we must speak—such could be the motto of writings about the Holocaust, fiction and non-fiction. The betrayal starts with numbers and adjectives. Numbers, since when one speaks of the "six million" who died, one crosses the limits of emotional intelligibility. Adjectives, since the words "tragic," "horrific," or even "evil" are not strong enough. Nouns are not very helpful either; terms like "camp," "selection," "resistance" evoke imagery that obscures rather than illuminates reality of the times.

Language is an universalizing tool; words we use immediately evoke experiences we can relate to. Describing what happened during the Holocaust means describing experiences we cannot—and ultimately ought not—relate to. This basic challenge may explain why "Auschwitz" has acquired such symbolic potency, for it is, for Westerners at least, an essentially untransferable term; what it speaks of is only the Holocaust. (In Poland, though, this does not apply; for one, the camp's name Oswiecim is also the name of a town close by; more importantly, as there were many Polish prisoners in the camp, the connection with Jewish suffering is not there.) The choice of Auschwitz may be historically problematic, in that it was the site of a great deal more than the extermination of the Jews. But it reflects the fate of memory more than history; in Auschwitz, there were survivors, many of whom went on to write about it—Elie Wiesel, Primo Levi, Charlotte Delbo, and others. The search for the right words has led in many different directions, from minimalist simplicity to elaborately metaphorical expression; writings on the Holocaust exhibit an immense range of styles. Critical analysis of those writings is by now a large field of scholarship. Yet as critical standards develop, and a certain degree of academic consensus is established, it also becomes increasingly clear that the basic question about proper ways of remembering is not likely to be settled, at least not at the center.[4]

Where a semblance of agreement emerges is at the margins, now not only of literary endeavors but symbolic production in general. The growing supply of pornography and kitsch,[5] if anything else, prompts loud protests from within and outside academia. Both categories are inherently difficult precisely to define, of course, but the strength of visceral reaction against eroticizing Nazism, for example, may not need definition. Yet if the little cottage industry in Nazi paraphernalia is something most people would find troubling, the wide use of "Hitler" to describe political opponents warranted few comments indeed during the Gulf War.

The negative standards, quite naturally, gain more public exposure. Outside the group of specialists, few people are familiar with the reflection on remembering the Holocaust. When the line of decency is crossed, however, and the debate moves to the popular media, vast numbers of nonspecialists learn the line exists. This selective attention may partly account for a general perception of Holocaust remembrance as solid, established, unproblematic. Coupled with the undeniable growth of films, books, memorials, and courses, the impression is easily created that if anything, this memory is all too well taken care of. In relative quantitative terms, this is quite true. Even with *glasnost*, we are still far from having a similarly extensive memory base about mass murders in the Soviet Union, to take the most immediate comparison. But in terms of finding the right ways of remembering, the multiplicity speaks of the continuous search, a search in which what some see as overexposure is yet another attempt at finding answers. With memory of the Holocaust, it appears that all of the basic questions are left open, from who is to be remembered to who is to remember, from when to where and how. For the analyst, it might be all too natural to adopt one of the developed approaches as *the* right one—and that includes myself. But demanding as it may be, if we are to be faithful to the phenomenon we study, we ought to recognize the full diversity of remembrance proposals. At issue is not some form of relativism, but rather an acknowledgment that, at least for now, few standards exist. It is the search that matters.

The who/when/where/how questions can rarely be neatly separated. To take one of the more difficult challenges—honoring the heroes—at issue here is a whole web of problems. Defining heroic behavior on the part of non-Jews during the Holocaust seems straightforward enough; those who aided Jews at the risk to their own lives are indeed granted special recognition by the State of Israel. What about Jews who did the same, faced with much higher odds?[6] There, the recognition is only beginning to emerge, as if helping one's own people would not quite qualify for heroism. The attempt to preserve the traditional order of things has led to immense concentration on honoring the Warsaw ghetto fighters; the date on which the uprising in the ghetto began was also chosen (after considerable debate) as the official day of commemoration of the Holocaust in Israel and then the Diaspora. This emphasis troubles many; Marek Edelman, today the only surviving leader of the uprising, speaks with force about the equality of heroic death of those with arms and those herded on the trains.[7] Indeed, when the ghetto fighters are described as "those who died with dignity," as they often are, the dignity of memory is at risk. Ought one then to abandon the very notion of a hero? Or, perhaps, should we grant the honors to all who perished? But if we do that, those Jews who collaborated with the Nazis come to receive the same status as others.

Remembrance without heroes is also at high risk of anonymity. Recognizing how easy it is to bracket the "six million" out from emotional involvement, many of the people working in the area have made a concerted effort to give the numbers individual faces. Even among historians, still not very keen on describing the fate of ordinary men and women, there has been a remarkable movement towards the particular; filled with individual stories, Martin Gilbert's book on the Holocaust represents one of the possible choices;[8] the collection of oral histories, intensified now that the survivors grow older, represents another. Written memoirs follow that pattern, and the immense impact of the television series *Holocaust* and *The Diary of Anne Frank* earlier points to its resonance with human capacity to remember.[9]

Empathy alone does not, though, make for understanding. And, remembering the Holocaust does not just mean honoring its victims. It is once we are outside the comparatively "safe" area of memory of suffering that the challenges grow exponentially. Intellectually, the "not to remember the past is to repeat it" idea compels a search for explanations. Morally, this very search implicates wider and wider circles of humanity. Remembrance becomes more and more uncomfortable, disruptive of our sense of the order of things.[10] And even if one accepts that it was Auschwitz that had disrupted forever the secular and the sacred order, it is not at all clear that remembering Auschwitz should mean the same. In other words, we have an obligation to our present and future as well as to our past, all entering the negotiations about the "proper" legacy.

Elsewhere in this book, I look at some of the debates surrounding the definition of a "proper" place for memory of the Holocaust. Here, in keeping with the overall theme, I would like to reflect on the more basic issue of the "proper understanding" of that past. How such understanding is understood informs both the work of discovery and the communication of results. Whether for academic research, educational practices, or artistic endeavors, "understanding" is the most crucial of tools. The construction of collective memory employs different types of understanding, from dry scholarly knowledge to a visceral sense of the past, each with different claims to truth and authenticity. Ordinarily, they complement each other; ordinarily, people's expectations and responses are very much informed by the distinct modes of understanding possible within given formats. We might like historians to add a touch of poetry to their writing, or a film about the American Civil War to be based on facts, but we do not question their respective principles for putting together a "reality of the past" (intellectual debates notwithstanding).

Memory of the Holocaust defies those general rules in a number of ways. Neither scholars nor artists appear confident that they *can* "understand," all the while they work to convey meaning of the events. The lines separating knowledge and visceral feelings are often blurred. Expectations attached to formally different modes of remembrance cross over as well. And more than once, memory workers acknowledge that their task is an impossible one.

Most affected by the challenge is the community of scholars. For them to admit that, ultimately, understanding is not possible, is to contradict the fundamental rules of scientific inquiry.[11] As a sociologist, I am all too aware of the common solution in my field to the predicament—and that is to avoid the subject. Within the discipline, studying the Holocaust—and genocide, and state-sponsored violence—occupies a tiny, marginal spot on the agenda.[12] And the results of the few studies that had been done are not very encouraging; it seems that standard sociological questions do not fit well with the task at hand.[13] Recently, there began some efforts to reformulate the questions and to invite wider participation from sociologists;[14] it remains to be seen whether the shift can affect the core of the disciplinary theory and practice.

Social sciences, in general, despite their claims to understanding human behavior, have so far paid scant attention to the Holocaust. Implicitly or explicitly, what happened to Jews during the Nazi period is treated as an aberration, an exception, a departure from all norms—and as such not warranting more than special case type of analysis. Individually, political scientists or psychologists have done some exemplary work in the area, but the subject remains marginal.

Persisting on the margins of social sciences allowed studies of the Holocaust largely to avoid confrontation with the basic issue of "understanding." When covering a very specific and small aspect of the whole, it is possible to avoid it. For at least one prominent historian, Michael Marrus,[15] it is indeed necessary to avoid it if the work is to get done at all; advocating a form of return to "history as usual," Marrus sees the earlier, bold efforts to face the challenges of Auschwitz as commendable but impractical in the long run. Professionals should not be awed by what they study, they should not be disarmed by a sense of ultimate incomprehensibility. The argument is for more, not less, studies in the area but also for a certain bracketing of emotions; the scaling down of aspirations becomes a precondition for growth. Much along those lines, I recently heard a history professor calling for total exclusion of visual materials from courses on the Holocaust;[16] empathy with the victims, in his view, morally blocks the students from asking critical questions about their actions. Taking the argument for value-neutrality to its extreme, any form of identification with those who suffered is thus prohibited in the name of intellectual integrity. Emotional disengagement is what allows one to understand the Holocaust as one would any other historical event.

While most historians, by virtue of their craft, employ a degree of detachment from their subject, few would agree that studying the Holocaust is exactly the same as studying the Roman Empire, for example. Fewer still would argue for writing and teaching strategies devoid of empathetic dimension.[17] Historical accounts on the Holocaust struggle with the limits of both scholarly and emotive language; they vary widely in the balance between the two. Some offer insight into very specific areas, some propose large, synthetic interpretations, many operate inbetween. As we have already seen, there is also here a much more pronounced than usual emphasis on the fate of individuals. What is virtually universal is the acknowledgment of the challenge; whether focusing on such broad questions as "how was it possible?" or the more particular ones like "what was known?", historians adopt a certain humility in their claims.

Indirectly, too, this humility is very much evident in the degree of cooperation with other thinkers, representing often radically different heuristic approaches. Philosophers, theologians and artists are given equal, if not at times superior status as interpreters of the Holocaust. Hannah Arendt, George Steiner, Elie Wiesel, Primo Levi, Richard Rubenstein, Roy and Alice L. Eckardt—these are only some of the nonhistorians that the historians have listened to most attentively. This unprecedented degree of mutual cooperation, respect, and exchange of ideas is, I believe, the best indication of how demanding is the task of "understanding Auschwitz." The fact that not only disciplinary lines are crossed, but those traditionally separating art from science, is a testimony to the challenge, but also to the willingness to confront it.

I would not wish to overromanticize the endeavor. Intellectuals, being human and greatly attached to their projects and ideas, are particularly prone to petty squabbles. With careers and reputations at stake, debates can become nasty or the system of mutual support too cosy. Those working in Holocaust studies are not immune to such general pressures. But, comparatively speaking, it is the spirit of cooperation that prevails. And yes, there is the sense of awe towards the subject matter, a certain added seriousness to the proceedings (at meetings and conferences, for example). There is also the rather practical factor allowing for inquiries to be largely unencumbered by personalized competition—the very marginal status within respective disciplines. With some exceptions, academics here cannot function as full-time Holocaust specialists; thus they have more independence when pursuing interests in the area, and a much less competitive position vis-à-vis their colleagues.

Judging by my own experience, and drawing on many talks with others, I would like to add that treating one's work with Holocaust materials as always a part and not the whole is frequently a conscious individual choice, rather than institutional necessity. For reasons of psychological hygiene, as it were, one wishes to be able to come and leave. Looking into the abyss is emotionally demanding; there is the fear of developing a certain fascination with the horrific on the one hand and of becoming numb on the other. The option open to surgeons of rudely joking about patients under their knife is not a possibility here. The best one can do is to recognize one's own limits and act accordingly.

It is equally important, although harder in practice, to recognize the limits among one's audience. If all memory workers dealing with Holocaust materials face their own reluctance to be immersed in the traumatic past, they draw strength from their very commitment to do the work. Whatever the sources of such commitment, it is something deeply felt and not easily disturbed; long leaves from the subject reflect rather than weaken it. Among the people to whom the work is directed, however, such is not the case. Beyond the relatively small "community of memory,"[18] the obligation to remember the Holocaust very much needs to be constructed along with the resources. Delving into traumatic experiences of no personal relevance is not something we naturally or willingly do. And indeed, for quite a long time, most North Americans and many Europeans were not asked to.

Earlier in our discussion, I suggested that the problematics of remembering the Holocaust implicate all of the basic questions, the whole what/when/where/how nexus. It is time to focus on the subsidiary dyad, as it were, the issues of who is to remember and why, issues which today very much inform the search for the right ways to secure a public presence for that memory.

For many years, the main goal of memory workers, scholars, writers, artists, curators, has been to make remembering the Holocaust *possible*. The task, as we have seen, proved very difficult, but if the search for the right ways to remember continues, it has already allowed for the construction of a rich memory base. There is a great deal of work still to be done. At Auschwitz, for example, an international commission is currently discussing major modifications to the structure of the museum exhibit, in response to serious criticisms from many quarters that the legacy of Auschwitz cannot be found on the site itself.

In other places throughout the changed Central and Eastern Europe, too, there are both local initiatives and international efforts to fill in the void left by Communist regimes; "victims of Fascism," once the standard phrase, gradually become Jews again. Beyond the physical restoration of memory markers, there is a renewed effort at historical documentation, now that many Soviet archives have been opened. We may also expect more gathering of oral testimonies and more writings to emerge from the area.

In other countries, too, the creation of basic records is not at all complete. Yet while the work continues, and is likely to continue for quite some time, its goals have been gradually redefined now to include making remembrance of the Holocaust *necessary*. Most notably in the United States,[19] where since 1985 a federal program has been in place to sponsor and encourage state and local initiatives, memory of the Holocaust would now be granted an altogether different public status. From integration within school curricula to the construction of the Holocaust Memorial Museum in the heart of Washington, D.C., Americans, especially young Americans, are now asked to remember. In Canada, a parallel shift has occurred, though limited for now to the educational sphere. The work here, too, is far from complete—and far from unproblematic.

Some of the challenge is readily apparent. Teaching on the Holocaust—in the classroom or in a museum—is a formidable task, intellectually as well as emotionally. Educational solutions must be found to problems persisting at the base, such as understanding and language. Many a complexity may have to be lightly passed over for the sake of pedagogical effectiveness. There are limits of time and space, necessitating choices at each stage of the process, choices which could easily distort the overall "message." To go back to our example of defining heroism and resistance, if a special teach-in for high school students consists of a lecture by a Jewish partisan and a film about ghetto fighters, all under the theme of "resistance," it is all too easy for them to leave, ignorant of what the majority of Jews were doing to resist—which was to survive with dignity, to retain a self. At the particular teach-in I attended recently in Waterloo, Ontario, one of the educators involved tried to repair the situation with a brief introductory comment on how meaningless are our established concepts. The statement was clear to me, but I doubt it had much resonance for the young people in the audience. It was not until the second part of the day, when they met, in small groups, with survivors, and could ask informal questions, that I sensed the program acquired some meaning. For those young students, whose experience in life is so distant from virtually all facets of the trauma in Nazi Europe, a survivor provided the needed human connection.

Teachers very much recognize this need for bridging the distance. Inviting survivors, or when that is not possible, reading their individual testimonies appears a favored solution.[20] It works in so far as students become capable of imagining themselves in the situations they discuss. Self-examination is not the only goal of Holocaust education, but it is an important component here. Facing up to one's own attitudes to the Other, acknowledging the potential for good and evil in oneself, thinking through many a moral dilemma—such are, broadly speaking, desired results of the lessons.

The bridging that thus occurs is of a special universal-to-individual quality. What disappears, and what calls for different strategies and sensibility to reappear, is the in-between historical specificity. It is in this area that most problems arise. It is one thing to speak of the Holocaust as a distant reality that we can all learn from as humans, it is an altogether different matter to speak of the Germans, Jews, Poles, Ukrainians, Italians—and yes, Americans and Canadians. The desire to be faithful to historical truth must now be balanced against measures of caution; at issue is moral responsibility in the very concrete terms of one's people or one's country; at issue, too, is the potential for generating conflict and prejudice. The relevance to students' experience acquires a political dimension. Canada's dismal record in accepting Jewish refugees from Nazi Europe can easily become an argument in the dispute over current immigration policies. The Arabs' sympathy for the Nazi cause might enter the present Middle East conflict agenda, as could Holocaust echoes in Israel. The struggle for independence in the Baltic republics—or Croatia—may lose some of its appealing glow.

The list could continue on, but I think the point is made—remembering the Holocaust is not politically neutral. And yet, there are compelling reasons to make it so if it is to have a secure public presence in North America, in and outside the classroom. A telling lesson here comes from Canada, where during the mid-1980s, proposals for new legislation allowing for trials of war criminals sparked a serious clash between (organized) Jewish and Ukrainian communities.[21] Prior to the conflict, activists from the two communities had just begun efforts to improve the traditionally hostile relations; in the wake of a very public debate, those efforts appeared doomed for some time to come. In letters to the editor, many uninvolved Canadians expressed dismay at dwelling on historical grievances in general, citing the dangerous developments in the Sikh/Hindu relations as another case in point. A polity, the argument went, whose citizens come from all corners of the globe cannot afford any encouragement to the "old country" hatreds. Spelled out was a principle usually well hidden in broad generalities—that remembering the Holocaust ought not to interfere with the goals of ethnic harmony.

I live in Kitchener, Ontario, a city where many people are of German origin, some quite recent. When Ernst Zundel, a West German immigrant to Canada, went on trial in Toronto for publishing materials denying that the Holocaust ever happened, the local newspaper became a forum for expressing concerns with the possible damage to the image of Germans as a whole. Interestingly, it was not Zundel's actions—and he had quite an elaborate tough-man media personality as well—that troubled people; the very exposure accorded to Auschwitz, day after day of the long trial, did. One should add that within the Jewish community as well, voices were heard objecting to this type of publicity; since the judge decided then that the historical facticity of the Holocaust would be argued in court, the deniers were seen as having won the battle no matter what the verdict. Both sides believed the impact of the extensive media coverage would be significant and, for different reasons, did not trust the journalists. As it turns out, neither antisemitic nor anti-German attitudes received any boosts from the trial, as revealed in later surveys.[22] But the concerns that they might are not so easy to dismiss, as those concerns, whatever their merit, influence also the future presence of the past.

The idea that, today, public discussion of the Holocaust may incite rather than warn against antisemitism may at first appear as a case of strange reasoning. Yet, in Canada at least, this was a widely shared sentiment during the years which saw both the debates on war criminals and successive trials of Zundel as well as another revisionist.[23] In the classroom setting, teachers too are aware that for at least some students the question "why the Jews?" will draw in many below-the-surface prejudices. To answer this question in the depth it deserves is difficult in a newspaper or a course. And what makes the task especially problematic is yet another dimension of dealing with the Holocaust in its full historical specificity—the religious one. Here too, there may be compelling reasons to minimize the impact of remembrance.

The challenge of Auschwitz is twofold. One is universal, the "where was God?" Both Christian and Jewish theologians have struggled with the answers; traces of the question are also to be found in much of Holocaust literature and art in general. The other challenge is specific—and directed to this worldly realm of Christianity. What was the role of the churches, the dogma, the teachings in making the death sentence for all Jews possible? The companion question is no less morally troubling—what did Christians, as Christians, do to prevent the killings?

In an increasingly secularized public domain, including the educational system, it is possible to avoid discussing the fundamentals of belief. What is not possible to avoid altogether, as long as the question "why the Jews?" is posed, is the critical examination of the Christian heritage. And this brings lessons of the Holocaust, inadvertently, into the center of politically charged current debates about the proper place of *that* cultural legacy. Teachers who may feel under siege for wishing to preserve a Christian presence in the classroom (in Ontario, policies of the public schools explicitly prohibit it, for example) would have understandable reluctance to dwell on what is essentially an indictment of Christianity. We should add to this the ever-present potential for offending students' sensibilities, and the relative scarcity of resources originating with the Christian churches,[24] all working against the full disclosure of the religious dimension of the past. The strange idea that exposure to the Holocaust could encourage antisemitism does not appear so strange any more. Jews, after all, must have done *something* to provoke the wrath.

The building of bridges to the students' own experience that would be historically specific is no less problematic in the secular domain. Beyond specific political resonances we discussed above, there are the fundamental beliefs in progress and rationality implicated here. And not only are the questions troubling, but they remain much more unsettled than others. The assignment of responsibility for what happened to the Jews to "modernity" is still debated, both in general terms and in the particulars. The linkages between the Nazi project and antecedent ideas retain a certain provisional quality, all the while more work is being done in this area. For educators, what may be most immediately problematic is less the continuing debate than the implications of posing the questions at all. In a society based on the idea of progress, and in the classrooms dedicated to the dissemination of knowledge, to point out that the Holocaust might not have been possible without both *is* demanding.

For some people, that challenge is precisely the reason why the Holocaust should be studied, now also at the university level. Doctors— or anthropologists-to-be—ought to learn what their knowledge could be and was used for. Aspiring social engineers—and chemists—ought to see the potential results of their efforts. In short, warning signs, if nothing else, are called for within the academia.

So far, university curricula have proved rather resistant to such self-questioning reflection,[25] much more so, it seems, than those in the seminaries. Speaking as a scholar, this disturbs me, yet I can also appreciate the acute problems inherent in telling one's students not to trust their teachers. At the same time, I would hope that with the general shifts in public attitudes engendered by ecological concerns would come greater readiness to face the responsibility of science through lessons of the Holocaust as well.

The transition from memory-as-possibility to memory-as-necessity raises, as we have seen, the issue of justification. In the North American context, several options may be available and are indeed being tried out, with a definite preference shown for universalizing the significance of remembering the Holocaust. In other contexts, the options may be far fewer, but the challenge of finding the "right" reasons to remember remains.

Poland, which I studied most closely, illustrates the difficulties encountered in the wide zone of bystander communities where Jews had been subject to persecution (as opposed to those in the free world). In the country where so many of the European Jews perished, remembering the Holocaust may at first appear not to need any justification. Such is not the case, however. At stake are two distinct modes of remembering, each requiring a different rationale. Mourning the Jews, in particular the Polish Jews, calls for including them in the national family—and this means reversing the principle of exclusion which had been in operation both before, during and after the Holocaust. Learning from history, on the other hand, calls for acceptance of large measures of collective responsibility, something that Poles generally have been very reluctant to do. For decades, memory of the Holocaust functioned, officially and unofficially, as part of memory of Nazism, and thus very much together with the memory of Polish victimization, effectively removing the issue of responsibility. The prevailing view of the "Final Solution" as completely accountable within the history of Germany served further to narrow the potential lessons. Not seeing themselves implicated as Christians or as Europeans allowed Poles to remember the Holocaust without reflecting on it. And even today, when Poles are being asked to remember *and* to reflect, the appeals rest on the direct, physical connection with Auschwitz. The moral self-questioning which is called for, extending over the whole of recent Polish-Jewish history, is presented as necessary for national health, as it were. In this way, remembering the Holocaust is justified as part of a larger effort to reevaluate Poland's relations with minorities, we might add, a politically urgent effort in the new Europe.

The gradual shift from treating the Holocaust as one among many Nazi crimes to recognizing its uniqueness might eventually lead to less Poland-centered reflection. But in a country so directly implicated in that history, it might indeed be still too early to dwell on issues of universal significance. The moral accounting has only begun.

That remembering the Holocaust is also, if not prominently, a form of moral accounting is a general proposition, of course, applying well beyond Poland's borders. What the Polish case exemplifies perhaps better than others, though, is the great difficulty of arriving at sound criteria of judgment. Here too, the experience during those dark years poses an immense challenge to our established order of things. Put simply, not having been there weighs heavily on our ability to set the moral parameters, almost to the point that we might resist the attempt altogether.

Poland was the only European country where any action to aid Jews was punishable by death; in the case of hiding a Jew, this meant death to the whole family. Facing such severe consequences ought largely to account, as many Polish writers have argued, for how few Jews were actually saved, the other part of the explanation being the very physical difficulty of providing refuge to some three million mostly unassimilated Jews. The reasoning is plausible until one realizes that many other and often rather mundane infractions were subject to the death penalty—the smuggling of food, for example. And that despite the dangers, underground activities of all kinds flourished.

But if Poles disobeyed the Nazis in numerous ways, they did that with the full societal approval and indeed encouragement. Such was not the case as far as helping Jews was concerned; *after* the war, many of the rescuers preferred to remain silent about their actions. Neither the civil nor the church authorities appealed for or sanctioned aid to the Jews. When the first organized effort began and such an appeal was issued, most of Poland's Jews had already been killed.

This is not the place to draw this moral balance sheet in full, of course. I only wish to illustrate some of the problems involved in apportioning responsibility on the basis of "historical facts." To appreciate choices which were available—and the choices actually made—one needs to proceed through many a layer, from the well-documented laws of the Nazi occupation all the way to the much less tangible realm of attitudes and ideas. What compounds the difficulty is the very knowledge we acquire in the process. It is all too easy—and I am now speaking in general terms—to be guided by what we know when passing moral judgments. Yet people who lived at the time operated within a necessarily different set of parameters; what they "knew" is often hard to reconstruct but we must try. Hindsight and contemporary sensibility, so important for our understanding of the events, can prove serious obstacles to moral accounting.

Beyond that challenge, which may be said to be part and parcel of any historical inquiry, lie challenges unique to the Holocaust. The world of camps and ghettos was not a "normal" one. For us to appreciate choices confronting a man on work duty in the gas chambers of Treblinka is ultimately impossible. Not knowing what it is like to be hungry for months and years, do we have the licence to judge those who were?

As with many questions about remembering the Holocaust, this one too remains open. For some people, including survivors, assessing actions of the victims in moral terms is itself indecent. For other people, also including survivors, it is a compelling need if we are to learn from the past. And again, the intuitively drawn lines become visible in public debates, such as one sparked by Hannah Arendt's statements on the victims' complicity.[26] Some of the memory shorthand, too, betrays definite moral perspective—most prominently, the image of "sheep to slaughter"—leading to critical reexamination of the assumptions we hold. Overall, though, there is little consensus of how much moral accounting should the victims be subject to—or on how to proceed.

The situation is clearly different, though no less problematic, as we move to perpetrators and bystanders. It is different, since there is a wide consensus on the need to draw balance sheets. Where the problems center is in two areas. First, as exemplified here by the situation in Poland, there is the complexity of issues involved. In the case of Germany, which may initially appear to be a great deal more clear cut, the sheer quantity of studies dealing with various sectors of society attests to the difficulties. Compounding those difficulties is the often unacknowledged but no less strong awareness of the present day implications of the analytical results. As we mentioned earlier, memory of the Holocaust is not neutral. The assessment of moral responsibility on the part of historical actors can rarely be separated from contemporary realities. There is the very concrete continuity, let us say between the I. G. Farben company that supplied Zyklon B gas to Auschwitz and the I. G. Farben today that, somewhat manipulating the rules, builds new headquarters in Berlin. And there is the symbolic continuity of both institutions and communities, the continuity which forms the base for much debated claims of "collective responsibility."

The elapse of time does make it easier to confront the morally challenging past, yet it may also work to create a gap of relevance, as it were. It is characteristic, for example, that among the people actively involved in recent debates about the Holocaust, both in Germany and Poland, most belonged to the generation of war children, a generation with personal memories but also no direct responsibility. All the continuities notwithstanding, will the next generation care enough to remember? And if it remembers, will it be a troubling memory? Is it not possible to morally neutralize the impact of Auschwitz?

Observing the recent developments in Germany, Austria, France, Poland, I would argue this is not a theoretical concern. Where memory, on moral grounds, *is* a necessity, it is also a burden. If completely to forget may not be possible, finding ways to remember which least challenge the collective self appears a thriving practice.[27] To come back to Berlin for a moment, where a new museum of national history is under construction, visitors there will be able to see the "Nazi room" as one among many. Already a few years ago, German readers could find out that theirs was not a radically different legacy in view of Stalin's crimes and the continuing list of other mass atrocities in our times. They could read it in the press, as well as in a bestselling novel by a Polish writer who won unprecedented acclaim in Germany.[28]

As a line of moral reasoning, this one came under heavy attack, most notably from Jurgen Habermas, provoking a long and heated debate.[29] My sympathies, as is likely already clear, are definitely with the critics. Yet in an analytically crucial way, the linkages so formed between Auschwitz and the *gulag* and Cambodia and . . . ought not to be dismissed. As I said at the outset of these reflections, for students of remembrance, these traumas *are* linked in that they all challenge our capability to construct memory. I see the challenge of Auschwitz as the ultimate one, but the issues discussed here resonate on other memory terrains as well. If I leave it up to the readers to hear such resonances, it is mainly in recognition of my own limitations. To formulate meaningful questions about the vicissitudes of remembrance requires, quite simply, a total immersion in the specific histories, both of the events to be remembered and the ensuing efforts.

The lesson I would like to conclude with here is rather a general one. As students of remembrance, we continuously use critical standards when analyzing how the job is done, often without much questioning of our own tools. Looking closely at an area where the normative principles are all open to dispute serves us a note of caution. We may be wrong, wrong in thinking that we know what is the right way to remember. At the very least, we ought to consider the possibility.

## Notes

1. For the most comprehensive (and compact) survey of these questions, see Saul Friedländer, ed., *Probing the Limits of Representation: Nazism and the "Final Solution"* (Cambridge, Mass.: Harvard University Press, 1992).

2. Rainer Kolmel, "A Holocaust Memorial in Berlin?" in *Remembering for the Future: Jews and Christians During and After the Holocaust* (Oxford: Pergamon Press, 1988), 1755-67.

3. See Zev Garber and Bruce Zuckerman, "Why Do We Call the Holocaust "the Holocaust"?: An Inquiry into the Psychology of Labels," in *Remembering for the Future: Jews and Christians During and After the Holocaust* (Oxford: Pergamon Press, 1988), 1879-92.

4. Sidra DeKoven Ezrahi, *By Words Alone. The Holocaust in Literature* (Chicago and London: University of Chicago Press, 1980) exemplifies this concern in respect to literature. Ilan Avisar, *Screening the Holocaust: Cinema's Images of the Unimaginable* (Bloomington and Indianapolis: Indiana University Press, 1988) treats the issue of filmic representation. Robert Skloot, *The Darkness We Carry. The Drama of the Holocaust* (Madison: The University of Wisconsin Press, 1988)

addresses the challenges specific to theater. (All three have been selected here for their international comparative scope.)

5. For an extensive discussion, see Saul Friedländer, *Reflections of Nazism: An Essay on Kitsch and Death*, translated from French by Thomas Weyr (New York: Harper and Row, 1984).

6. Nechama Tec brought this issue to attention in "Altruism and Rescuing Jews," a paper presented at the Annual Scholars' Conference on the Church Struggle and the Holocaust, Philadelphia, March 1989. She continues research in this area.

7. Hanna Krall, *Shielding The Flame: An Intimate Conversation with Dr. Marek Edelman, The Last Surviving Leader of the Warsaw Ghetto Uprising*, translated by Joanna Stasinska and Lawrence Weschler (New York: Henry Holt and Company, 1986).

8. Martin Gilbert, *The Holocaust: The Jewish Tragedy* (Glasgow: Fontana, 1987).

9. For a further discussion, see Judith E. Doneson, *The Holocaust in American Film* (Philadelphia: The Jewish Publication Society, 1987).

10. For the most extensive collection of papers addressing this issue, see *Remembering for the Future: Jews and Christians During and After the Holocaust*, papers presented at the International Scholars' Conference held in Oxford, July 10-13, 1988 (Oxford: Pergamon Press, 1988).

11. Reflections in Istvan Deak, "The Incomprehensible Holocaust," *The New York Review* (September 28, 1989):63–72, exemplify this problem.

12. See Frank Chalk and Kurt Jonassohn, *The History and Sociology of Genocide: Analyses and Case Studies* (New Haven: Yale University Press, 1990).

13. For example, one of the most ambitious works here is Helen Fein, *Accounting for Genocide: National Responses and Jewish Victimization during the Holocaust* (Chicago: University of Chicago Press, 1984). As a comparative analysis, it is valuable indeed. Yet as a basis for case-by-case historical inquiry and understanding it represents a modest beginning.

14. See, especially, Zygmunt Bauman, *Modernity and the Holocaust* (New York: Cornell University Press, 1989).

15. Michael M. Marrus, *The Holocaust in History* (Toronto: Lester & Orpen Dennys, 1987).

16. Now published, Jacques Kornberg, "On Teaching the Holocaust as History," in *Montreal Institute for Genocide Studies: Occasional Papers* (Concordia University, June 1991):1–11.

17. See, especially, Zev Garber, with Alan L. Berger and Richard Libowitz, eds., *Methodology in the Academic Teaching of the Holocaust* (Lanham and London: University Press of America, 1988).

18. I am borrowing this term from Robert N. Bellah, Richard Madsen, William M. Sullivan, Ann Swidler and Steven M. Tipton, *Habits of the Heart: Individualism and Commitment in American Life* (Berkeley: University of California Press, 1985). For a further discussion, see ch. 3.

19. See Judith Miller, *One, by One, by One. Facing the Holocaust* (New York: Simon and Schuster, 1990).

20. This is based on several discussions at the Annual Scholars' Conferences on the Church Struggle and the Holocaust.

21. For a full account, see Harold Troper and Morton Weinfeld, *Old Wounds: Jews, Ukrainians and the Hunt for Nazi War Criminals in Canada* (Markham, Ont.: Viking, 1988).

22. See Gabriel Weimann and Conrad Winn, *Hate on Trial: The Zundel Affair, the Media, Public Opinion in Canada* (New York: Mosaic Press, 1986).

23. See also Steve Mertl and John Ward, *Keegstra: The Issues, The Trial, The Consequences* (Saskatoon, Sask.: Prairie Books, 1985).

24. I thank Roy and Alice L. Eckardt for many a discussion on these issues.

25. See, for example, reflections in Robert N. Proctor, *Racial Hygiene: Medicine Under the Nazis* (Cambridge, Mass.: Harvard University Press, 1988).

26. Hanna Arendt, *Eichmann in Jerusalem: A Report on the Banality of Evil*, rev. ed. (New York: Penguin Books, 1965).

27. For an excellent analysis of this process, see Alain Finkielkraut, *Remembering in Vain. The Klaus Barbie Trial & Crimes Against Humanity*, translated by Roxamme Lapidus with Sima Godfrey (New York: Columbia University Press, 1992).

28. See Iwona Irwin-Zarecka, "Challenged to Respond—New Polish Novels About the Holocaust," in Alan L. Berger, ed., *Bearing Witness to the Holocaust 1939–1989* (Lewiston, N.Y.: The Edwin Mellen Press, 1991), 273-83.

29. See Richard J. Evans, *In Hitler's Shadow: West German Historians and the Attempt to Escape from the Nazi Past* (New York: Pantheon Books, 1989).

# PART II
# Dynamics of Relevance

# 3

# Communities of Memory

The term "collective memory" accommodates a great variety of
territorial claims. At times, it is used to describe the heritage of the whole
of humanity, at times, it becomes a national property, at still other times
it is said to bond generations. For students of local and regional traditions,
the "collective" designates relatively small groups of people; for students
of the media, the "collective" could encompass a multinational audience.
Such vagueness, while understandable considering how open the concept
is, does pose analytical challenges. At issue is not only a methodological
confusion inherent in mixing different levels and types of inquiry; more
importantly, the apparent adaptability of "collective memory" to
whatever research circumstances may lead to glossing over some key
empirical questions about the relationship between private and public
remembrance. Thus as we justifiably pay more attention to how the past
is mediated, framed, represented, we may be assuming too much as to
the relevance of both that past and that mediation. In other words, as we
learn more about the practices and principles of memory work, we may
be leaving behind ordinary individuals who rather selectively attend to
the now rapidly growing and diversifying storehouse of public memories.

In an effort to remedy the situation, let us take the opposite path for a
while, and reflect on how the actors themselves come to draw boundaries
of sharing in remembrance of times past. What are the communities of
memory and how do they come into being? How do they matter, for those
within as well as on the outside?

In its most direct meaning, a community of memory is one created by
that very memory. For people to feel a sense of bonding with others solely
because of a shared experience, the experience itself would often be of
extraordinary if not traumatic quality. Soldiers who came back from the

trenches of World War I, veterans of the war in Vietnam, survivors of the atomic bomb, escapees from Pol Pot's Cambodia, survivors of the Holocaust—all these groups remained apart in their visceral, often untranslatable memory of horror. The experience they shared could not be truly shared with others, at least not at the same level of understanding. And a sense of recognition, immediately apparent when survivors meet each other is too of exceptional quality.

Viewers of Oliver Stone's *Born on the Fourth of July*, a film capturing for the wide public what going to Vietnam and coming back were about, would be very much made aware of the divide between "us" and "them." In Japan, the language and social practice separated out those "tainted" by the bomb.[1] Holocaust survivors, as their numbers are now declining, express great anxiety about the approaching disappearance of authentic witness, again stressing the abyss between those who were there and those who were not.

What is "there," though? In the case of Holocaust survivors in particular, the community of memory appears to have constantly shifting boundaries. For the very term "survivor," while in principle applicable to any Jew who stayed alive until liberation, in the practice of remembrance tends to focus, at times exclusively, on those who came back from "*l'univers concentrationnaire*."[2] Within memory of the Holocaust, Auschwitz, Majdanek, Treblinka stand apart, as if in clear recognition that the experience in the camps was unique among the unique. At the same time, as more writers and artists of the "second generation" work through the meanings of living with the memory of the Holocaust, the community bonded by that memory grows to include all the empathetic witnesses as well. The direct connection between experience and remembrance is now not severed, rather, it is redrawn to capture the complexity of effects of that experience beyond individual memories.[3]

The shifting of community boundaries proceeds even further, though. For as the Holocaust assumes a centrality in the reflections of some prominent Christians, they too may be said to belong to that community of memory. In a sense, the bonding initially created by living through a trauma extends, with time, to those for whom remembrance of that trauma acts as a key orienting force for their lives and public actions. What underlies that bonding, though, or what defines the community through its many transitions, is a shared, if not always explicated, meaning given to the experience itself. Thus if the invisible divide around the survivors can never be fully bridged, remembrance which retains this divide as one of its important structuring principles can allow for survivors to join others.[4] Personal relevance of the traumatic memory, and not personal witness to the trauma, here defines the community.

That it is the meaning given to the event, rather than the event itself which may create a community of memory is very much in evidence when we consider the absence of remembrance on the part of key witnesses to the destruction of European Jewry—the Poles. In theory, people who lived around Auschwitz or Treblinka during their years of operation, who could forever smell the stench of burning bodies, who saw the trains return from the camps empty, in short, people who came a lot closer to the abyss than anyone but the victims themselves, ought to have had traumatic memories of what happened. Some do. But by and large, the Polish witnesses and later, the Polish memory workers affecting the public domain, never produced bonds of remembrance that would reflect their experience of the Holocaust. Two reasons may account for this, I think. First, for the majority of Poles, it is their own victimization during the Nazi occupation that represented a formative trauma; indeed, the prominent place accorded to both private and public remembrance of the war's Polish victims and heroes continues to focalize national sentiments, now that the memory of Soviet occupations is reconstructed as well. Secondly, the disappearance of the Jews, did *not* constitute a trauma for Polish society, either at the time or in the decades that followed, however abhorred were the means to achieve it.[5] If the Holocaust first figured prominently within the Communist canon of public commemoration, then to be appropriated as a Polish loss, none of this manipulatory work held much relevance for the public at large. It is only recently that Poland's opinion makers of various political persuasions, together with a group of concerned youth, began to speak of the fate of Polish Jewry as a *loss*. And this belated mourning, as it were, still preserves (with a few exceptions) the nontraumatic quality of being witness by clearly separating the "Final Solution" from the experience of the Poles. Defining the Holocaust as something that did not implicate the Poles themselves makes the event important, but not relevant.

That a community of memory cannot be artificially created by imposing an "objectively" traumatic meaning on events subjectively experienced otherwise is perhaps best illustrated by the vicissitudes of

German memory of the Nazi era. The "unmasterable past" is only unmasterable to those morally challenged by it, and feeling so challenged by no means reflects the actual "weight" of one's actions.[6] As scholars increasingly turn their attention to the role of specific sectors of society in the overall success of the Nazi project, it also becomes increasingly clear that remorse or even regret are rare among the direct participants. The unanticipated depth and scope of reaction to the American series *Holocaust*, shown on West German television in 1979,[7] was a sharp reminder of the failures of a long, concerted educational effort at exposing the Nazi crimes. And the popularity of *Heimat*, a sixteen-hour German series on memory of the past, produced in direct response to *Holocaust* and excluding any traces of Auschwitz from its vision of the past, is quite indicative of what the public would like privately to remember.[8]

At this point, it could be argued that perhaps expecting a community of memory to form around a *moral* trauma is expecting too much from ordinary humans. Indeed, it is often the victims of traumas who most immediately and most "naturally" bond together. And yet, even within the generally grim picture of normalizing Nazism, there are significant counterforces to reckon with. The children of the Nazis, both literally and metaphorically, often *did* ask questions. German filmmakers, writers, and artists did produce works that troubled the national conscience. The effort to reformulate German identity, especially as the West and East unite, has been challenged by those keen on not burying the past. A minority, yes, and quite unlike a community, the people of conscience cannot be altogether ignored.

The even more convincing evidence to the potential of moral trauma as a source of bonding comes from the United States. The experience of soldiers in Vietnam as it is transmitted and translated for the public by some of the most outspoken veterans cannot be reduced to its morally troubling dimension. Yet neither can it bypass the moral terrain, both in remembrance of actions in Vietnam and that of coming home. Based on the life story of one veteran and made into a widely popular film by another, the saga of the man "born on the Fourth of July" is a clear illustration of how the two moral questions combine in the merging public memory. The man was haunted by what he did in Vietnam; the film is haunting in its presentation of the return to a rat-infested veterans' hospital and to widespread hostility from the neighbours. It is true that the "healing of America" that many see as having begun with the unveiling of the Vietnam War Memorial in Washington is more about what Americans inflicted on each other rather than their actions in Vietnam, but one ought to consider here the other image superimposing itself on the memories of the war, the image of "boat people." With time, in other words, the moral charge of remembrance has not disappeared, it acquired a great deal more complexity. With time, too, it is the second generation which increasingly enters the community of memory while searching for its own ethical answers.

As memory of this century's other great trauma—the Soviet *gulag*—is gradually reconstructed, it becomes apparent that the communities of memory emerging from "there" are varied and often distanced from each other.[9] Being a Ukrainian, a Pole, a Jew, a Russian—all victims—was important during the life in the *gulag* and continues to be so in remembrance. Bonds of solidarity that cut across ethnic lines have not completely disappeared, but they have become exceptions to the general rule of identifying with one's kin, then and later. At the same time, writings from and about the *gulag* testify to the insidious dynamics of totalitarianism rather than further inspiring a sense of national belonging; remembrance is both a local project and a universal one, with clearly defined political aims. Those who came back from the *gulag*, then, are naturally reentering their old communities of memory, all the while testifying to what is now openly acknowledged as centrally relevant to the victim nations. In this way, the *gulag* experience finds its place within collective memory of already bounded and bonded ethnic communities. What still remains to be seen is how the moral challenge of the *gulag* and Soviet-style rule in general can find its place in those memories without radically disrupting the vision of unified civil society.

Such communities of memory bonded by traumatic experience do often become absorbed by the wider national or ethnic collectivity. In the process, their very presence might be enough to secure remembrance or to redefine collective identity. Much more likely, though, it is through a transition from unspoken bonding to outspoken (and frequently institu- tionalized) activity that the community of memory acquires public resonance. Many Holocaust survivors or Vietnam war veterans lead strictly private lives, coping alone with their memories. But others, especially as the years go by, find it essential to record their experience, to create memorial markers for those who had died, to talk to the young, to join groups or associations. In effect, they then create communities *tout court*, engaged mainly (but not exclusively) in the work of remembrance. Another form that this community involvement may take—and equally important from the point of view of contributing to public memory—is one of cooperation with established *local* organizations. If the spectacular success of veterans' efforts can be seen in the impact of the Wall in Washington, the less nationally visible initiatives count as well; the "small town America" is, after all, where healing may be needed the most.

Survivors of the Holocaust are in an unique position in this regard, since their local communities no longer exist. Faced with the impossibility of return, survivors would join in with others who had emigrated earlier from their towns and villages to create "Memorial Books." Over 500 of these books now exist, in North America, France, Argentina, and Israel. Recalling the life as well as death of Jewish communities across Eastern Europe, "Memorial Books" vary in their scholarly sophistication or historical scope; they all serve as memory markers, a substitute for the nearly nonexistent graves.[10]

Recently, with the greater hospitality to Western (Jewish) visitors throughout Eastern Europe, the work of remembrance has returned to its more traditional forms, always, though, on a scale unable to match the scope of destruction. Jewish graves are being found and restored, memorial plaques attached to what once were thriving communal centers, synagogues-turned-warehouses become historical landmarks. The sacred grounds, even if only in small proportion, are rendered sacred again. It remains to be seen, of course, whether such efforts translate into remembrance on the part of the *now* locals; they have already, though, helped in the grieving of the Jews themselves.[11]

If traumas pose a special challenge to remembrance—and create special bonds among those who were there—they are definitely not unique in their power to generate a community of memory. Indeed, what these tragic experiences share may be found in a variety of events devoid of the ultimate encounters with death and evil, but still carrying enough "formative force" to become the base for collective self-definition. There is the element of great adversity, both to the human spirit and human ingenuity; there are moral choices to be made, challenges to traditional ways, often fear of the unknown. There is, in short, the intensity of human drama in its many dimensions, the out-of-ordinariness of experience.

And it does appear that such are indeed characteristics of those historical events we have come to see as *generational* markers: great world wars, the Depression, 1960s.

Generations too are communities of memory, even though theirs may be a much more heterogeneous relation to the past, reflecting the diversity of individual experience of key events. Numerically larger than any of the survivor communities (indeed, often inclusive of those), generations sharing in formative memory are also not "phenomenologically separate" from others; however different their values and attitudes may become from those of people coming after, full empathy is a possibility.

Generations so understood, it should be stressed, are not just "age cohorts" sharing in the similar social circumstances at different stages of their lives. Rather, they are comprised of people whose age may vary widely, but who would all be strongly affected in their outlook by a particular time in history. Children who grew up in the communes are as much a part of the 1960s' generation as their then-young parents and not-so-young college professors who took the side of rebellious youth. With time, of course, what was once a formative experience may be superseded by another or rendered irrelevant by individual life choices; generations may grow, split up, shrink in size. For a community of memory in flux, as it were, generation is an anchor, not a trap for self-definition.

If traumatic, tragic experiences by their very nature engender a great deal of memory work, both on the part of those who were there and those concerned with securing remembrance, the formative drama that begets a generation may live on by sheer force of the effect it had on individual lives. This is not to say that public remembrance will not result—or not matter—but only that even without articulation, through commemorative ceremonies, for example, *private* memories acquire public relevance. People who grew up during the Depression do not ordinarily set up monuments to the hardships they had gone through. Rather, they tell stories, and perhaps even more importantly, act on their then-acquired view of life, work, and money.

Much has been written on the profound effect World War I had on European cultures and mores.[12] To see that effect as confined to public remembrance of the war itself would be to miss most of it. Precisely because it was such a formative time, memory of the war did not have to be directly evoked for it to remain relevant. The very strength of that memory lies in its multifaceted "translation" into discourse about present and future.

Generations, then, are not primarily communities of remembrance. Shared memories are shared reference points, often not actively attended to yet retaining their formative quality. Generations leave us more than records of their experience or monuments to their heroes. They leave changes in the cultural landscape.

Generations as communities of memory rarely become communities *tout court*. Their size, internal diversity and often great geographical spread, when added to the fact that the past informs but does not define individuals' lives, make "generational institutionalization" highly unlikely. When some form of group formation occurs, it would be on a much smaller than generational scale, often springing from a sense of camaraderie with people one became close to during the dramatic times. Veterans of specific army formations or underground units active in World War II did create an organizational framework for remembering. Civilians did not.

Within their local communities, though, members of the same generation may indeed become socially separate even when not organized. The notion of a "generation gap" aptly reflects what often happens when values and attitudes clash. And the fact that intrageneration communication is frequently a great deal easier points again to the importance of sharing tacit understandings of the past and present.

To complete this picture of communities of memory formed by individuals with not only common experience but a shared sense of its meaning and relevance, let us now consider the opposite end of the sociological scale, as it were. A great deal of our daily interaction takes place within various communities of memory allowing us the comfort of feeling at home with people we are with. And even when we are not actively attending to the shared memories, their very existence provides for a sense of belonging we all seem to need. Indeed, without the sharing of memories, it is difficult, if not impossible to conceive of social bonding, on whatever a scale.

If collective memory is understood as we understand it here, not as a collection of individual memories or some magically constructed reservoir of ideas and images, but rather as a socially articulated and socially maintained "reality of the past," then it also makes sense to look at the most basic and accessible means for memory articulation and maintenance—talk.[13] Family dinners and gatherings for special occasions are a prime time for the construction, reconstruction, and repair of familial memory; a guest who is a stranger, no matter how welcome would he be made to feel, ends up left out. And if that guest is not to remain a guest, he needs to patiently sit through the old stories until he too can be a part of the new ones. A new worker joining a company team will too be immediately treated to institutional tales, but cannot join the "community" until there be tales involving his own mishaps and successes.

These communities of memory often outlive the actual sharing of experience; one need only think of class reunions. Living separate lives, the once-friends may no longer share anything but their memories, and there are times when this proves insufficient to counter the differences of the present. Often enough, though, a brief exchange of favorite old stories brings back the bonds, however altered by the passage of time. Photographs, home movies and songs from the past all help in the process, as would a return to the original physical environment.

Class reunions or visits with friends from times long gone can be very disappointing, of course. Bonds of shared experience, when such experience *is* ordinary, are often fragile. People's priorities and ways of making sense of the past change, so that talking may become a confirmation of separation rather than a maintenance job. Not validated, individual memory recedes, if not disappears altogether.

Do such small and fragile communities of memory matter in the overall picture of the dynamics of remembrance? Would not their immersion in the ordinary, everyday happenings make them potentially irrelevant to the realm of public discourse? After all, families, school buddies or work colleagues rarely go public with their stories, unless they already are public with their lives. And yet, precisely because theirs are private memories, with high degree of significance for the everyday living, these memories can and often do preempt the publicly articulated ones.[14] In Germany, for example, it is very much on the home front that a positive, even nostalgic picture of the Nazi era could be preserved. At the very least and most common, the "reality of the past" constructed in the individual's immediate circles would be providing the key base line for the reception of, indeed, receptivity to the socially sanctioned offerings. At its strongest, the private maintenance of remembrance may directly counter the officially given version of the past; the now explosive "recovery of memory" in the once-Communist countries is but one testimony to how familial stories can successfully resist ideological encroachments.[15]

The significance of such small communities of memory is not limited, one should add, to the realm of recent, directly experienced past. Although stories told by participants and witnesses to the events may carry more vibrancy and detail, families especially are also actively preserving memories of times and people long gone. In Poland, for example, the longing for independence survived, despite all the official manipulation, largely because so many families could talk about and remember struggles going back to the nineteenth, if not the eighteenth century.

Added to such direct ways that the *contents* of privately constructed memory may have an impact on the receiving of public offerings should be now the more subtle and pervasive influences on the individual's value system in general. Just as the members of a generational group need not actively attend to their formative past for that past to "live on," families or friends too may act on the principles embedded in their shared stories without constantly re-telling them. And these principles ("do not trust the government" being but one example) contribute a great deal to how people attend to and interpret public discourse, that about the past included.

Not enough is empirically known about the dialectics of mediated, framed remembrance and that maintained in the relatively private spheres. And just as students of popular culture argue vehemently about its impact on people, it may take a long time before there develops an analytical agreement on the dynamics of collective memory. What the work already done shows is that neither "the past" nor remembrance of it can be deduced from public discourse alone. The "realities of the past" as they pertain to individuals are not carbon copies of publicly available accounts. They are often worked out within smaller and larger communities of memory, their shape and texture reflecting a complex mixture of history and biography. In other words, how people attend to the past, if at all, and how they make sense of it is very much grounded in their experience. At the same time, and allowing for this, the public framing of remembrance does matter. Beyond providing resources to work with, public discourse may validate (or discourage) particular ways of seeing the past.[16] It may also create an altogether new community of memory, where bonding extends well beyond individuals' own experience.

All the communities of memory we discussed so far are natural, in a sense that they come into existence through people's sharing in living through events as well as the telling. Collective memory, though, is not reducible to such immediacy of links with the past. Often, it is the telling itself, the ongoing articulation of the "reality of the past" that forms and informs a community. For that matter, the past so told need not be real at all to offer the basis for communal solidarity. All that is needed is active remembrance, communally shared and deemed important for the community's self-definition. Rituals and the structuring of a yearly cycle serve that function very well.

In both the Jewish and the Christian tradition, collective memory of the key "events" of religious significance is built into the observance of festivals, into the prayers, into the calendar itself. The Jews are indeed often referred to as a "people of memory,"[17] since virtually all of their holidays are commemorative ones, referring to events at very different historical distance in a unified yearly series of ritual (and stories). It was only in the nineteenth century that "Jewish history" as such became a legitimate subject of inquiry for Jews. And even at its most modern and secular, Jewish self-definition is heavily referenced by remembrance— of the Holocaust and the creation of the State of Israel.[18] Some of what is yearly commemorated did happen (for example, the destruction of Jerusalem Temple), some has to be accepted on faith by believers. But to its very core, this is a community of memory which has managed to survive for centuries because of it.

Both the perennial modern debate around the question of "who is a Jew?" and the varied answers offered by Jews reflecting on their identity point to an increasing importance of sharing in memory obligations, if not in memory itself. The displacement of religious observance from the center of the Jews' lives often results in granting remembrance an ever more sacred status. Seen in this light, the outrage felt by some Jews at other Jews' "betrayal" that follows breaking the community ranks (especially in North America) is perhaps the best indication of sentiments involved in what may appear as ideological squabbles. And the ease with which the past comes to be invoked as justification for problematic decisions in the present (especially in Israel) testifies to the continuing significance of memory for the community.

If the case of the Jews is perhaps the most dramatic evidence to the strengths of collective memory, it is also highly instructive as to the mythical structure needed when remembrance is to sustain a people. There is the "myth of the origin," something that anthropologists have uncovered in virtually all human societies. There are heroes, who provide the essential exemplars of core moral beliefs. There is the highly selective memory of outside forces affecting the people's fate. And, perhaps most importantly, there is the narrative of shared suffering, greatly strengthening the sense of moral obligation to the communal past.

Collective identity does not have to rest on a narrative of victimization, of course. The "glorious past," when such exists, carries its own appeal. Yet history supplies us with some very convincing examples of the rallying power inherent in a shared memory of oppression, power not matched by that of success stories. Indeed, for remembrance of victories and progress to be meaningful at all, it must contain its own "dark" reference points. A mixed narrative, then, is needed even under the best of circumstances.

If we look at this century's two most cruel regimes—Nazi Germany and Stalinist Russia—for all the differences between them, we may be struck by the parallels in their uses of publicly manufactured memory. At the very center, there are stories of extreme victimization: Germany's losses in World War I and the injustice of the Versailles Treaty,[19] the post-Revolutionary war in Russia and then, the Great War's tremendous hardships. Both employ the figure of a savior: Hitler and Stalin. Where they part is at the point of introducing elements of glory; for the Nazis, references to the mythical past structured the mythical future; in the Stalinist vision, the bright future had to hold on its ideological own. The key similarity, though, is in how these narratives actually worked in social practice. Beyond "true believers" who might have indeed adopted the whole package, ordinary men and women identified primarily with the victimization story, all the more so for the strong biographical connection.[20] There is a troubling lesson here, a lesson well learned by those mobilizing small and large communities for action: nothing may serve the purpose of solidarity better than living memory of suffering at the hands of. . . . And how this ". . . ." is filled depends more often than not on politically and ideologically driven choices, where mythmaking can be at its strongest; one need only to think of the Nazi image of the Jew.

Once the suffering recedes further into the past, beyond the immediate experience of community members, the need for active memory work clearly increases. But whether sustained by privately told stories or solely by public remembrance, the narrative of victimization has to be first plausible to the individuals called upon. That this is not always easily attainable, especially when the community of memory is being created anew, as it were, may best be seen in the history of large and international social movements in this century: the workers' and women's. Again, for all the differences between them—and for the great ideological diversity *within* both—they have shared the broad promise of liberation from oppression, and the considerable difficulties of making the promise appealing to their constituents. The challenge has been twofold; first, people need to accept that their lives are indeed defined by their being workers or women, and then, they need to adopt the narrative of oppression and liberation as their own. On both counts, individuals' loyalty to other, more natural communities may prevent their accommodation of the movement's claims. And on both counts, efforts must be made, through inquiring, writing, and telling, to provide the prospective members with varied and moving stories, exemplifying the struggle. Beyond that, there is the needed work on remembrance proper: the choice of rallying dates for ceremonial observance of the movement's values and goals, the attending to one's heroic figures, commemorating of key victories and defeats. (The appropriation of this symbolic activity by the "workers' state" should not obscure its more natural dynamics here.)

In neither case, producing a stock of shared memories is in and of itself sufficient to secure members' loyalty; the vision of liberation and equality carries its own heavy responsibility. Yet without an articulation of the past, first of oppression, then of the struggle, full identification with the movement would be impossible to achieve. That it is often so difficult to achieve, beyond the relatively small core of activists, need not reflect the weaknesses of the constructed narratives. Rather, it is reflective of the strengths inherent in the smaller, older, and personally relevant communities of memory.

Framing an experience as that of oppression is, of course, greatly helped if there already exists a shared sense of trauma or suffering. Indeed, when we think of the notion of "victimization," the two elements appear inseparable. A closer look, though, allows for recognition that two quite different dynamics of remembrance are at work here. Japanese Canadians, interned, relocated, and stripped of property during World War II, shared for many years a near silent memory of their suffering. It took the efforts of their children and grandchildren, imbued with the very

Canadian (and recent) ideas about citizens' rights, to define the war experience as one of injustice and government-sanctioned oppression, and to demand apology and retribution.[21] It is as if suffering itself survives as a visceral memory, while its explanation, still deeply felt, is more a result of ideological work, the work of framing remembrance in categories of victim/oppressor. For the people involved, what they went through is all too real, but it is also open to changes in definition.

We have already seen how such openness can be exploited for vicious political purposes (the Nazi idea of the Jew); we should perhaps accept that even in its benign forms, designating the oppressor carries exploitive potential. There is indeed only a fine line, often crossed in political arguments, between sombre remembrance of the victims and capitalizing on the emotional charge of memory for immediate communal returns. Across Central Europe and in the former Soviet Union, it might be impossible for some time to come to separate commemoration of the regimes' victims from the ongoing political manoeuvring. Memory of the Holocaust, for all its inherent resistance to simplification (as this is an event many see as defying explanation), has been used and is likely to continue being used to score smaller and larger political points. As morally troubling as this exploitation of human suffering is, it also attests to the awesome powers of memory in the maintenance of communal solidarity as well as spear-heading communal action.

If the memory of victimization can so well serve the cause of communal unity, it is not only because of its particular emotional strength. Structurally as well, the self-definition as a victim clearly marks the boundary between "us" and "them" in ways only matched by ties of kinship. To construct a sense of community, one almost inevitably needs the presence of the Other; the oppressor serves this role very well indeed. It is no coincidence that the radical segment of the feminist movement is the one most resembling a community *tout court*, for it is also the one clearly identifying men as the (enemy) Other. In many parts of the world, intensification of ethnic warfare follows a redrawing of boundaries according to narratives of victimization;[22] there the two bonding forces cross and combine in politically complex scenarios. It is certainly saddening, if not tragic, that we humans persist in acutely dividing "us" from "them"; for students of collective memory, it is also imperative that we understand the resources drawn upon in this process.

In most countries today, the state borders do *not* define the boundaries between "us" and "them." Ethnically and culturally homogeneous states are a rarity, and even when few minorities are present, regional divisions still matter. Nationalist dreams notwithstanding, the citizens' loyalty to the state cannot thus rely on their membership in a community of memory; indeed, such membership often poses a challenge to state unity. At the same time, without some form of a common historical narrative (together with all the patriotic symbolism it entails), the state cannot achieve legitimacy as a political entity.[23] Added to that is the challenge of accommodation to the historical shifts in the country's borders and thus also power and population. In the Western world, recent decades have further complicated the situation with the continuous influx of immigrants (and illegals) from Asia, Africa, South and Central America, all putting into question the established visions of society.

Drawing on the experience in Canada, a relatively young country, but also one where the increasing diversity translated into state policies of multiculturalism (back in 1971), can be instructive here.[24] Canadians, so it seems, have had a permanent "identity crisis." French Canadians, most of whom live in Quebec, have progressively moved toward a self-definition as "Québecois," a distinct society within both Canada and North America, bounded by language and history. English Canadians, on the other hand, tend to articulate their difference in terms of the Other—the United States—and in narratives of social values rather than historical experience. Often referred to as "two solitudes," English and French Canada struggle politically as well as symbolically to maintain a unified front.

The official policy of bilingualism, often challenged on both sides, was to reflect the idea of different-but-equal Canadians, or rather the presence of two founding peoples. But then, shortly after that vision was put into administrative practice, another one emerged—that of *multiculturalism*. Now all the ethnic groups within Canada were to be respected, if not encouraged, in their differences. Advocated as both a necessity (in face of increasingly non-European immigration) and a form of "enrichment program" for the country, multiculturalism gradually earned in political stature. At the end of the 1980s, the idea was indeed accepted by the majority of Canadians. Constitutional debates of that period showed, though, that the practice of multiculturalism may be another matter altogether. First, its incompatibility with the older French-plus-

English formula became rather apparent, especially in Quebec which was not yet ready to dilute its hard-won Frenchness. Then, more and more questions were publicly raised about the limits to tolerance, be it of bullfighting or of traditional Sikh garb. Finally, the policy came under much sharper scrutiny from social scientists, recognizing the immense conflict potential built into the vague definition of "cultural."

As long as multiculturalism appeared contained in colorful ethnic festivals and culinary delights of Toronto or Vancouver, the idea of "Canada" appeared safe. But when it began to be taken politically seriously by various ethnic communities of memory and translated into claims of historical justice, both vis-à-vis Canada and the old world Other (by Ukrainians and Jews, for example), the frail base for future Canadian unity emerged in sharp outline.

It is true that many of the ethnic groups in Canada today have had no contact with each other prior to their arrival there; when disputes arise, these are then rooted in cultural differences alone. But a significant portion of the "Canadian mosaic" is made up of peoples who did have (some still do) turbulent experience together, where mutual hostility and apprehension became interwoven in the fabric of their collective memories.[25] And if the vision of equality to which they are now asked to adhere provides a theoretical end to animosities, the encouragement to retain ethnic culture may be spelling the exact opposite. An unhyphenated Canadian historical narrative may simply prove too weak in competition with communal traditions (especially, once again, when these rest on a vision of victimization).

If Canada can be seen as an unique social laboratory for working out the balance between the useful and the damaging[26] collective memory, it is also an illuminating example of the more universal trends in the formation of communities of memory, away from strictly ethnic ties. Canada is a vast country, but like many smaller ones, it is a country of regions. Some of these regions are certified political entities, with considerable powers (the provinces), others retain separate character both physically, sociologically and symbolically (Northern Ontario, for example). Regional identity, as any dispute shows, is strong. It reflects differences in the landscape, way of life and, yes, the ethnic composition as well. As such, it has more of an everyday relevance to people. It is a heritage of manageable size, as it were. And the symbolic fabric of that regional heritage is much closer at hand than "Canadianism." Historical landmarks (which in the Canadian context means dating back fifty years or more) are now increasingly recognized as needing preservation; urban planners are asked to respect the original character of spaces. The days of unfettered growth appear to be gone. Artifacts from the past find their place in local museums—and living rooms. Local traditions are being revived, at times reinvented. The emphasis is on tangible reminders of the past and their integration into the rapidly changing present.[27] In short, in the wake of modernization, with all the accompanying uprootedness, there is a concerted effort to restore and maintain both local (of a town) and regional traditions. In the process, new inhabitants are welcome to share in—but not transform—the older community of memory.

Whether the Canadian experiment at accommodating the whole broad range of loyalties and cultural anchors succeeds, it is too early to tell. On the one hand, if we were to draw lessons from many centuries of European history, a locally based communal identity appears not only sustainable but also open to multiethnic membership. Not to idealize the picture, since tensions and conflicts along religious and ethnic lines were indeed common, the pre-1918 "middle Europe" in particular exemplifies how the attachments to geographically small and culturally mixed "home"—be it Vienna or Vilno—can be a viable option. On the other hand, though, what we have seen in many corners of Europe in recent years points to a tremendous rallying force of arguments for ethnic purity. The violence in ex-Yugoslavia, the disenfranchisement of minorities in the Baltic republics, and the calls for redrawing of borders issued by Hungarian nationalists are but some testimony to the fragility of local communal bonds. And the fact that so many of the advocates for a new order of solidarity evoke what might be called "racial" memories, often jointly with stories of victimization, sadly confirms our earlier observations as to the power inherent in such appeals. When seen from Sarajevo, the challenges facing Canadians obviously pale in comparison. Yet both here and there, and, one might add, in the United States as well as Western Europe, the stakes may be remarkably similar—and high. Will the peoples' sense of a shared past be used to create inclusive and manageable political entities? Or, will the varied communities of memory become exclusionary, strife generating, and ultimately irreconcilable detractors from any possibility of societal peace?

These are, admittedly, "big" questions. As students of the dynamics of collective memory, we may be best advised to stay with the smaller ones. The very complexity of the patterns we have found within the experience/community/identity nexus, the great variation in ways in which communities of memory are constructed and maintained, and finally, the different weight these processes carry in social and political life, all point to the need for scaling down the inquiry. And yet, it is those 'big' questions which remind us of the priorities on the analytical agenda. The bonds that collective memory can create as well as those it can destroy are more than a matter of definitions.

## Notes

1. In part, the reaction was guided by the very human fear of the unknown effects of radiation; see Robert Lifton, *Death in Life: Survivors of Hiroshima* (New York: Basic Books, 1968).
2. For a further discussion of this problematic, see Emanuel Tanay, "On Being a Survivor," in Alan L. Berger, ed., *Bearing Witness To The Holocaust 1939–1989* (Lewiston, N.Y.: The Edwin Mellen Press, 1991), 17-31.
3. See, especially, Alan L. Berger, "Bearing Witness: Second Generation Literature of the *Shoah*," in *Modern Judaism* 10, 1 (Feb. 1990):43-63.
4. A compelling account of this dynamic may be found in Lawrence L. Langer, *Holocaust Testimonies: The Ruins of Memory* (New Haven and London: Yale University Press, 1991).
5. On this point, see also Iwona Irwin-Zarecka, "Poland, After the Holocaust," in *Remembering for the Future: Jews and Christians During and After the Holocaust* (Oxford: Pergamon Press, 1988), 143-55.
6. See, for example, Peter Sichrovsky, *Born Guilty: Children of Nazi Families*, translated from German by Jean Steinberg (New York: Basic Books, 1988).
7. See Anson Rabinbach and Jack Zipes, eds., *Germans & Jews Since the Holocaust: The Changing Situation in West Germany* (New York: Holmes & Meier Publishers, 1986).
8. For a study of *Heimat* in the broader context of West German cinema, see Anton Kaes, *From Hitler to Heimat: The Return of History as Film* (Cambridge, Mass.: Harvard University Press, 1989).
9. The following section relies on materials found in several Polish periodicals. I am also indebted to John Jaworsky for sharing his findings on the national identification among prisoners of the *gulag*.
10. See Jack Kugelmass and Jonathan Boyarin, eds. and trans., *From a Ruined Garden: The Memorial Books of Polish Jewry* (New York: Schocken Books, 1983); Annette Wieviorka and Itzhok Niborski, *Les livres du souvenir: Mémoriaux juifs de Pologne* (Paris: Editions Gallimard/Julliard, 1983).
11. From my discussions with a number of survivors who had visited Poland in the last few years, often bringing along their children, it seems the very voyage has a sacred quality. This theme also appears in Jack Kugelmass, "The Rites of the Tribe: American Jewish Tourism in Poland," in Ivan Karp, Christine Mullen Kramer, and Steven D. Lavine, eds., *Museums and Communities: The Politics of Public Culture* (Washington: Smithsonian Institution Press, 1992).

12. See, especially, Paul Fussell, *The Great War and Modern Memory* (New York and London: Oxford University Press, 1975) and Modris Eksteins, *Rites of Spring: The Great War and the Birth of the Modern Age* (Toronto: Lester & Orpen Dennys, 1989).

13. For a good discussion of the dynamics of reminiscing, see Edward S. Casey, *Remembering: A Phenomenological Study* (Bloomington and Indianapolis: Indiana University Press, 1987).

14. Empirically rich studies of the private/public interplay may be found in Raphael Samuel and Paul Thompson, eds., *The Myths We Live By* (London and New York: Routledge, 1990).

15. Not all stories here are of success. See Alain Brossat, Sonia Combe, Jean-Yves Potel, Jean-Charles Szurek, eds., *A l'Est, la mémoire retrouvée* (Paris: Editions la Découverte, 1990).

16. For an interesting (autobiographical) analysis of the complexities at play, see Alain Finkielkraut, *Le Juif imaginaire* (Paris: Seuil, 1980).

17. See, especially, Yosef Hayim Yerushalmi, *Zakhor: Jewish History and Jewish Memory* (Seattle: University of Washington Press, 1982).

18. For a critical view, see Jacob Neusner, *Stranger at Home: "The Holocaust," Zionism and American Judaism* (Chicago: The University of Chicago Press, 1981).

19. For in-depth discussion see George L. Mosse, *Fallen Soldiers: Reshaping the Memory of the World Wars* (New York and Oxford: Oxford University Press, 1990).

20. See Bronislaw Baczko, *Les Imaginaires Sociaux: Mémoirs et espoirs collectifs* (Paris: Payot, 1984).

21. H. David Kirk, "Acculturation and Protest among Canadians and Americans of Japanese Ancestry: A Note on the 'Loyalty of Disloyalty,'" paper presented at CSAA meetings, Winnipeg, June 1986.

22. See Donald L. Horowitz, *Ethnic Groups in Conflict* (Los Angeles: University of California Press, 1985).

23. See, especially, Benedict Anderson, *Imagined Communities. Reflections on the Origin and Spread of Nationalism* (London and New York: Verso, 1983).

24. The following section draws on a senior seminar on multiculturalism, held in 1991/92; I thank my students for their valuable input. A research project in this area, although not carried on to completion, provided me with insights as to the "politics of science."

25. To take but one example: among the most recent immigrants who settled in Toronto, there are large numbers of Caribbean blacks, Southeast Asians, and Poles. For the latter, this is their first real exposure to people of different skin color (Poland being a racially homogeneous country). Yet when the same Poles encounter Toronto's Jews or Ukrainians, the past matters.

26. At stake, as well, is the very definition of "useful" versus "damaging"—a highly politicized terrain.

27. On this dynamic in the United States, see Michael Kammen, *Mystic Chords of Memory: The Transformation of Tradition in American Culture* (New York: Alfred A. Knopf, 1991).

# 4

# Conflicts

In its common usage, the expression "collective memory" suggests a consensus. And yet, the social construction of "realities of the past" is frequently a site of intense conflict and debate. Would this mean we are stuck with a concept that is analytically misleading so much of the time? I think not, as long as we recognize that the consensus implied in the name is the *ideal* that memory workers aspire to and willingly struggle for, especially under adverse circumstances. Collective memory is not a given, not a "natural" result of historical experience. It is a product of a great deal of work by large numbers of people, all securing (mostly) public articulation for the past. For this reason alone, we should not be surprised to see differences of perspective and opinion as well as sharp, principled disagreements. But of course there is more to the story. Collective memory is a precious resource, after all, for maintaining social bonds and claiming authority, for mobilizing action and legitimating it. Indeed, it is one of the most important symbolic resources we have, imbued as it often is with quasi-sacred meanings and capable of evoking very powerful emotions. If, in many social contexts, collective memory appears underemployed, as it were, this should not prevent us from acknowledging its potential force. And one of the best ways to appreciate what that force is, is to look closely at the dynamics of conflict.

In this book, I frequently treat debates about the past or about remembrance as especially rich reservoirs of data, with their high degree of articulation of different framing principles making for analytically easy access. Here, our task will be to go beyond this admittedly pragmatic approach as we raise questions about the texture of conflict itself. We would still be learning *from* instances of conflict, but this time, we are also interested in learning *about* them. And, in keeping with such a shift of focus, we would now be looking at memory-as-a-contested-terrain in many of its different forms, where sharply articulate debates occupy only a portion of the overall picture. The open, public and, one should add, recorded disagreements retain their utility value, but are now made to acquire specificity vis-à-vis other expressions of conflict.

In both social and analytical practice, the loud debates appear to function primarily as "tips of the iceberg." When protesters gather in front of the Royal Ontario Museum in Toronto, incensed by what they see as a racist portrayal of Africans, at issue is as much the exhibit itself as the long-felt oppression by the white society.[1] The public display becomes an *occasion* for speaking about problems well beyond memory. And the significance of the debate is not lost on the participants—or observers.

Why "Into the Heart of Africa" triggered such an intense controversy is an empirical question; aside from the qualities of the exhibit, we would need to know more about the people and institutions involved. There is no inevitability of conflict, I would argue, or no easy way to predict that this rather than that memory production will serve as a site for articulation of opposite views. At times, when the producers themselves frame their work as "controversial," we may somewhat safely assume that a debate would result; there are no guarantees, though. At times, it is the symbolic importance of the work that generates or at least intensifies the debate; the construction of the Vietnam War Memorial in Washington might be a case in point. But again, not all major memory markers are subject to such controversies; the Vietnam War Memorial in New York, to pursue our example, was built entirely on consensus.[2] The ability to capture public attention, especially in this media-saturated world, matters. And so does the availability of other channels for discussion of what are often very complex issues; under the Communist regimes, which did not look favorably, to say the least, at any questioning of the system, debates about an otherwise obscure historical novel would often serve as a substitute for the real thing.

To say that memory disputes happen when something hits a sensitive public nerve may be part of the explanation; however, most of the time, we only know this *after* the fact. The recent controversy over the symbolism at the site of Auschwitz is highly instructive here.[3] The key word is "recent," for while occasional criticisms have been voiced by Jewish observers over a long period of time,[4] it was only in 1987 that concerted, organized, institutional effort began, aiming to rectify the absence of Jewish memory at Auschwitz. The Polish side, especially the Catholic Church officials, were perhaps understandably baffled. Not only did they not appreciate what "Auschwitz" meant to Jews, at the more immediate level they simply could not comprehend why they were *now* taken to task. In other words, the raw nerve which was clearly struck by the presence of a convent and a large cross should have been so struck long ago, they reasoned. And indeed, "objectively speaking," the timing of the dispute remains a puzzle. It is very likely that what ultimately prompted the vocal reaction was the few Jewish activists who took this matter to be their high priority. What we are left with, analytically, is the troubling "human factor."

Because memory disputes implicate big issues and often high social as well as political stakes, when they are subjected to analytical scrutiny, the focus is on substantive matters at hand. To further our understanding of the dynamics of collective memory, it would also be important to explore their more "formal" qualities. If we cannot, with any degree of accuracy, predict the onset of disputes, we might be better equipped to account for their staying power. The work that goes into maintenance of conflict on the public agenda, the work of articulation through organiza-tion and media channels, these are perfectly amenable to sociological questioning.[5] And one of the advantages of posing such questions as who does what, where and when is that we may gain the much needed corrective as to the social significance of the dispute itself. There is no doubt, for example, that the issues of German identity and history addressed during the mid-1980s in a very public dispute among West German intellectuals were of key philosophical importance. And we can learn a great deal from these polemics, not only about each participant's position but more broadly about the predicaments facing German society as a whole.[6] Yet whether this dispute had any impact beyond the rather narrow circle of intellectuals, we do not know. It was conducted in the popular magazines, which would suggest some degree of relevance for the educated readers. A few years later, though, when the two Germanies united and the whole question of national identity returned, it was as if the earlier debates had left only weak traces. When confronted with the increasingly violent attacks against foreigners, with all their Nazi echoes, public opinion leaders would appeal for calm in a language of the nation's *reputation.* Mostly missing was the reflection on the now dual legacy of Hitler and Communism.[7]

It may well be that as students of public discourse, justifiably attracted to memory disputes as occasions for articulating ideas about the past, we are prone to see such articulation as more socially important than it actually is. The written work, after all, remains our most valuable guide to thoughts and feelings; we justifiably pay attention when we are given a chance to examine what would otherwise be hidden from us. And those writing the words clearly believe they matter. When controversy ensues, there is an ever greater sense that the writings matter; arguments, responses, claims, counterclaims, when printed for many to read, amplify this perception with each new item appearing. The issues in dispute become more and more complex, the analysis becomes more and more challenging. It is natural then to feel that the task is done once the difficult interpretive procedure is over, once we have explicated the various positions and connected them to larger philosophical or ideological patterns. It is not natural, I would suggest, then to question the relevance of the exercise. And yet question we must, if what we aim to understand are the *dynamics* of collective memory. The public disputes, more often than not, challenge the established wisdom, by critically exposing it as well as crystallizing the alternatives. As such, they have the potential to *change* the existing ways of remembrance; indeed, changing people's views is often an explicit goal of the participants themselves. An analysis that stays strictly within the realm of ideas can tell us what is being disturbed and how, but it cannot gauge the extent of change. For this, we need to turn our attention to the wider social context in which the debate is taking place. We also might have to wait and reexamine the state of affairs a year or two or more after the public confrontation. All along the way, we would be looking for signs of either a shift in the ways of remembrance or of the more likely continuing if now diffused presence of conflict. In short, although memory disputes occur within a limited span of time, the analysis of their significance calls for a longitudinal, historical approach.

Such an approach is ever more necessary when the conflict itself is of a long duration. Just as we learn the most about ways of remembrance from the empirically grounded "histories of memory," we cannot understand the dynamics of conflict without the "thick descriptions" offered by the case studies. At the current stage of analytical endeavors, it is too early to formulate many highly general rules. Rather, what I will aim for in the remainder of this chapter is a set of general *questions*, a set of concerns and issues much deserving of further exploration.

It is useful to remind ourselves first that the analysis of memory conflicts is not just, or primarily, of academic interest. In the fall of 1991, when I am writing these lines, the bloodshed in Yugoslavia, the modest beginnings of a peace process in the Middle East, the great uncertainties as to the future of what once was the Soviet Union, the strengthening of neo-Nazi voices in Germany, all in their own way force a reminder on the scholarly community. I am not an idealistic believer in the power of academic words; at the same time, though, I do feel that social scientists in particular ought to do better in terms of illuminating the tremendous force inherent in what we politely call "historical grievances." Reading the enlightened appeals to reason, I cannot help but think that we are again missing something, that as long as we do not alter our models of human action to allow for what Serbs and Croats were actually doing, we are destined for comfortable insignificance.

Not all conflicts about the past result in people's killing each other, of course. But that considerable numbers do ought to at least alert us to the possibility, to the very real potential for violence. Nor do historical grievances exhaust the list of disagreements between the warring sides. But, again, the fact that they often figure so prominently on such lists demands serious recognition, and an inquiry going beyond the comforting notion of ideological smokescreens. All too often, I think, we are ready to see talk about the past or appeals to memory of compatriots as useful propaganda techniques, as something that political activists cynically apply to motivate "the masses." I am sure some are doing just that, yet the very effectiveness of such strategies points to their resonating with deeply felt emotions. It is this emotional intensity that so clearly varies in degree when we look at different memory conflicts, that  demands foremost analytical attention. What is it, we need to ask, that makes people *care* so much about "their" past?

I am putting quotation marks around the possessive here to signal one of the key qualities collective memory appears to acquire in conflict situations—the identification of communal boundaries with distinct visions of the shared past. For Serbs and Croats, the most divisive period is that of World War II and its aftermath; the two sides have radically different, if not opposite ways of recounting the events. As I listened to

Polish and Jewish voices describing life during the 1918–1939 period, both ordinary people and historians would be painting such different portraits of the times that the very idea of a shared past seemed almost absurd. And yet it is precisely because a certain historical terrain was coinhabited that most memory conflicts arise in the first place. (The dividing lines need not be ethnic or national, one should stress at this point. In France, they might be ideological; in the United States, often regional in nature.)

What this implies is that analytically as well it is wise to look for the sources of the conflict and the roots of its emotional intensity in the historical experience itself. The "grievances" are usually not about times of prosperity, peace, and happiness. Indeed, many of the continuing conflicts about the past implicate periods of intense social and political upheaval, if not war. The Turks refusing to acknowledge genocide of the Armenians, the French struggling with the memory of the Vichy period, the peoples in the former Soviet empire reckoning with the Communist legacy—these are but a few examples of long-term disputes originating in the past, however much propelled on or off public agenda by the vicissitudes of the present.

The question such historical dependency raises, though, is one of its explanatory power. Yes, knowing more about the conflict at source helps us to appreciate the depth of emotions involved. But no, it cannot alone account for persisting relevance of that past. For each example of struggles that are remembered, we could, after all, cite a counterexample of struggles long forgotten. This is one reason for my stressing the need for more empirical studies, as they could shed some inductive light on the question. My educated guess is that we would find the persistence of conflict to be highly context-specific in cultural, social, and political terms.

Before more case histories are written, though, it is both possible and necessary to refine our analytical tools. Neither "conflict" nor "persistence" of it are homogeneous phenomena. As the discussion of memory disputes already suggests, conflicts manifest themselves in many different ways, calling upon us to use different methods for gathering data as well as different explanatory strategies.

To begin, some conflicts are more manifest than others, in the sense of acquiring *public* articulation. Where the public sphere is tightly controlled by the state, as was the case in the pre-Gorbachev Soviet

Union, the fabrication of consensus about the past created a barrier difficult for researchers to penetrate. We now know that retained under the allowed surface were many traditional ethnic grievances, for this is what has emerged with the policy of *glasnost*. But to have known that during the previous era, with virtually no access to the people themselves, would have been hard indeed.

While totalitarian states are an extreme case of silencing the private sphere, theirs is not an unique monopoly on public discourse. In democratic societies we also find large sectors of the population not having a voice in the public forum. If the recent efforts at "empowerment" of marginal groups are any indication, these groups would often harbor memories sharply at odds with the established canons. *Now* manifest, the conflicts are being exposed and studied. But once again, their presence is not new and this ought to alert us to the need for paying more attention to the publicly invisible.

At the other end of the analytical spectrum are conflicts firmly entrenched within both the "infrastructure" of collective memory and the cycles of communal remembrance. In France, for example, the public sphere provides room for commemorating Petain, the head of the Vichy government, as well as the heroes of the resistance; there are books extolling the virtues of each Republic and books attacking them; there are parades celebrating storming of the Bastille and there are the splendors of Versailles. If at different times one perspective on the past may be privileged over another, there does not seem to occur any complete disappearance of the many cleavages that have been accumulating over decades, if not centuries.[8] In a situation such as this one, an analyst might be faced with an overabundance of material and the exercising of caution would mean the careful weighing of what is or is not socially important.

Tracing the vicissitudes of conflict over time implicates primarily questions about such public articulation—its forms, channels, intensity, or periodic disappearances. But it also—and rather prominently at that— implicates questions about time passage itself. The degree of experiential distance from the events under dispute has a strong bearing on the meaning and the relevance these events would carry for people. We now know, for example, that challenges to the prevailing silences on the issues of moral responsibility and the Holocaust came about—in West Germany, in France, in Poland—when the *children* of those directly involved were growing up. For a troubling past to become an openly contested terrain, it might indeed be necessary that a certain distance be first established. On the other hand, that past is still not too far removed from the lived experience; the children questioned their parents, metaphorically, if not literally, speaking. Time positioning such as this one—between individual memory and full detachment—is a likely source for efforts to reevaluate the past, efforts with strong potential for generating conflict.

On the other hand, the passage of time is an important factor to consider when looking at those conflicts where an experiential connection no longer exists. Just as collective memory does not follow any chronological order of priorities, its contested elements may too be found close to or far indeed from the present. And just as consensual remembrance rests on specific framing of the significance of the past, for a conflict to persist or emerge, there must exist a particular understanding of its relevance. What makes conflicts over a past long gone especially interesting to analysts is exactly this need for defining and redefining relevance. Once outside the experiential realm, the past does not naturally generate passions of the kind we encounter in memory disputes. Thus, to come back to our earlier question of what makes people *care* so deeply about their past, it is very much a question about the social construction of feelings.

Within the restricted terrain of direct personal experience, we may expect that actual conflicts would carry on into the realm of collective memory, or that emotions at source would be informing those to emerge later. Even then, a public intervention into those private feelings can reshape them, or at the least affect their impact. For example, as one watched the developments in Czechoslovakia after the fall of the Communist regime in 1989, with President Havel first appealing for forgiveness for all involved in the apparatus of oppression and then, in October of 1991 acquiescing to sign a new law which sets a complex system of punishments in place, it was not hard to imagine the effect of such a public licence on private hatreds.[9] Havel was clearly in a predicament there, opposed to any retribution, yet required to respond to pressures from below, his initial attempts at emotional management of conflict proving quite unsuccessful.

The jury, in Prague and elsewhere in the post-Communist world, is still out as to which of the private feelings would be in the end allowed to shape public memories of the regime. What is already apparent, though, is the complexity of the picture. Also, as the ranks of once united oppositionists split—as most notably occurred within Poland's Solidarity movement—the neat division into "us" and "them" that defined the lines of memory conflicts along with all others gives way to a very untidy situation indeed. And the now open channels for public debate, together with the challenges of electoral politics, almost guarantee that social engineering of people's emotional stance towards their recent past continue.

I do not wish to suggest that individual experience is irrelevant to this process, nor that feelings could be created by public declaration only. There *are* limits to what people would accept as the definition of what just happened to them. I am suggesting that the most immediate links to the past, the most deeply felt personal memories, become subject to public framing and reframing just as much as those distant and detached. The fate of collective memory is not sealed at source.

With the "realities of the past" far removed from any personal experience, we are far more likely to question the maintenance mechanisms of conflict. When dealing with cases of social turmoil, we expect it to affect people for some years to come; indeed, it is these instances of consensus emerging on the ruins of conflict that would be most puzzling us. But to understand why people still care about the American Civil War or the French Revolution—or, to take the more recent example, about Christopher Columbus—we can no longer draw on the direct experiential connections. In the case of debates around Columbus's legacy, we cannot even draw on the kind of linkage I suggested earlier, that is to a significant conflict in the past, at least in the sense of events that Columbus himself would have participated in. Does it mean that historical experience does not mean anything? Are the struggles over memory simply a reflection of the current issues and priorities, with history serving as a convenient substitute (or additional) ground for fighting contemporary battles?

It might be tempting indeed to answer "yes" here, to see the past as rich but raw material used to express, justify or defeat particular ideological positions. Such an approach, though, begs the question of why is it the past, or rather the construction site of different "realities of the past" that is so used.

In keeping with my advocacy of an empirically grounded approach, I would argue that the best way to answer this question is to look at how it is answered in social practice. What claims being made about the pasts long gone allow them to acquire (or retain) significance in contemporary conflicts? The key word here is "in," for it is rare indeed that a conflict about the past be only about the past. If vocal public disputes feature as "tips of the iceberg," the more diffuse debates are equally immersed in larger issues, concerns well beyond those with historical accuracy. And it is these larger issues, or the matters at stake in memory conflicts, that would be mostly responsible for the involvement and the intensity of particular feelings. Evoking national pride is quite different from tacit recognition of ideological principles, and defending the sacred is quite different from defining a political agenda. The matters at stake, in other words, frame how and how much people care.

Let me reemphasize at this point that such framing of emotions applies both to events within the living memory of the participants as well as those distant in time; the distinction itself is obviously subject to continuing change due to the passage of time. If I am focusing here more on strategies allowing the pasts long gone to retain significance, it is only because those are more analytically visible, as it were, not as clouded by the "natural" feelings stemming from people's experience. But as the example of Czechoslovakia aimed to suggest, questioning such emotional framing of the recent past is a path very much worth pursuing.

When exploring the processes of sustaining memory conflicts, it is also useful to remind ourselves that our subject is indeed *conflict*. People come to care a great deal about their past in a whole variety of contexts and situations; some of these, like memory projects are discussed elsewhere in the book. But what concerns us here is a rather different quality of emotional involvement, inherent in the very presence of conflict. At its most analytically basic level, the caring for the past is always coupled here with having someone challenge your vision of it. How such challenges are socially defined may indeed hold the keys to the dynamic of conflict itself; at the very least, it informs the issues which matter.

Whether or not a memory conflict acquires a powerful presence on the public agenda is not simply reflective of the importance of issues at stake. As I suggested earlier, the vicissitudes of conflict would be very context-specific, so that our knowledge of its significance would serve as a piece in the whole puzzle.[10] At the same time, though, it is an indispensable piece of knowledge, something we need especially urgently when trying to predict (and prevent) outbursts of violence. All other things being equal, some challenges to one's vision of the past represent more of a threat than others and thus carry the potential for defense going beyond verbal arguments. Even when not actually resorting to arms, people who feel threatened do not make good candidates for civic cooperation with those who pose that threat.

At a first glance, we seem to have moved far away indeed from our initial questioning of the debates surrounding the commemoration of 1492. And yet, some reports from South America already suggest (a year early) the very real possibility of violent protest on the part of Indian activists. What to the readers of the *New York Times* may be an intellectually challenging exercise resonates rather differently among victim groups. Their grievances are not solely historical, of course, but there is a sense of continuity between what is defined as "cultural genocide" in the past and the present lack of repentance. To celebrate Columbus becomes a highly symbolically charged act of denial of responsibility, a threat to the basic sense of justice.[11]

That the ideal of justice figures so prominently in memory conflicts of grave intensity is not coincidental. When killings, expulsion, oppression go unacknowledged, when these bring rewards rather than punishments, when those responsible are allowed the comforts of forgetting, the wounds remain open. The passing of time does not heal these wounds; the fact that people who had committed the crimes are long dead does not seem to matter. If the historical moral accounts have never been settled, in other words, time collapses.

Commentators often express surprise that people in Ireland still care about what happened in the twelfth century, or that Jews persist in holding the Ukrainians responsible for the pogroms of the seventeenth, or that American blacks continue to speak of slavery in language of the lived experience. It is as if the past, once gone long enough, should somehow become neutral. Had justice been perceived to have been rendered, this would be indeed a reasonable expectation. But when it is not, the length of time which has passed may be in fact compounding rather than lessening the grievance.

In the memory conflict I studied closely, that between Poles and Jews over the issue of responsibility for the fate of Polish Jews during the Holocaust, I also found expressions of surprise. This time, it was not about the "still caring" factor; it would be too early for that. But many Polish observers were deeply upset that Jews appeared to care more about the wrongs committed by Poles than those by the Nazis themselves.

There was outrage over such blatant reversal of moral priorities. Missing until very recently was any recognition that the persistent denial of responsibility on the part of the Poles, especially when contrasted with the considerable efforts at moral accounting in West Germany, was the key to the Jews' reaction.

The lesson here is an important one; it is not the "absolute weight" of historically inflicted pain which matters. Rather, it is how people *perceive* the consequences, mostly in terms of justice rendered but also justice attempted. The implication, at the level of social practice in the present (and the future), is that whenever possible, we should not allow moral wrongs, on a large as well as small scale, to go publicly unnoticed. When not confronted, discussed if not acted upon, the wounds do not heal, just deepen.[12]

Analytically, this concern translates into the need for more indepth studies and thus understanding of the types of discursive practice which would help conflict resolution. Not all "talk" serves the cause, not all "silences" impede it. The settling of moral accounts is not a purely symbolic or discursive matter, of course. Native Canadians, for example, while speaking in rather conciliatory terms about the legacy of European conquest, have in 1991 demanded no less than self-government. A redistribution of power, territorial concessions, financial retributions, all can and do enter the morally set agendas. To some people, these are the matters that count, not the symbolic gestures of one kind or another. And yet, as one hears of another bomb attack on a Turkish official, the Armenian activists behind it call for a simple admission of guilt, nothing more. We may abhor the tactics, but we also ought to recognize that, in this case at least, the symbolic justice is the first priority.

When studying historical grievances in general, we would be well advised not to impose our sense of priorities on the subject at hand. Too often, the conflicts themselves are mired in misunderstanding of what people care about, misperceptions as to the nature of particular "group interests." An inquiry into strategies of conflict resolution can easily turn into ineffective advocacy, unless we bring such understandings and misunderstandings to the surface. In short, it is the participants' definitions of justice (and injustice) which count, not ours.

All this is not to say that as scholars we remain *morally* neutral; the grievances we study compel moral judgments and we should be aware of the ones we make. Rather, I am calling for a critical neutrality of a different kind, one which makes us more sensitive to the ways moral accounting actually proceeds.[13] We have a great deal to learn here and deciding beforehand that struggles for historical justice are "really about X" (as defined by our favorite theory) would be very counterproductive.

So far, we have been looking at grievances almost exclusively from the perspective of the victimized groups, those who seek justice. To have a fuller understanding of the dynamics of memory conflict, we now need to raise some questions about the other side, those called upon to respond. The emotional temperature, as it were, of a conflict is a product of *both* sides' involvement; the defining of matters at stake, while more explicit on the part of the victims, is not their exclusive property. And indeed, if we see the challenge to one's vision of the past as a key element in conflict situations, it is crucial to explore the meanings such challenges acquire.

Struggles for historical justice are not symmetrical in the sense that both sides see them as such. Those Americans (or Italians, Spanish, Portuguese) who defend the idea of celebrating the memory of Columbus and his accomplishments do not necessarily deny (nor need to) that the Native Americans had suffered greatly. What they are defending is Columbus's "good name" and, by extension, the good name of Western civilization. The debates, coming as they do after some years of heated discussions about America's cultural heritage, link directly to those larger issues of collective identity. To commemorate 1492 solely as the beginning of genocide is to deny any worth to American society, to its cherished values and myths. It is a threat to the core of the collective self. Even those who see 1992 as an opportunity to reevaluate the past, to engage in moral accounting—in the name of justice—cannot bypass that issue; in their appeals, America emerges as strong and healthy enough to be able to confront the dark chapters in its history. Thus the challenge to America's sense of self-worth can be made to testify to it, provided serious memory work is done. In that way, the conflict over Columbus's legacy could ultimately be accommodated within the existing structures of sensibility.

In this particular case, the potential for accommodation is high, I believe, primarily because American public discourse has traditionally allowed considerable room for self-criticism. It is also important that as the legacy of 1492 is being debated, the voices heard come from rather diverse quarters and not just a two bounded communities. The visions of the past brought forward are not homogeneous either, rather, they split and crack in complex, often ideologically unpredictable ways. Indeed, a student of this conflict, ten years from now, will be facing quite a task of identifying its politics.

In societies where the "national honor" has greater symbolic potency, and where self-criticism might not be a common or valued practice, we would expect the challenge represented by historical grievances not to be as amenable to accommodation, if at all. We can also expect the rhetoric of conflict there to be much more explicitly about collective self-worth and reputation. In other words, the defining of calls for justice as threats, usually from outside, to the communal well-being and dignity is likely to be out in the open, used as the rallying points for social support in ways rarely encountered on the American scene. This was a pattern I observed in Poland, where mentions of the troubling record of antisemitism would be greeted with personal attacks on the messengers for "smearing the country's good name." A similar dynamic operated in Austria a few years ago, when the international outcry about Kurt Waldheim's past was defined as an attack on Austria's reputation, effectively preventing internal debates. In Japan, the strong reluctance to allow public discussion of its record of atrocities is also presented as a matter of national honor. The boundaries between "us" and "them" are clearly drawn, with critics from within often identified with outside forces, or directly accused of betraying the national community.[14]

When honor and self-worth are at stake, the potential for conflict resolution may itself lie with the ways these are understood. It is possible to redefine national honor so as to accommodate a critical reevaluation of the past. In Poland, for example, several intellectuals have been arguing in recent years about exposing the morally problematic chapters in the country's history in the name of a healthy collective identity; to speak of antisemitism or the cruel treatment of Germans and Ukrainians in the aftermath of World War II would thus now be seen as an honorable task, as something not only ethically correct but politically useful as well. For Poland to have good relations with its neighbours, the reasoning goes, and to retain international respect, it must deal honestly with the past, however much it hurts. So far, the advocates of self-critical moral accounting remain a minority, but as the ideological divisions within society multiply, their voices gain more public resonance. In effect, when different stances towards the past become parts of political "packages," the conflicting visions of history acquire new legitimacy. The "us" and "them" is no longer about patriots and outside intruders; the cleavages move within the national community.

What is also interesting in the three cases of evoking national honor we mentioned here is that Poland, Austria, and Japan present themselves as *victims* of history under dispute. The challenge of assuming responsibility for past wrongdoings, coming from another victimized group, is thus doubly problematic. It calls for a total stepping out from one's identity, no less. At stake is no longer "only" self-worth, but the basic organizing structure of collective memory, at least of the contested past. Where victimization defines a much longer "stretch" of self-definition— as it did in Poland, with German and Soviet occupation in 1939–45 connected on one side to more than a century of partitions and struggles against Russia, Prussia, and Austro-Hungary, and on the other side to the imposition of the Communist rule—the resistance to any challenge of the idea is ever greater. The evocation of honor and betrayal is not a rhetorical strategy there, it reflects deeply felt emotions. And the gradual displacement of that language by the vocabulary of ideological competition may be a reflection of newly discovered strengths as an agent in history.

When we look at memory conflicts, as I suggested earlier, we ought to treat their rhetoric seriously. Explicit references to national honor on the one hand and to being victimized on the other tell us a great deal about the basic moral obligations brought into play. Conflicts about the past divide people and often bond the opposing sides; it is thus important to know of previously existing communal boundaries. Are those reinforced or redrawn by the memory conflict? How do definitions of "us" and "them" emerge and possibly shift? Would ideologically grounded visions of the past be as firmly defended as those expressing allegiance to one's family and kin?

To pursue this line of inquiry is not an easy matter; what one is attempting to "measure," in effect, is the degree of sacredness of memories. If some conflicts about the past are benign, as it were, an expected feature of sociopolitical life, other disputes engender hatred, if not violence. How close a particular confrontation comes to one or the other end of this continuum largely depends, I think, on the obligation one feels to the contested memory. It is true, as we observed here, that the "caring for one's past" is a social construct. But it is also true that the process implicates emotions which are already, experientially, there.

Caring for one's kin—and for their memory—is a strong base to build upon, in a way that political affiliations might not be. And "kin" is indeed a pervasive image used to bond people, whether or not they are actually blood related. It is this sense of kinship, of the past as direct ancestry, that may account for particular potency of some memory conflicts—and the relatively benign nature of others.

Once again, we can learn a great deal about this implicit dynamic from instances of its public articulation, in this case, from conflicts about the very nature of moral obligation to memory. In North America, for example, there is now an ongoing debate between Native Canadian and Native American leaders and professional archaeologists (together with museum curators) as to the "proper" treatment of ancient Native remains.[15] What these Native cultures define as sacred (in the strongest sense of the term), those espousing the Western scientific ethos see as valuable data. What one side defines as ancestors (in the broadest sense of the term), the other treats as universal property. Contested here is not so much a vision of history as the basic moral obligations to guide the work of remembrance.

Another area of inquiry that could serve to illuminate the differences between ideologically grounded memory conflicts and those implicating the-past-as-sacred is the still much to be explored history of dissidence in the countries under Communist rule. We know that, generally speaking, the state-imposed official version of the national past had been a direct assault on memories preserved by tradition and private tellings. We also know that even under the most adverse of circumstances, certain courageous people persisted in keeping forbidden records—or attending to forbidden graves. Finally, we are beginning to appreciate the scope and variety of strategies applied to smuggle oppositional memories into the public sphere, from writing and reading "between the lines" to imaginative uses of literary classics. To trace the choices made when defending "historical truth," especially when those choices translated into potentially harsh punishment by the regime, would be to gain a firmer understanding of different ways of caring about collective memory. There are some valuable lessons to be learned here about what is and what is not perceived as sacred.

The risks taken by individuals struggling against the Communist regime's assault on their memory were not uniformly high, of course; much depended on the sociopolitical situation at the time as well as the nature of counterremembrance involved. Telling stories among family and friends—perhaps the most effective method of preserving the unofficial narratives—carried less risk than working to secure public record through writing; poets in the Soviet Union of the 1970s faced the *gulag* for composing the forbidden lines, while a filmmaker in Poland at that time would only see his "wrong" work put in a Party vault. Recognizing those differences is important, "risk" being a context-specific category. When retracing the priorities set for oppositional memory work, we would also need to factor in the difficulties of access to resources. In the Soviet Union, unapproved typewriters were illegal for a very long time, with paper in a chronic short supply; in the late 1970s, the Polish authorities allowed private import of video recorders. Clearly, what people could and could not practically do had an impact on their choices.

To assess the nature of moral obligations involved, it would be especially important—and methodologically challenging—to locate the many private expressions of oppositional memory. The yearly pilgrimage to an unmarked grave of those killed by Security Forces, for example, speaks of the sacredness of that memory in a way a scholarly article in *samizdat* could not.

The vicissitudes of conflict between the state and civil society under Communist regimes may be unique for the sharp inequality of power and resources. Yet what they illuminate especially well is an universal dynamic of *investment*. Caring about one's past, or at least caring enough to defend it against challenges, requires the individual to invest in that memory, intellectually, emotionally as well as in more pragmatic ways. When we pose the question of what is at stake in disputes over the past, we would thus also be interested in the nature of such private engagements. Even debates that appear as purely intellectual exercises can—and often do—acquire moral dimension; being "right" or "wrong" about the meaning of history is both a cognitive and an ethical category. People on the opposing sides of a dispute judge each other in those terms; as the words used are so frequently the same, it is important for analysts to appreciate their separate realms of reference.

In the context of brief and general reflection on the dynamics of memory conflicts, it would be impossible to give justice to the full variety of issues, facts, figures, interpretations and "lessons of history" which become subject to debates. As the many examples mentioned throughout the book indicate, virtually all aspects of remembrance are open to dispute, both during the construction of collective memory and its subsequent uses, revisions, dismantlings. Conflicts are not departures from the norm, in so far as they occur frequently and commonly. But they are special. For analysts, they offer a wealth of data, making the invisible ideas and feelings appear in highly articulate forms. For the participants, investing in their "realities of the past" is also qualitatively distinct from the more passive, if not indifferent modes of remembrance. The challenge, as I argued here, is better to understand the distinctiveness of memory conflicts and especially their potential to destroy human trust if not human lives.

## Notes

1. Discussions with Harriet and Andrew Lyons, anthropologists who studied this controversy, have been of great help to me.
2. Judith Balfe, unpublished paper.
3. I am relying here on my own analysis of statements found in the Polish press, and especially those in the lay Catholic weekly *Tygodnik Powszechny*. See also Carol Rittner and John K. Roth, eds., *Memory Offended: The Auschwitz Convent Controversy* (New York: Praeger, 1991).
4. See, for example, Pierre Vidal-Naquet, *Les Juifs, la mémoire et le présent* (Paris: Maspero, 1981).
5. A case in point is Norma Field, *In the Realm of a Dying Emperor: A Portrait of Japan at Century's End* (New York: Pantheon Books, 1991).
6. See, especially, Charles S. Maier, *The Unmasterable Past: History, Holocaust, and German National Identity* (Cambridge, Mass.: Harvard University Press, 1988).
7. Brigitte Young, presentation on the situation in Germany, Wilfrid Laurier University, November 1992.
8. See Henri Rousso, *The Vichy Syndrome. History and Memory in France since 1944*, translated by Arthur Goldhammer (Cambridge, Mass.: Harvard University Press, 1991).
9. In Poland, efforts to put a similar law into place resulted in a change of government in June 1992; as of March 1993, three new proposals are still hotly debated. And, in a truly bizarre twist, it is President Walesa himself who has been seeking an official confirmation that he did not work as a Communist secret agent. The stakes, in short, are very high.
10. For a study of "ethnic politics" exemplifying this approach, see Harold Troper and Morton Weinfeld, *Old Wounds: Jews, Ukrainians and the Hunt for Nazi War Criminals in Canada* (Markham, Ontario: Viking, 1988).
11. Implicity recognizing this principle, the government of Canada did forbid any offical festivities in 1992.
12. It appears that in 1992, South African public debates on the future of their past centered on exactly this issue.
13. The discussion of Spain during the Civil War in Bruce Lincoln, *Discourse and the Construction of Society. Comparative Studies of Myth, Ritual, and Classification*

(New York and Oxford: Oxford University Press, 1989) exemplifies both the challenges and the high returns of this approach.

14. See, especially, Norma Field, *In the Realm of a Dying Emperor: A Portrait of Japan at Century's End* (New York: Pantheon Books, 1991).

15. I thank Ron Grimes for first bringing this issue to my attention. For more discussion, see Ivan Karp and Steven D. Lavine, eds., *Exhibiting Cultures. The Poetics and Politics of Museum Display* (Washington: Smithsonian Institution Press, 1991).

# 5

# Presence of the Past

How relevant is the past? *politically* How much public presence should it have? How much presence does it have? When posed in such broad terms, these questions may well be unanswerable. Yet they are also very basic to any understanding of the dynamics of collective memory. Indeed, if often implicitly, concerns with the presence of the past are at the core of these reflections. In this chapter, I would like to give them the more explicit attention they deserve.

One of the most analytically challenging issues here is that of *selection*. If the terrain of collective memory is vast and varied, it is also structured. To uncover some of the principles at work in this structuring of remembrance, we may have to first scale down the inquiry, though. Recognizing just how complex the processes are that account for presence of the past at the level of society-at-large, let us then begin with questions about smaller units. What aspects of the past do families, friends, colleagues, attend to?

Many a familial or institutional tale serves primarily as a warning and a lesson. When I was growing up, for example, a story of my grandfather's brother who managed to lose all of his extensive properties in gambling was a grand and colorful piece of family lore. Somewhat less impressive, but used for similar purpose were stories of my own bad behavior as a small child; these, no longer directly relevant to my troubles as a teenager, acquired the anticipatory quality of guidelines for parenthood. When a new employee enters a work setting, much of his "learning the ropes" relies on careful listening to the warning tales of past mishaps. The experiences framed into those useful stories need not be particularly traumatic; indeed, remembrance of traumas follows a very different logic. Their appeal rests on the clarity of moral as well as pragmatic lines,

87

for not only is "good" separated from "bad" but also the consequences of action are well defined. Hypothetically, fictional accounts could work just as well here, and some indeed do.[1] But the historical reality behind the tale adds greatly to its force, anchoring the tale, as it were, in familiar surroundings. Not all bosses are created equal, so that getting to know this one's idiosyncracies is a lot more helpful than generalized advice. And while we tend to think of moral norms in universal terms, these too are practically worked out in smaller settings.

A similar mixture of moral and pragmatic guidance may be found in the second type of frequently told stories about the past—the inspiring tales of accomplishment. Once again, although fictional figures—or public persona—serve just as well to illustrate the paths to success, attending to the family's own history adds in flavor and specificity here. The very meaning of "accomplishment" can best be worked out in those tellings, and it is something that varies greatly. Positive feelings generated in the process are of value in and of themselves, too. Remembrance becomes an aid, in effect, in weathering the present.

Beyond drawing on the past for lessons, for a reconfirmation of the moral order as well as its redefinition, a less instrumental approach may also secure a presence for remembrance. Not focusing on specific narratives and concrete individuals, going back in time through reminiscing, usually warmly, about the days gone by is something we often do for its own sake.[2] The pleasure derived from such reminiscing has a great deal to do with our social nature; bonds between people, formed in shared experience, demand renewing through the telling. Many a social occasion is indeed designed partly to evoke reminiscence. And the travel industry taps into this process as well, by providing us with the physical means to go back. The past as a cosy home, however imaginary or sentimentalized, *is* nice to return to.

Indeed, if we look inside people's homes, it becomes apparent that for most of us, comfort translates into the presence of a past. Whether it be in photographs or a collection of rocks, reminders of where we had been are all around us. What we include in our "memory household" is subject to deeply felt rules of selection, as many a quarrel between two people moving in together can testify. To outsiders, the choices made may be unintelligible, or categorized under the heading of "taste" which does not give them justice. To ourselves, the whole process is not visible either, until the time comes that we have to move—and pack. Then, the symbolic "nest" we have constructed, about to be dismantled, demands our attention if not fullfledged justification for its existence.

Within our memory households, there are both autobiographical reminders and elements of the much more distant past (greatgrandparents' chest, for example), with a special place often reserved for objects evoking people dear to us who are no longer there. Highly individualized—even when using common tools such as photographs—these symbolic nests are extensions of our self. Being deprived of them, even if only temporarily, can result in a deep sense of loss. Not demanding our active attention, most of the time, a memory household offers an anchor, the comfort of continuity and identity.

If the contents of our memory household tend to accumulate quietly over time, they can also be subject to more dramatic and direct change. Individual growth may call for a break with the past (or, more likely, with a part of it), in which case certain reminding fixtures are deemed to disappear.[3] There are times when the presentation of self demands considerable dramaturgical skills in rearranging, hiding, highlighting only the appropriate memory markers. And there are times when experience itself is too disruptive to our sense of self to be granted any permanency of reminders. Those could also be times for a renewed search of the past for comfort and solace.

The work involved in the construction and maintenance of our memory household is often quite invisible. The form of presence we grant to our past is also, for the most part, not compelling. Glancing at the familiar objects around us can direct our thoughts to the past, but it does not have to, and indeed, much of the time, it is not supposed to. Getting on with our everyday routines would be next to impossible were we to dwell constantly in the past. On the other hand, without the supports of our private "infrastructure" of memory, we may feel quite disoriented or even threatened in our identity.

On a societal scale, memory work continuously going on *is* visible. But precisely because it is visible and justifiably commending our analytical attention, its dynamics can overshadow the quieter, uncompelling presence of the past. For even in places where the crowded public discourse emphasizes concerns with the present and the future, or among peoples with what we may see as a low level of historical awareness, the past does not disappear. Not attended to, not dwelt upon, not subject to major disputes, "realities of the past" stay in the background nevertheless. Always potentially retrievable from the extant "records," be those a stretch of buildings or a book, meanings attached to the past lose some of their clarity and potency, but they can be filled in again when an occasion arises. Urban neighbourhoods in many North American cities provide a terrain rich in such "dormant" collective memory; ordinarily not evoking warm remembrance for their inhabitants, they can do just that for people who left the places behind decades (or generations) ago.[4] This process of retrieval may involve individuals, or it may be a collective undertaking, in which case a new frame of remembrance is likely to emerge. Declaring an old courthouse in the Bronx an historical landmark, with all the renovation, plaques, and ceremony this may entail, differs thus from leaving it quietly to speak of the old days.

Remembrance too has its own "infrastructure." Parts of it might be continuously in use, while other parts remain unattended for long stretches of time. And over time, the meaning attached to both often changes. A book which, when it appeared sixty years ago, had the power to define experience in the trenches of World War I for millions of readers, *All Quiet on the Western Front*, is hardly read today. But when it is read, and especially when it is being analyzed, it is taken as a memory marker of a different kind altogether, a sign of its own time.[5] This phenomenon of a sedimentation of meaning is not uncommon in the process of retrieving abandoned pieces of the memory's "infrastructure." It is a way of preserving some of the original symbolic texture while looking from a current perspective. And if historians and critics do it with a whole armature of specialized knowledge, visitors to a pioneer village recreating the life of Ontarians in the nineteenth century proceed in a very similar fashion indeed. Whether applied to something which in its time served to evoke memory, in other words, or to something which only now is designed to do that, the mixing of original and contemporary meanings secures a new presence for the past.

From the point of view of individuals, a great deal of the collective memory markers retain such dormant presence. Public attention, though directed towards a larger share of the extant "infrastructure," still leaves much outside its sphere of immediate relevance. For analytical purposes, that which is left outside becomes muted. If not given a public voice at some point, it is in danger of disappearing from view altogether.[6] When speaking of the presence of the past, we should recognize this serious limitation to our analytical endeavors. We can also expect that as the study of collective memory matures, we will learn more about its dormant qualities.

The idea of memory households that offer comfort and an anchor, all the while leaving much of the past contained there dormant, becomes particularly useful when we reflect on the now broader questions about remembrance and *collective* self. If how much presence is given to the past varies, from community to community and across historical time, a part of this variation, I think, lies with the very materials that are used to build the common memory household.

North American visitors to Europe often comment, with awe and some regret, on the ease of visceral contact with the past when in Rome, Athens, or Paris. When I left Warsaw and came to Canada as a young adult, my establishing of links with the new country took the form of exploring its vastness and beauty. When asked, my Canadian friends too would point to the Ontario lakes or British Columbia forests, rather than any historical buildings, as their key identity references. As the now strengthening movement for "heritage preservation" testifies, many people might consider *both* the natural and human-built environments as important for communal self. Yet the tangible, visible differences in the length of a shared history matter. How we relate to the past, or more specifically, how much the past is made to serve as a base for collective identity, may well reflect simply what is available.[7]

And yet we know that even when visible memory markers are present in abundance, remembrance of the past they are marking is not automatically guaranteed, nor is its meaning constant. Memory too has a history, so that what once testified to imperial glories may be later relegated to colorful curiosum (or, as in the former Soviet Union, to a memento of oppression). Jewish cemeteries and synagogues, while very much there throughout Eastern Europe, command attention of only a few passers-by. How, if at all, they serve as memory markers depends on new significance they acquire as parts of national (and international) heritage. Large migrations that followed the end of World War II resulted in massive disconnections between historical landscapes and their "owners." Again, markers that meant a lot to Germans in Breslau mean little to Poles in Wroclaw.

The scarcity of available, tangible resources can be compensated for with other means, of course. If Americans have only a few monuments to their conquest of the West, movies do the mythic work just as well.

Literature about the lost homelands in Europe not only preserves their image in nostalgic tones, it also gives them cultural significance well beyond that of historically concrete sites; myths emerge almost naturally here, as the sense of loss acquires permanence.[8] The narrative of "this is where we come from," in other words, draws strength from the physical reminders of the past, but is not dependent on them. Visual, emotional as well as intellectual referents of memory-of-the-origins must exist in some form; what that form is varies greatly.

How the relative absence of physical markers is compensated for, if at all, depends largely on how important memory-of-the-origins becomes, for different peoples, at different points in time. And that, in turn, may depend on the more specific framing of remembrance in relation to collective identity.

Elsewhere in this book, we discuss how the shared past matters for communities of memory, large and small. The recognition of powers inherent in collective memory for the construction and maintenance of collective identity should not obscure from view the often problematic relation between the two. Collective memory is only *one* of the forces that bond people together; even within the notion of "tradition" included are values and common ways of doing things which transcend any specifiable time in the past.[9] Goals, aspirations, fears, as well as ties of kinship can draw strength from collective memory—but they do not have to.

For people struggling to maintain their identity against historical forces of conquest, oppression or dispersion, their (often mythical) past acquires great significance. The stories of grandeur, of victories against adversity, of sheer perseverance—all offer both solace and inspiration. Among Canada's Ukrainians, for example, the dream of national independence, kept very much alive by successive waves of emigrants, rested on an historical narrative both strongly felt and strongly defended from any antisolace criticisms by others (in this case, mostly Jews and Poles who also had roots in the land).[10]

In the countries of Central Europe that were subjected to Soviet domination, and whose memories were being ideologically assaulted in truly Orwellian manner, the past served as the key battle terrain for rescuing national identity.[11] For Western observers, the explosion of commemoration during the brief first reign of Solidarity in Poland bordered on inexplicable obsession, especially in the context of dire economic situation.[12] And yet, the vivid presence of remembrance, in all its powerful symbolism, was a very logical result of suddenly freeing access to the public sphere. Battles long fought in private or between-the-public-lines moved into the open. When collective memory had to go underground again (with the declaration of martial law in 1981), its potency only grew. Yet when the political situation dramatically changed at the end of the decade, spelling the beginnings of democracy, something quite remarkable happened to remembrance as well. The past, especially the previously forbidden past, acquired an enormous share of public discourse. Many Poles, also beyond intellectual circles, began to voice protest.[13] Why? Because a country in the midst of a grand economic experiment (and crisis), building the foundations of its polity and international relations, was now seen as held back by too much attending to its past. Resurrecting political programs from pre-World War I era, which might have worked as training for democracy under the Communist regime, was often deemed sheer madness in the new circumstances. The highly negative perceptions of Poland's neighbours, maintained by memory (in the case of Germans, both private and public), would now be judged as the most serious impediment to any successful integration with Europe. Lessons drawn from history, in other words, became counterproductive.

This particular dispute over the significance of memory had many interesting twists. Just as in other countries of the region, for example, local authorities in Poland took to the changing of names with great zeal. Streets, city squares, (whole towns in Germany), schools, hospitals, were given new-old patrons without much deliberation or thought, it seemed. Whole chapters of perfectly good history were destined for oblivion, as any connection with the Left became suspect. The often public smashing of monuments, especially those of Lenin, completed the picture of a great will to erase all markers of the Communist past. Again, some observers, sensitive to the irony of Orwell-in-reverse, began to protest.

Though the word itself was discredited by its previous usage by the regime, "normalization" of collective memory was being appealed for. It was as if the special place accorded to remembrance before had to in itself become part of memory. Normality, in congruence with democracy, destined the past to a much more limited sphere of public observance and public knowledge. It is not that memory is not to matter, far from it, but it is not to be the sole determinant of the present and the future.

The pains of transition from an all-encompassing frame for remembrance to one reducing it to size are understandable. At stake here is a redefinition of collective identity itself. A parallel process, though in the opposite direction, as it were, may be equally difficult. In Germany, or rather in West Germany a few years before unification, an intense public debate, with historians at the center, put into question the place of memory in that country's identity.[14] After the postwar decades of drawing on the constitution and thus a pledge to democracy for the idea of "Germanness," voices of doubt were raised as to the implicit prohibition on remembrance. The Germans, of course, were asked by everyone "never to forget" the Nazi regime, but they were also reprimanded for any celebration of national heritage showing signs of nationalist longing (which did cover a great deal of territory). Now they asked how were they possibly to become a "normal nation" without recourse to the whole of their history. This question may not have an answer, at least one that would be morally acceptable. But we may expect that Germany as a great European power will gradually enlarge the scope of a publicly celebrated past. We can only hope that the wound of 1933-1945 will not be easily healed in the process. For while framing remembrance of that period as "inspiring" appears to outsiders as impossible to accomplish, the already achieved privatization of memory, allowing for the "suffering" frame to emerge carries the potential of doing just that.[15]

The dilemma posed by German history—that of the integration of its horrifying chapters into what should essentially be an inspiring narrative—is the most acute version of a problem shared by many a collectivity. What is to be done with remembrance engendering shame, doubt, or feelings of guilt? How much presence should be granted to a morally problematic, challenging past? Can one be asked to commemorate mistakes and failures?

One of the key arguments used to justify the lessening of attention to the Nazi crimes (in Germany and elsewhere, in disputes over war criminals in particular) is that the sheer passage of time removes that past from the sphere of direct communal responsibility. One of the key arguments *for* the continuing emphasis on the Nazi period is that with the passage of time, moral lessons acquire ever greater universal significance. On both sides, the increasing distance in time appears to reframe remembrance, from that of concrete individual actions to one of general cultural background. That for some people, such reframing spells the end of the need to confront the past is understandable. It reflects a conception of moral responsibility oriented around specific historical actors and their deeds. In such direct terms, young Germans, born long after the war, indeed cannot be held accountable. That for other people, the growing distance in time spells exactly the opposite is equally understandable. For it reflects the idea that moral responsibility carries a large indirect component, so that all people identifying themselves with the "Western civilization" ought to confront what their culture had produced. And, among the "all," people brought up in Germany face an especially urgent task, as it was in their country where different (and differently shared) cultural forces combined to enact the "Final Solution." In effect, then, while the passage of time makes dealing with the past easier in that one is no longer compelled to question one's own parents, the presence of that past becomes a great deal more pronounced, more widespread, as it were. The moral challenge, too, addresses itself, albeit in different forms, to a great deal more people.

In that process of distancing and generalization, the burden of the past is not lessened. If anything, the moral questioning in the face of the Holocaust acquires new and often heavy weight when it begins to incorporate historically specific actions and their less tangible social context. To take but one example: in France, where the record of helping and resisting the implementation of the "Final Solution" is mixed indeed, the hard memory work, raising very troubling questions, is not about facts and figures. Rather, it involves a highly critical exploration of the intellectual and emotional heritage on the Right—and the Left—of attitudes towards the Jew, an exploration going back into prerevolutionary times.[16] Issues of direct responsibility do not disappear from the agenda, but it is their historical contextualization which largely accounts for their significance as a moral challenge to French society in general.

What we have here is an effort to integrate the undeniably difficult chapter in France's history through a construction of complex ideological linkages, and thus making the past immediately relevant to the present. As much as this effort may be undertaken in the name of moral necessity (and memory obligations), its public acceptance, however grudging at times, rests on its immersion in contemporary politics. Implicitly as well as explicitly, the dwelling on history many would prefer to forget is made possible, if not justifiable, by the present. It is also very much helped, however paradoxically, by the growing popularity of extreme xenophobia espoused by Le Pen's National Front; the idea of ridding France of "target populations" acquires more than historical resonance.

In the case of Germany, the sheer enormity of the Nazi crimes, together with continuing, albeit fluctuating, international pressure renders the Nazi period difficult *not* to confront. More frequently, though, the vicissitudes of remembrance of troubling past follow the model encountered in France, that is the needs of the present. At its very basic, "troubling past" must first be so defined for it to be confronted. To gain a presence on the public agenda, it also needs to be deemed important, important beyond the generally weak justification of moral necessity. Some people may, of course, be deeply sensitive to the moral propriety of their community and pursue the challenging task of confronting the impropriety on its own merit. But for a community of memory as a whole, engaging in moral accounting cannot be expected to follow from high standards alone. The additional, and often more than sufficient motivation, is provided by pragmatic necessities of the present—or by an active solicitation from those wronged in the past.

Recognizing that the morally troubling past is nearly always a record of doing harm to *others*, it is not at all surprising that the prime challengers to the communal sense of well-being would be its victims. On an international scale, the prime example of the (so far unsuccessful) challenge to remembrance has been the Armenians struggling for an acknowledgment of their genocide by and from the Turks. Victim groups, such as Native Indians in North America, may be joined by other people of conscience, of course; still, it is with their claims that the memory work begins. In other instances, victim groups' voice may indeed be overpowered by that of morally troubled perpetrators themselves—the anti-imperialism rhetoric of protest in the West comes to mind. But whether on their own, or with the help of the community's righteous non-Other, the victims' narrative of victimization is the one focused on. In that sense, the initiative and ultimately control over the framing (or reframing) of remembrance belongs on the outside of a community of memory. (This might explain why the whole process is arduous and long-lasting, as well as how its success depends on the degree of self-criticism rarely encountered in social life.)

A critical examination of one's record towards the Other gains a great deal more acceptability when initiated by shifts in patterns and goals of coexistence. As Central and Eastern Europe sheds the Communist yoke, it becomes clear that for the region peacefully to enjoy a future, a great many past scores must be settled.[17] In most of these countries, minority populations have not been treated well; once again, the prospects of democratic rule are very much dependent on the extent of moral accounting. And if in much of the region, Jewish presence is minuscule, the apparent popular appeal of antisemitism testifies to the need for confronting the Holocaust, meaning not only the records of indifference or cooperation with the Nazis but also (and perhaps more significantly) the records of postwar violence and hostility to survivors.

On that last point, one may ultimately count only on the good will of Gentiles, rather than pressure from the Jews, though the efforts of Israel and Western Jewish organizations cannot be discounted here. But as far as relations between the Czechs and the Poles, or the Hungarians and the Rumanians, or the Ukrainians and the Poles, be it across or within the shifting national borders—these are all subject to critical reexamination under tremendous political pressures. Theoretically, it would, of course, be preferable to engage in moral accounting in less stressful circumstances. But practically, the well-established patterns of remembrance have little chance of being displaced unless a great deal is at stake politically. Even then, as the recent record shows, admitting to one's people's oppressive treatment of others does not automatically follow appeals for mutual understanding. But it is a start.

Whatever the dynamics behind the public reevaluation of the past, at issue here is a major challenge to the narratives of collective identity. At times, it is a challenge to one or two components of the narrative; often, it is a more serious one from a counter-narrative which is effectively being produced in the process. The significance of the challenge is not lost on those involved; the arguments for continuing with the unpleasant task of critical examination of the past are strong arguments, couched in terms of moral, political, social necessity. And even if no direct action in the present is called for (such as reparations to those wronged, for example), many a subtle shift in recounting the past acquire strong symbolic qualities. To take but one example: when Ukrainians living in Poland are permitted to use Ukrainian names again for their villages and hamlets, there is no mistake as to how important the gesture is as a step towards accommodating a Ukrainian presence in Poland's recent past.

Whether the challengers to the communal sense of well-being come from within or from without, the element of *empathy* with the Other is a key orienting force in the process. Seeing the past from a different perspective is a challenge, even when no morally troubling questions arise. It is in the nature of collective identity that it provides an extensive interpretive grid for classifying people and events in the world, past and present. To ask people to understand the Other's views is to ask for an often difficult imaginative leap, for a stepping out of comfortable patterns. To make it possible, resources must accompany broad appeals and editorials from opinion makers. The Other's own voice has to be heard, the Other's own past must acquire a presence.[18]

In recent years, Poland, more than perhaps any other country in the region, has set to recover its Jewish heritage. Starting with the principle of long-shared history, Polish intellectuals framed the process as both a fulfilment of a moral obligation and an enrichment of national culture. Books, articles, exhibits, movies, plays, lectures, and seminars—a veritable deluge of resources, available for the very first time in Polish-Jewish history—exposed the young people in particular to a rich Jewish culture. Yet it also, inadvertently at times, exposed them to a very different perspective on Poland's history. And this proved to be as much of a challenge as the very direct questions about the country's role in the Holocaust. The whole structure of seeing the Jew as an inferior Other (and thus confirmation of the superior Pole) risked collapse. It did not. But the accommodation with the distinct, if not disturbing, telling of the past has proven problematic. One of the strategies used has been to make the distinct appealing in and of itself—to make the Jew exotic and unthreatening. Another consists of indeed reexamining, piece by piece, the accepted historical record to arrive at more balanced accounts. Selective listening, involved in both, is an invaluable aid in the process. Poles, it must be recognized, are in a rather unique situation in that they exercise total control over reframing of remembrance; the Jew is an invited guest.

If the case of Poland and the Jew is unique in the extent of control on the part of host memory, as it were, it also exemplifies a common pattern of attending to the past for ideological (rather than more directly political) reasons. The interest in things Jewish began with—and was encouraged by—an effort to define Polish society as pluralistic and this, by all key political actors on the then Communist stage. Attitudes towards the Jew became a form of "litmus test" for the quality of self-definition. In the circumstances where Jewish presence was minimal, it was the memory of the Jew that gained prominence. The choice of that memory was not coincidental—its symbolic significance for the Poles' collective identity *is* high—but the very decision to propel the discovery of Jewish heritage bore little, if any, relation to history itself. Rather, in what appears to be a general pattern, the granting of presence to a particular past followed its newly defined "fit" with current concerns and debates.

That the past is often called upon to respond to ongoing shifts in collective self-definition is very much in evidence in North America today. Canadians, having introduced the idea of theirs being a multicultural society back in 1971, can now not only read a fast growing series of books about the different ethnic communities, but are also being confronted with an equally fast growing list of grievances from groups wronged in the past.[19] The recovery of historical record, while widely accepted as essential for building a solid foundation for the new Canadian identity, is thus by no means unproblematic. The very focus on diverse histories is hard enough to accommodate with the idea of national unity, but especially so when the narratives speak of oppression. The challenge, for all the contextual differences, appears to parallel what we encountered in the case of Poland—how is one to balance the need for comfort, and thus the pleasingly exotic Other, with the demands for the not so pleasant self-criticism. (The American reader is asked here to reflect on this dynamics in American terms.)

The key lesson which emerges here is that the relation between collective memory and collective identity can be and often is problematic. Yes, on whatever scale of human bonds, we do draw strength from the shared past. And yes, history offers a great deal of comfort, inspiration and the essential anchoring for the self. But history can also be a burden, a troublesome obstacle to the sense of common identity and well-being. Even families face this predicament, trying as they might to erase memories of abuse, for example. The presence of the past, for all its fit within the current agendas, is often disquieting. It is not surprising, then, that questions about the "correct" role of remembrance in public life are so frequently subject to intense debate. However implicitly, ordinary people and opinion makers alike do recognize that much is at stake when granting presence to a past. As students of collective memory, we are well advised to listen to their voices in order better to apprehend how and why the past is deemed meaningful, if at all.

# Notes

1.  See Raphael Samuel and Paul Thompson, eds., *The Myths We Live By* (London and New York: Routledge, 1990).
2.  See, especially, Edward S. Casey, *Remembering: A Phenomenological Study* (Bloomington and Indianapolis: Indiana University Press, 1987).
3.  For an insightful discussion of how individuals "rewrite history," see Erving Goffman, *The Presentation of Self in Everyday Life* (Garden City, N.Y.: Doubleday, 1959).
4.  See, for example, Irving Louis Horowitz, *Daydreams and Nightmares: Reflections of a Harlem Childhood* (Jackson: University Press of Mississippi, 1990).
5.  See Modris Eksteins, *Rites of Spring: The Great War and the Birth of the Modern Age* (Toronto: Lester & Orpen Dennys, 1989).
6.  This was partly the motivation behind the multivolume *Les lieux de mémoire*, edited by Pierre Nora (Paris: Gallimard, 1982-93).
7.  For comparative materials, see Benedict Anderson, *Imagined Communities: Reflections on the Origin and Spread of Nationalism* (London and New York: Verso, 1983).
8.  In post-1945 Polish literature, for example, a special place is reserved for works about the eastern lands "*kresy*"; Czeslaw Milosz' writings are representative here. Similarly, many German authors—most prominently Gunther Grass—secure presence for their lost eastern homeland.
9.  See, especially, Paul Connerton, *How Societies Remember* (Cambridge: Cambridge University Press, 1989).
10. Harold Troper and Morton Weinfeld, *Old Wounds: Jews, Ukrainians and the Hunt for Nazi War Criminals in Canada* (Markham, Ont.: Viking, 1988).
11. See Alain Brossat, Sonia Combe, Jean-Yves Potel, Jean-Charles Szurek, eds., *A l'Est, la mémoire retrouvée* (Paris: Editions la Découverte, 1990).
12. See, especially, Lawrence Weschler, *The Passion of Poland: From Solidarity Through the State of War—The Complete* New Yorker *Reports on Poland* (New York: Pantheon Books, 1984).
13. The subject was a major concern, of articles as well as letters to the editor, in *Polityka*, a popular weekly.
14. See, especially, Charles S. Maier, *The Unmasterable Past: History, Holocaust, and German National Identity* (Cambridge, Mass.: Harvard University Press, 1988).
15. For a further discussion, see Anton Kaes, *From Hitler to Heimat: The Return of History as Film* (Cambridge, Mass.: Harvard University Press, 1989).
16. See, for example, Zeev Sternhell, *Ni droite ni gauche: L'idéologie fasciste en France* (Paris: Seuil, 1983).
17. For more discussion, see Iwona Irwin-Zarecka, "In Search of Usable Pasts," *Society* 30, 2 (January/February 1993):32-36.
18. For further reflection on this dynamic in North American terms, see Ivan Karp, Christine Mullen Kraemer, and Steven D. Lavine, eds., *Museums and Communities. The Politics of Public Culture* (Washington, D.C.: Smithsonian Institution Press, 1992).
19. By the early 1990s, this would include Native, Japanese, Chinese, Ukrainian, Jewish, Italian, as well as black Canadians.

# 6

# Memory in Future Tense

Tempting as it might be in these turbulent times, this chapter does not set out to predict the future of remembrance or otherwise. Rather, it is a reflection on the ways future—as a vision—enters the process of constructing and framing "realities of the past."

Analytically as well as for pragmatic reasons, studies of the dynamics of collective memory concentrate on the relationships between the past and the present. Whether when tracing back specific histories of memory or when looking at the contemporary scene, our data, our concerns, the theoretical parameters we use, all quite naturally fall within the past/present nexus. And yet, while trying to understand why people do what they do to secure or disrupt remembrance, we need a place for their sense of the future. At its most fundamental, much of memory work is done "for posterity." And beyond such a general role as an orienting force, there are times when a very specific vision of the future frames the utilization of the past. That those specific visions emerge in specific historical circumstances allows for their analysis to pursue familiar questions about the sociopolitical context. But it also necessitates opening some new lines of inquiry, precisely to account for the directness of connecting the future to the past. It is, after all, not at all obvious why looking forward ought to implicate looking back.

Let us begin with the more diffuse and often implicit role assigned to the future in the construction of collective memory—that of an audience. When historical buildings are being preserved, monuments erected, new museums built, the sizeable costs involved in such endeavors are rarely justified on the basis of the present needs of the community. Envisioned as long-term investments, these memory works are to enjoy meaningful life for decades, if not centuries after their original audiences are gone.

Yet a reflection on what this implies does not automatically enter the considerations of planners and designers, beyond the immediate demands of physical durability. Most often, the attitude seems to be that what is being produced today will function as "witness to the times" (both the present and the past) in much the same way the older memory works have done for us. It is an attitude of a certain resignation to the inherent unpredictability of the future; it is a recognition of continuity in the human condition, one which translates into modest hopes that the work at hand indeed endures. The future generations, while very much the intended audience for the current endeavors, are too much like us to make a difference. And we are, one should add, not all that different from the generations which came before us.[1] Remembrance, in this view, emerges as a fairly stable quality of human affairs, something we help secure but not something we tinker with much.

This tried and traditional approach is being gradually challenged by developments within the artistic and academic communities, and especially those affecting the discipline of curatorship itself.[2] On a recent visit to the new Canadian Museum of Civilization in Ottawa-Hull, I was sharply reminded of the need to include "future" within the analytical parameters of studying collective memory. Opened in 1989, this is a self-consciously different museum, a "museum for the global village," according to its designers. It is a museum with an explicit (and published)[3] vision, not only of its purpose—this being the promotion of intercultural understanding—but also of its future users. Drawing on careful demographic and sociological analyses, as well as the experiences around the world in staging historical displays, be it in museums or theme parks, the Canadian planners opted for a multimedia combination of pedagogy and entertainment. The operative premise here is one of profound *discontinuity* between what worked yesterday and what would work tomorrow, all the while the changes occurring in the present are seen as viable indicators for planning for the future.

Beyond designing an essentially user-friendly museum, curators in Ottawa went a step further. Prominent in their statement of vision is the recognition of what might be broadly termed a postmodern dilemma— the need for a museum *not* to claim authority on historical truth, all the while constructing legible exhibits about the past. What is at stake here is no longer the practical demands of attracting visitors—the Canadian Museum of Civilization offers both a large hands-on children's section, a grand store with objects attesting to the "experience" (curators' term) and the world's largest movie screen. Rather, it is a new philosophy of memory work, combining efforts by the museum staff with those of visitors. In the future, the assumption seems to be, people will indeed be responding very differently to treasures from the past and thus new, more interactive strategies are required. If some of the old ways of museum displays might be retained for a while, the orientation of present thinking and planning is definitely forward.[4]

Considering the sophisticated terms used to describe this museum as a "process" and a "vision," I found it somewhat ironic that the key exhibit serving as a showcase for both the museum itself and the "Canadian civilization" is unabashedly ahistorical. Artifacts, house frontals, totem poles, and other ritual objects, originating with six different tribes on the northwest coast, are placed together with no regard for where or when they came from. The result *is* spectacular, not least because of the grand scale and the interplay of light. But is a beautification without context what is meant by "intercultural understanding"? Apparently, while the idea of Native Canadian display introducing visitors to the museum was there from the start, the specific choices reflected the fact that the only Canadian attraction warranting three stars in the Michelin tourist guide is a Haida village on the west coast. No comment.

It might be argued that for a publicly funded institution, in these times of fiscal restraint, not to prepare for the future would be folly. It will still need to be shown, in the years to come, that the museum's vision of a "postmodern visitor" is a viable one.

The Canadian Museum of Civilization is clearly not an isolated case. To what extent the ideas of postmodernism would be affecting memory works destined for popular consumption is still an open question. Elsewhere in this book, I have pointed to the generally greater self-consciousness on the part of memory workers that comes with current preoccupation with the meaning of "history" and "truth." What I think calls for much further inquiry is the issue foregrounded on the drawing boards at the museum—the impact of imagining the future audience. Clearly, not all memory work, conscious of itself, integrates a vision of the future. We may also expect such visions that are active to vary greatly, in content and longevity, as it were. And we know far too little about historical precedents for the current predicaments. In short, there is a great deal of empirical work to be done.

Imagining the future audience affects not only the finished products of memory workers; on a much broader scale now, it guides many of the activities aimed at securing the raw materials to be used in times to come. Again, museums, in their role as official collectors, play an important role here, selecting, labelling, storing, and altogether making certain artifacts available for future students as well as exhibitors. Archives, too, the traditional guardians of documentary evidence, expand their capacities to include an evergrowing range of material. The key force operating here appears to be the technology itself. With the development of computer data bases, our ability to store information has grown exponentially. In a sense, the opening of a possibility to record just about everything that was printed—and said or shown—in the public sphere can make the very idea of selection redundant, other than as a sign of fiscal restraint. With the growing interest that *we* have in the lives of ordinary people in times past comes an implicit expectation, too, that our everyday life is worth recording. If we often find it extremely difficult to reconstruct such historical ordinariness, our efforts today should make the task a great deal easier in the future. Recognizing that much of contemporary publishing and film is technically incapable of long-term endurance leads to innovative technical solutions. The only problems appear to be of a practical nature, with scientists invited to assist in improving our capability to store and record. The competing narratives that inevitably result from such an open approach to memory keeping are for the future generations to sort out.

Such a picture of abundance and equal opportunity built into the process of recording our times is of necessity an ideal one. Even in countries that are technologically advanced and committed to democracy, financial considerations alone prompt the establishment of priorities, priorities often informed by the political agendas. In Canada, for example, the allocation of funding to various ethnic communities as well as to the central "bank" of Native Canadian artifacts follows from the relatively recent official sanctioning of multiculturalism as the country's defining principle. If pornographic movies are indeed part and parcel of the North American everyday life, I have yet to hear of supreme efforts to preserve them for posterity on a par with those devoted to early silent features. The principle of computer storage does not yet extend to the whole variety of small, alternative presses however interesting their publications to future historians. In as much as the key institutions assigned the task of record keeping remain for the most part publicly funded, we may safely assume that setting of their mandates will not leave the political sphere.

What is likely to change, though, with various technological devices becoming more accessible to the public itself is the impact of privately produced records. Ironically, just as the public memory keeping extends in the direction of the everyday, what "little people" themselves select to pass on resolutely retains the out-of-the-ordinary quality. But that too may change; one sees more video cameras, for example, used on not so special occasions. To what extent will the institutional guardians of collective memory allow the presence of the public's own products, we simply do not know yet.[5] If the popularity of reality oriented television shows is any indication, though, it is as *consumers* that individuals might ultimately decide.

Once again, some telling lessons might be drawn from the planning process behind the Canadian Museum of Civilization. The operative vision of the future visitor is one of a demanding consumer of information, a person very much attracted to displays about the past, but highly impatient with less than entertaining packaging. Allowing for different degrees of interest in detailed knowledge, for different types of desired museum experience, and for the differences between Canadian and foreign visitors, this introduces complexity into the picture yet does not interfere with the basic premise. In the "global village," people are expected to be drawn to cultural histories, their own as well as others'. The current trend of serving the past as a tourist attraction is expected to continue; in this respect, the museum is in hard competition with theme parks and Disney's empire and ought to act accordingly, enter marketing. But the consumer is also expected to demand the museum to retain its unique status of a "depository of national memory"; indeed, the planners anticipate an increased interest in the collecting and storing of artifacts with a design of a special glassed-in "people mover" to allow a closer look at these behind the scene activities.

Consistent with the projected needs for proper packaging is the emphasis on the emotional aspects of the museum experience. Beyond the general recognition that any educational goals are best attained by combining intellectual and emotional cues to the past, there are specific procedures for mood-production to be built into the exhibits. With a push of a button, for example, visitors would be able to recreate the "authentic" smells or noises of a setting. (In the fall of 1991 when I was there, such gadgetry was not yet installed, emotional simulation being reduced to mainly visual effects of site reconstruction of a, by now, traditional variety.) Introducing live performances and more hands-on activity displays is to serve a similar purpose of emotional engagement. Intercultural understanding, it is stressed throughout, cannot be produced without empathy. Appropriately invoking McLuhan's legacy, the "museum for a global village" is a multimedia experiment in the engineering of feelings.

In most museums, it is the "aura" of the artifacts themselves that makes for an emotional impact on visitors. The Canadian planners resolutely set to break away from such quasi-sacred atmosphere. At the same time, though, it is the museum—its splendid architecture, its position across the river from Parliament Hill, its structural elements—that is assigned the aura-producing task. The entry via Grand Hall, for example, is described as a "ritual of initiation," with the design of the Hall praised for the awe-inspiring grandeur.

This vision of the future of the past is thus an interesting mixture. History becomes a nice place to visit,[6] rendered all the more comfortable and entertaining with sensory stimulation. But the museum experience is to be even more special than it is today, a viable alternative to going on an exhilarating ride in Disneyworld. That at least some history is not the least bit entertaining remains completely outside the optimistic frame. Translated into practice, this does mean a celebration of Canada's Native peoples' heritage without even a hint of the long and troubling history of their subjugation.

What I found particularly telling in this design "for the global village" was the recognition of an increasing *commercial* value of the past. However one feels about it, I think that students of collective memory are well advised to take notice here. Beyond the often remarked on appeal of nostalgia in fashion (or movies),[7] we might be witness to a larger cultural shift, with profound implications for the vicissitudes of remembrance. In the advanced, Western world at least, and especially in North America, the last two decades saw an enormous growth of local heritage societies and both practical and legal efforts at securing historical preservation. Genealogy is a fast growing enterprise as well. Many a popular book, play, movie or television production speaks of the past. And yes, the tourism industry is increasingly responsive to the demands for historically oriented adventures. The past, in short, becomes an attractive commodity.

There are a number of plausible explanations offered by cultural critics as well as more casual observers. The one I find perhaps most convincing points to a shift in visions of the future, from the optimism inherent in the belief in progress to the uncertainties implicated in questioning, if not altogether abandoning that belief. Once the idea that "new" is not automatically "better" takes root in ordinary people's perception of their lives, it is possible for the "old" to acquire positive appeal. We know that, historically, in times of rapid and threatening social change, the longing for old order is almost guaranteed to emerge; the Nazis taught us, too, that such a longing can be a revolutionary force and perfectly at ease with modern technology. What makes the situation today rather different from the previous challenges to the vision of progress, though, is the pervasiveness of the questioning, both in political and in social terms.

Politically, seeing progress as a threat or an enemy is no longer confined to the realm of conservative thinking. The environmental movement, most noticeably, and the calls for empowerment to women and minorities more implicitly, all carry the call to reevaluate the relationship between technology and power. Ethical debates, sparked by new scientific developments, implicate the whole political spectrum as well in introducing doubt about moral virtues of progress. Such debates—on euthanasia or reproductive techniques—resonate well beyond the circles of specialists. The very spread of new technologies for prolonging life, for example, makes it likely for ordinary men and women to have to face the dilemmas these pose. Similarly, as more and more people actually work with computers, they do not need experts to tell them of this being a mixed blessing. Discussions about the effects of television on our lives have long left the academic halls to engage families and friends. The renewed public concern with the quality of education is also a *public* phenomenon, however much it involves the specialists' sophisticated arguments.

It is not that people reject modern technological developments, far from it; the "new and improved" label still sells. But more and more people—as parents, patients, workers, commuters—begin to see the future as problematic. No longer restricted to the intellectuals' formulations, questions about progress acquire an immediate, lived relevance.

Other questions that have been acquiring such direct, lived relevance to many people in North America and Western Europe are those about cultural *identity*, theirs and the Others'. The time of massive demographic shifts in the ethnic composition of society, coupled with a widening public debate on their implications is also the time when the ideas of global economy and polity begin to penetrate everyday concerns (with unemployment, for example). On both fronts, the need for self-anchoring—on a manageable scale—increases. The local heritage preservation is perhaps the clearest expression of turning to the past for anchors. More generally, though, the commodification of history that we have observed may reflect a less tangible interest in affirming differences against the sameness brought on by globalization.[8]

Finally, the attractive packaging of the past must be seen as the marketing phenomenon it also is, responsive to the public demand yet also reinforcing it with the steady supply of goods. It is difficult to say which comes first, for example, the wish to visit historical reconstructions or Disney's ample provision of them. History *is* a virtually limitless reservoir of things interesting, beautiful, exotic and ours is not the first age to use the bounty.

What happens to remembrance, though, when it plays in the market place? On a limited scale, that of identity reinforcement, communal memory becomes strengthened; there is now both more "infrastructure" around and a keener interest in the past. Outside of that realm, however, outside the "realities of the past" firmly attached to their cultural context, it is a different matter altogether. For optimists, the "global village" allows for greater understanding of other people's heritage. I tend towards a more pessimistic view here, seeing the neat and tidy presentations of (historical) self as allowing us to feel better, to claim we have gained understanding without having to work at it. To go back to the Canadian Museum of Civilization for a moment, to the visitors admiring the beauty of Native Canadian artifacts, I would suggest this is only the first step towards appreciation of that culture, with no guarantees whatsoever that the next steps be taken.

Cultures, histories, memories are neither all pretty nor all inspiring, but this is exactly what they tend to become on the market. There may be nothing wrong with decorating our memory household with bits and pieces of other people's heritages (unless, of course, we are dealing with sacred objects), but it should not serve as the certificate of intercultural understanding. There is a great deal more involved in learning about and appreciating the Other than what can be offered on a brief tour.

When the past becomes a nice place to visit—and bring souvenirs from—and our role becomes that of consumers, certain ways of framing remembrance thus gain privilege over others. Education-cum-entertainment tends to displace critical thinking, while the beautification process further removes any troubling spots. The quantitatively larger presence of historical markers does not spell a qualitative increase in historical understanding. Memory is no longer a challenge or work to be done; consumer taste and preferences begin to replace cultural and political relevance. Ultimately, the attractive packaging may end depriving the past of its prime power, that of legitimation.

Such a scenario is not yet a reality. Exhibits of Native Canadian and Native American artifacts, for example, are being contested for their de-contextualized, sanitized image of history. But the potential, I believe, is there for history-as-commodity to gain a monopoly position on the market, restricting the critical approaches to the narrow area of scholarship and art.

Not yet a consumer product,[9] but very much an instrument for comfort and identity anchoring, such appears to be the role assigned to history in the countries emerging from Soviet domination. It is too early to tell, at this point, whether the ideal of the future-as-return-to-the-past is a viable one, in social and political practice. When the Russians dust off the symbols of their Tsarist grandeur, for example, their neighbours might not be the least bit impressed. When the Ukrainian government declares, in 1991, that it is not going to prosecute anyone implicated in the crimes of the Communist regime—for the sake of societal peace—it is not at all clear that the victims or the international community would be ready for striking the whole period off the record. For the once East Germans, a return to the past may prove most problematic indeed, as even the legacy of Prussia is not cherished by all. When the Polish leaders decided to name their newly democratic country the "Third Republic," with the Second being the 1918–1939 one, there was certainly no universal acclaim for this wiping out of decades of citizens' experience. In short, the forging of links to the "good" past by simply bracketing or removing the "bad" one may not work. That the attempts are even being made teaches us, though, something important about the memory demolition power inherent in visions of the future which rest on claims to identity and continuity.

A countervision, with predictably opposite implications, has begun to emerge, though. In it, Central and Eastern Europe are defined precisely as "post-Communist" societies, societies that cannot make any effective transition to functioning (capitalist) democracies unless the legacy of Communist rule is studied and understood. Often explicitly against the idea of return to the (glorious) past, this is a vision calling for scrupulous inquiry into the recent times. It appeals to people's sense of fairness, but also to their direct experience of the difficulties of transition. The slow-to-change work ethic, for example, is seen as one of the key problems and one of the key legacies of the Communist regime. The very immediate challenge of economic renewal is thus linked to a better appreciation of historical inheritance. The Communist past becomes an obstacle to overcome, but not to bypass. And from some quarters, such as the new Left[10] in Poland, come calls for a more balanced assessment of that past, allowing for a degree of celebration as well.

Whichever vision "wins" in the end, and I expect they will coexist in conflict for quite some time, the effects on current memory work have already been profound, a few irreversible. To take a simple illustration, the decisions as to the fate of secret police records made today define what history can be written tomorrow. And whether such records are sealed, destroyed, or catalogued largely depends on how people in charge see their future—and their past.

If the current developments in the post-Communist world offer an especially rich data bank for students of memory, the phenomenon itself is of course not unique. Countries undergoing profound political change, whether in the wake of a revolution, military defeat or liberation, usually stake new claims on the future. As they construct or reconstruct their identities, the past may be reframed on many levels, from giving it less (or more) importance to picking out useful narratives. And while such times of transition may not involve a great deal of actual memory work—there are other, more urgent tasks to attend to—the new visions of the future can set the parameters of work to be done. Beyond that, too, beyond the impact on the public management of the past, such new visions are likely to affect private attitudes as well. It then again becomes important to explore both forms of framing memories in the future tense.

For it is not at all certain that shifts in perception introduced "from above" would be immediately apparent "below." On a still more general note, it is clear that not all visions of the future implicate shifts in viewing the past. Even those that have the potential to do that may remain inactive, as it were, for a variety of social, political—and pragmatic—reasons. What our discussion suggests is not a "law" of memory construction whereby the future be given its due. Rather, it offers another way of seeing the framing of remembrance, useful for those concrete instances where the future actually matters.

## Notes

1. For an historical overview, see Michael Kammen, *Mystic Chords of Memory: The Transformation of Tradition in American Culture* (New York: Alfred A. Knopf, 1991).
2. Here, Ivan Karp and Steven D. Lavine, eds., *Exhibiting Cultures. The Poetics and Politics of Museum Display* (Washington, D.C.: Smithsonian Institution Press, 1991) and Ivan Karp, Christine Mullen Kraemer, and Steven D. Lavine, eds., *Museums and Communities. The Politics of Public Culture* (Washington: Smithsonian Institution Press, 1992) offer valuable resources.
3. George F. MacDonald and Stephen Alsford, *A Museum for The Global Village: Canadian Museum of Civilization* (Hull: Canadian Museum of Civilization, 1989).
4. See also Ada Louise Huxtable, "Inventing American Reality," *The New York Review* (Dec. 3, 1992):24-29.
5. The recent growth of highly accessible computer networks takes this question even further—will there *be* institutional guardians at all?
6. This idea is not new, of course. See, especially, David Lowenthal, *The Past is a Foreign Country* (Cambridge: Cambridge University Press, 1985).
7. See Fred Davis, *Yearning for Yesterday: A Sociology of Nostalgia* (New York: The Free Press, 1979).
8. It is significant that even on a smaller scale—that of European unification—the language of opposition is filled with references to local traditions.
9. Rapidly moving there, though, in these hard economic times. Tourists in Moscow can now purchase medals and other regime paraphernalia; historians can even buy KGB files.
10. The expression fits awkwardly, but it is also one used by the actors themselves. The position is shared by some ex-dissidents (including Adam Michnik, now editor-in-chief of the popular daily *Gazeta Wyborcza*) and some ex-liberal-Communists (grouped around the weekly *Polityka*), with support from many lay Catholic intellectuals. Attitudes to the recent past frequently serve as a political "litmus test" in an increasingly complex situation.

# PART III

# Dynamics of Memory Work

# 7

# Absences

Considering the vastness of the terrain of social life and how, of necessity, only limited space can be accorded to remembrance of things past, when is it useful to speak of "forgetting"? Taking our clues from memory practitioners, it appears that social forgetting is first and foremost that absence in collectively shared "reality of the past" that is recognized as such and deemed important to repair. Efforts to secure remembrance, so often framed as the work to prevent forgetting, also lead us in this direction, for it is again in anticipation of an absence that they are being made. This idea of social forgetting as something noticed and struggled against rests, of course, on the separation between those who accept such absent past as a given and those who do not.

To recognize that something is missing from collective memory is to place oneself at a distance from it; outsiders may have an easier task here, but it is often up to insiders to construct plausible alternatives to the once legitimate interpretation of the events. For example, as important as it is for the international community to scrutinize Germany's record of dealing with the Nazi past, it is the developments within Germany, within its educational system and cultural institutions, that are ultimately responsible for the structure of collective memory. Similarly, if the events at Tiananmen Square entered the Western record to a degree unmatched in the history of oppression in Communist China, this alone cannot guarantee that people *in* China do not succumb to yet another state-engineered amnesia; the battle against forgetting must be fought on the internal front as well.

Attending to an absence-which-ought-not-to-be also rests on a theoretically crucial, albeit often implicit principle: that which is not publicly known and spoken about will be socially forgotten. In sharp contrast to the rules governing individual remembering, where we allow for complex dynamics of unexpressed memories, collective remembering has to be out in the open, as it were. Beyond the experience inscribed in individuals' memories—and much of shared "realities of the past" lie beyond—there is a need for records, markers, stones, reminders, the full information base of remembrance. What this implies is that when speaking of social forgetting, we are best advised to keep psychological or psychoanalytical categories at bay and to focus, rather, on the social, political, and cultural factors at work.[1] An absence within collective memory may be psychologically motivated, of course, but it carries consequences well beyond individual mind and soul. An absence acts on people who may have nothing to forget individually as it makes parts of the past disappear altogether. Thus, to draw again on the German case, if it is illuminating to explore the psychodynamics of silence on the part of those who lived through the Nazi period, the result provides only one of the pieces to the picture of presences and absences in today's collective memory.[2]

The idea that when we speak of social forgetting we are speaking of a *noticed* absence implies, too, that collective forgetting, just as collective remembering, has its own history. What, at one point in time, seemed a perfectly natural lack of attention to details of the past, becomes, at another point in time, a significant omission. The absence of memory is just as socially constructed as memory itself, and with an equally strong intervention of morally as well as ideologically grounded claims to truth.[3] When groups whose experience had long been excluded from societal record fight against it being "forgotten," they are redefining that experience from one that did not deserve recording to one that does. Challenging the power structure of society—and a host of cultural assumptions—the work done to give historical presence to women, for example, rests on the initial recognition of a troubling absence. And this recognition is in no way inherent in the passage of time or the nature of women, it is a political act.

If noticing an absence in collective memory—and thus framing the realm of social forgetting—is often done out there in the world, there is nothing to prevent a lone analyst from coming forward with a critique of existing ways of remembrance. Indeed, many a work of historical investigation, by professionals or otherwise, opens with an explicit statement of purpose, that purpose being to restore to the deserving presence a fragment of the past. Once again, it is by giving a public voice to people once unknown or forgotten that an absence is both recognized and remedied. For students of collective remembrance, such investigations pose a challenge, though. Intellectual fashions in the academia and beyond, the understandable interest in enlarging historical terrain to stake career claims, the intrinsic appeal of novelty—all may provide a perfectly reasonable explanation for the effort. To speak of social forgetting we need more of a consistent pattern and more of a critical scrutiny mass. We need to be convinced that the now presented fragment of the past should have been part of collective memory all along. Few works pass this test. When they do, when they trace how once a shared and significant experience disappeared from the record, they are most illuminating indeed. The note of caution remains, however, not to treat all or even most of the exciting results of historical research as evidence of social forgetting; what we *now* deem important or interesting or worthy of remembrance is not an absolute standard.

The claim that an absence within collective memory is evidence of social forgetting is a strong claim. There are times when it is also an analytically counterproductive one, in that it may hide from view the very dynamics of exclusion one is working to illuminate. In my study of the place of the Jew in Poland's memory, for example, I opted for the term "memory void" instead. For as I was analyzing the history of Polish-Jewish relations, it became increasingly clear that it would be misleading to speak of forgetting in respect to experience that had been deemed irrelevant from the start. The nearly complete disappearance of Jewish heritage from Poland's records (until the early 1980s) had been a significant absence, but to account for it demanded moving well beyond the general notion of forgetting.

At stake here is not terminological accuracy, but rather the different requirements that analysis of the absences may impose on us. *Documenting* an absence within collective memory is distinct from tracing its origins and transformations. The first task is important for our understanding of the present and the future; the lack of basic resources for remembrance of certain aspects of the past severely limits, if not precludes collective remembering. In this sense, finding out what has been excluded from the record produces more predictively powerful results than other types of inquiry into the framing process. The dialectic between public offerings and private feelings and priorities collapses for but a few who do not need those public resources. (Or, as was the case in Poland, the socially created memory void around the Jew would be reinforced by privately held views on the subject.) Strengthened or not from below, the exclusion from the public record acts more totally than any inclusion could.

*Accounting for* the absences is another matter altogether. At times, explanations can be fairly straightforward, as in the case of political regimes which declared particular events or people nonexistent and proceeded to erase all memory traces accordingly.[4] The challenge then lies with questions about efficacy, for clearly the record of recent past calls for more intense efforts of silencing the witnesses than one removed from direct experience. Once outside of the Orwellian world, though, tracing of an absence may become a formidable task indeed, calling for an imaginative historical inquiry of its own.

Up until now, I have used the term "absence" in its literal meaning of something missing. In the limited number of cases, such usage is more than justified. Soviet history books and other forms of public discourse about the past have been, until recently, rather packed with omissions.[5] Studies looking at the treatment of the Holocaust in Western textbooks, too, show a great deal of gaps.[6] When I inspected popular books on Polish cultural history, the lack of any mention of the Jews (other than as victims of the Nazis) was glaringly obvious. Yet even in those cases, the idea that something is missing operates against the background of something else which is very much there. It is extremely rare to have a complete vacuum in the record, nor do we ordinarily expect that to apply when thinking about social forgetting.[7] If the famine during collectivization of the Ukraine indeed "disappeared," that whole period did not, rather, it acquired a definite—and positive—picture. If the memory of collaboration with the Nazis has had a rough time in securing public presence in France, this did not spell a blank over the war times, but rather a struggle with the "resistance myth."[8] Indeed, I would argue that most of the time, when we speak of forgetting, we are speaking of displacement (or replacement) of one version of the past by another. To use different imagery, when we set out to listen to historical silences, we are forced to listen to a great deal of noise.

In 1989, an internationally coordinated effort began to modify the textual and visual structure of the museum now on the site of the Auschwitz camp, so as better to represent the identity of mostly Jewish victims. Previously, the very word "Jew" was missing from the tablets commemorating the victims—or the guidebooks used by visitors. Rather, the people killed by the Nazis in Auschwitz were referred to by their country of origin, making it virtually impossible to appreciate the camp's central role in the "Final Solution." What existed, then, was not a void, but an elaborate "text" effectively silencing the Jewishness of the victims.

Tracing absences immersed in the "infrastructure" of collective memory is often a demanding task. It begins with—and cannot avoid—a conviction that the "reality of the past" at hand is at least incomplete, if not incorrect altogether. Such a conviction may well be at odds with one's intellectual understanding of the dynamics of remembrance, but without some, however provisional, sense of the factual base line, a critique of the material becomes impossible.[9] Recognizing that one is always making a judgment when studying social forgetting as to what is true and what is not may give us theoretical discomfort, yet it is not an unreasonable price to pay for illuminating a key field where social forces are played out. For it is the absences within collective memory that can tell us a great deal about the workings of power and hegemony.

This reasoning is not news to analysts of culture working within a critical perspective (broadly defined), such as that offered by feminism. The unmasking of specific absences, as well as inquiries as to the complex dynamics of silencing women in general are quite explicitly aimed at "correcting" our understanding of the past just as much as empowering women in the present. Similarly, when North Americans are asked to incorporate Native Indians' perspectives into the official historical canon, the goal is clearly political. Behind the analysis of absences— and exclusion—lie concerns with the legitimating power of collective memory.

An example from the other end of analytical—and political— spectrum proves illuminating here. For the last twenty years or so, the "revisionist" historians have worked hard to show that the Holocaust never happened, that it had all been a "hoax" created by Jews to secure international support for the creation of the state of Israel. The lines of power are drawn very sharply here, for the argument rests on the notion of Jewish control of the media and other means of memory production. To liberate the world from Zionist manipulators, their credibility is first put in question *as* Zionists, and then through the use of evidence contrary to their "truth."[10] In an admittedly rare case of the loud and clear manufacturing of forgetting, it is the powers-that-were that set to reclaim their privileged position, apparently exasperated over the losses.

The idea of displacement, of silences "all dressed up in words," helps to explain how well social forgetting often works. Our cognitive maps do not easily tolerate void and chaos, so that deleting whole periods of time from the record would likely produce discomfort or suspicion. In contrast, providing a plausible account of the past, while excluding even some key components, is a way of securing that it go unquestioned, at least until social circumstances drastically change. Thus, more often than not, when what is being forgotten are morally repugnant deeds, their absence from the record is more than compensated for by an alternative and morally comfortable vision. How plausible such an alternative vision is, how well it can be maintained, seems to depend both on its consistency with the orienting myths already in place in collective memory—and on the ability to neutralize the critics. The case of Austria, for example, where the victimological interpretation of its role in World War II admirably succeeded, even in the face of the Kurt Waldheim affair, is instructive on both counts. Forgetting the Nazi past worked well within the larger vision of the fallen empire, but it could not have been possible without cooperation from both the United States and the Soviet Union. Japan, with its minimal acceptance of dwelling on its own criminal record vis-à-vis the Chinese, relies heavily on the isolationist attitudes to neutralize criticism from outside. Parallels can be drawn here with Poland's rejection of its share in moral responsibility for the Holocaust; the very powerful idea of having been a victim of history in general and of the Nazis in particular offers comfort, while repeated critiques of "anti-Polonism," inherent in the Jewish perspective on the past, offers the out when questioned by Westerners.

On a different scale, it is only recently, with the increasing societal involvement in matters of ethics in science and technology, that the not-so-glorious chapters in the history of scientific communities are being brought to public attention and grudgingly incorporated into the professional training curricula. The atmosphere of scandal that still prevails when revelations about Heidegger or de Man reach the media may have a neutralizing effect of its own, in that the *ideal* of decency and neutrality is not disturbed.[11] But more and more people are willing to let the record show the scope of scientists' responsibility for the perpetuation of racism—and for the "Final Solution"—or to question their involvement in the nuclear arms race.[12] At a more intellectual level, too, social scientists in particular are now being taken to task for "forgetting" about genocide in their theories and research practice.[13] The picture that is gradually emerging points to the strength, once again, of an alternative vision where human beings are seen as rational and scientists are seen as more virtuous than most, a vision with wide societal support.

If forgetting about the morally troubling aspects of the past may be drawing additional strength from the widely shared reluctance to dwell on the negatives, the basic operational principle here is one common to the work of memory on the less charged terrain as well. That which does not fit within the established structures of thinking and feeling is very likely to be excluded from remembrance. And, once again, as such structures change, so the patterns of presence and absence are subject to modification.

More and more recent studies of collective remembering and forgetting take the form of case by case investigations of just such processes of change.[14] Recognizing the need to contextualize shifts in meaning assigned to the past translates into reconstructing the socially, culturally and politically complex trajectories. This empirically based approach appears to me as the most reasonable, at least at this stage of analytical time. For while the ideas developed here, as much as the theoretical roots of the work of others, suggest particular heuristic strategies, these cannot substitute for the richness of empirical material. The task, for now, is to formulate good questions, not abstract answers.

When tracing the dynamics of exclusion, we need to be especially careful, I would argue, not to close the inquiry by theoretical fiat. Resolving from the start to focus on the views and attitudes of intellectuals, for example, in recognition of their privileged position as guardians of collective memory may work in some cases, but not in others. The fact that a given narrative offered by historians worked to silence X, when given explanatory power, can effectively obscure the more significant role played by literature. Countries, communities, politics are not equal in the positions they assign to different storytellers or in the importance they grant to remembrance and historical truth. What in one context represents a significant omission may not do so in another; movies in North America warrant close analysis in a way that movies in then East Germany might not.

The study of social forgetting, then, necessitates empirical plausibility of its theoretical premises. Not only do we need convincing that a particular absence in collective memory warrants attention, we also should be persuaded that locating such absence in books rather than monuments, or, in films rather than parades makes sense. And this is only the beginning of retracing the process of exclusion, a retracing that is likely to bring forth a mixture of deliberate choices and tacit acceptance.

Recognizing that absences are often the result of displacement is of major help in what would otherwise appear as a daunting task. For we are better equipped, through the tradition of critical inquiry into the social construction of knowledge, to trace the patterns of remembrance that *are* in place. Mapping out both the details of specific narratives and a general outline of a "structure of sensibility"[15] these narratives fit into goes a long way towards explaining how alternative visions of the past never came to be. A student of Canadian history, for example, who ponders why the experience of radical democracy among the early twentieth-century farmers did not enter that country's sense of its past, offers a plausible explanation indeed by focusing on the consistent framing of "democracy" as involving parties and parliaments.[16] In this case, the idea of local autonomy can be shown to have been displaced through both the historians' and politicians' discourse. Similarly, when beginning in the late 1970s, French intellectuals embarked on a critique of the Left, they were both documenting a particular kind of social amnesia and the strengths of the positive vision of progress that had prevailed before.[17]

Case analyses such as those are often rooted in an ideological critique of the dominant interpretation of the past rather than an interest in the dynamics of exclusion as such. Still, they offer students of collective memory a great deal of valuable material on the intellectual itinerary of displacement. Once again, a certain amount of caution is in order, for the realm of ideas about the past need not be exclusively of such explicit, formulated nature. I too, when studying the fate of Jewish memory in Poland, had assigned high priority to the voices of scholars, writers, and opinion makers. Ultimately, though, I turned to visible markers of Jewish presence (or the lack thereof) in an effort to account for the children's virtual ignorance of that chapter in the country's history.[18] The disappearance of material traces could not explain the exclusion of the Jew, it was more of an indication of the process. But it could help explain how effective this forgetting had been, so close, after all, to the times of the Holocaust.

Although an analysis of displacement of one vision of the past by another is on heuristically most secure grounds when applied to actual texts, it can and it often must be extended to "texts" in their most open meaning. A building that was once a synagogue and now serves as a warehouse is just as much a site of displacement as a cross placed on Jewish memorial grounds. The section of Warsaw built on what had been the ruins of the ghetto, where only a few street names coincide with those from the past, silences that past just as effectively as the exhibit in the city museum which excludes any reference to Warsaw's Jews. Moving to another world, the imagery in *The Lone Ranger*, where the Wild West is a nature preserve, helps to forget the conquest of American Indians very well indeed.[19]

If opening one's analysis up to include the varied modes of remembering (and forgetting) is often a necessity, it is not without risks. Operating within the realm of written discourse, rooted in the long tradition of historical and sociological inquiry, has the great advantage of natural limits to our data, be they influential works of scholarship or literature. Once outside such demarcated terrain, the reservoir of potentially relevant material not only expands exponentially, but offers few clear clues as to limits or priorities. It may be relatively easy to show, drawing again on my previous work, the truncated vision of Jewish tradition as preserved in Polish literature and historiography, a vision which made references to the most basic of Jewish customs in *The Polish Jewry*, a book published in 1982, open to critique for the lack of proper "translation." It is a different task altogether to demonstrate that such a truncated vision received support in other areas of collective remembering, from film to local landscapes. Several analytical choices that had to be made at that stage stemmed less from a general theory of remembrance and more from a close reading of the particular situation at hand. Some of the choices had to follow purely pragmatic considerations of the availability of data. Assigning priority to one form of public discourse over another was also subject to change when a different type of displacement came into focus; looking at how Polish Jews became identified as Poles when victims of the Holocaust, I paid special attention to posters accompanying the many commemorative occasions, for example.

As varied as the forms of public discourse under consideration are, they still remain just that, forms of *public* discourse. When tracing an absence from the "reality of the past" still within experiential reach of a considerable number of people—as was the case with my analysis—there are good reasons to expect that the construction of remembrance would not necessarily draw on public resources. Instead, it is within the sphere of social tellings, familial tales and the like that much of the texture of the recent past would be formed. Especially in a country like Poland, with the Communist regime controlling such a wide range of public expression, attention had to turn to these other, hardly visible, forms of social discourse about the past. Yet, however analytically justified, such a turn would prove problematic indeed. On a very practical level, even a large team of researchers could not monitor enough of naturally occurring conversations to gain a fair sense of societal practices. To instigate talk about the past, while a tried strategy for finding out what people might think about a given issue, was not a viable alternative here either. Claude Lanzmann, when filming *Shoah* in Poland, did exactly that in various locales his crew visited.[20] The responses he elicited from Polish peasants and townsfolk were illuminating, but only their reactions to an intruding foreigner. There was simply no way of telling what they actually remembered—and forgot—when not prompted, not appearing before the camera.[21]

Some indications of the scope of social forgetting could be found in the behavioral sphere. With a few notable exceptions, the many markers of Jewish presence in Poland had been left unattended by the local residents. When not left to decay, Jewish tombstones would be used as pavement material, synagogues as warehouses. And, very much unlike the remembrance of the Polish dead which defied state prohibitions, honoring the Jewish dead fell strictly within the limits defined by the official stricture. The absence of mourning was most evident, however, in the developments immediately following the Holocaust. The returning survivors were not welcome, to say the very least; some 1500 lost their lives at the hands of Poles during the first two years after the end of the war.[22]

To the extent that social construction of remembrance relies on spontaneous storytelling, the widely shared perception of Jewish subjects as taboo offered perhaps the strongest support to the idea that the memory void existing in the public sphere was not being filled with private recollections. As a number of writers were breaking the silence in the early 1980s, they saw themselves as doing exactly that and often commented on the extreme difficulties inherent in talking about things Jewish. What emerged from their reflections was a generalized picture. Unlike in the West, where the emphasis would be on speaking about the Holocaust and the terms of discussion were both intellectually and theologically sophisticated, Polish commentators told of unease and emotional charge in the very mention of the word "Jew." Talk, any talk, about anything related to Jews, was seen as problematic. The language itself, or rather the connotations long attached to terms such as "Jew" and "Jewish" presented a formidable barrier to any normalization of discourse, *both* public and private.[23]

At the same time, the very persistence of the negative meaning of the word "Jew" *did* indicate the persistence of another form of talk, of the mythical identification of Jews with the forces of evil. The displacement at work here was thus not of the type where one "reality of the past" precludes another. Rather, the mythical Jew, conveniently adaptable to any and all historical circumstances, was finally being challenged by a host of historically specific real Jews.

What happened in Poland after I completed my study proved morally unsettling but intellectually illuminating. The vast expanding of public resources for remembering the Jews did not seem to alter the established patterns of private tellings. Outside of the small group of concerned intellectuals, largely responsible for the discussion of Jewish topics in the first place, the mythical Jew remained secure. During the 1990 electoral campaign for the presidency, the word "Jew" was widely used as the ultimate of weapons in discrediting one's opponents. Old conspiracy theories were revived and well. Star of David, added onto posters throughout the country, served as the symbol of enemy threat. Street talk, no longer constrained by the authorities, perpetuated the mythic image. Collective memory proved resistant indeed to intellectual tinkering.

While the "Poland and the Jew" case may be unique for its complex web of historical and political circumstances, the lessons that might be drawn from it point to a general dilemma facing those who are concerned with social forgetting. Inasmuch as the availability of public memory resources defines the potential scope of collective remembrance, filling in the blanks matters. But what appears to matter even more is dislodging the established patterns of thinking and feeling, patterns responsible for the gaps in remembrance. Countering an absence with an ever-growing informational base, in other words, provides only for the *possibility* of change within collective memory. The harder task is to make drawing on these new resources both emotionally and cognitively compelling, or to create a shared need to remember what had not been remembered before.

That task is harder not only because it requires a solid understanding of the roots, the history of particular forgetting, but also because what is to be constructed is much less tangible than knowledge or physical markers. To justify the new ways of remembering, whether on moral, intellectual or emotional grounds, is often to undermine some very cherished cultural values and beliefs. It can also be, as I remarked previously, an explicitly political undertaking. On all counts, many of the basic principles guiding collective life may come under attack. If remembrance tends to maintain social identity and order, working against forgetting is often a radical challenge to both. As such, it is likely to meet with resistance and opposition, even when (or perhaps especially when) the new "infrastructure" of memory is in fact allowed to be constructed.

Our discussion so far, with its heavy emphasis on recognizing, accounting for and ultimately repairing the absences in memory, offers only one side of the normative picture. Social forgetting, it is high time to note, can be and frequently is seen as something both needed and desirable. Beyond the very general idea that too much concern with the past may be counterproductive for collective well being, there are the more specific, culturally inscribed, principles that frame forgetting in a positive way.

Although the idea that we often should "forgive, but not forget" appears at first as a rule explicitly *against* forgetting, its practical application, both for better and for worse, tends to blur the distinction. When Vaclav Havel, as the new president of Czechoslovakia, appealed to his countrymen not to "dig up the dirt" in each other's past, he supported that appeal with a morally unassailable admission that he too was responsible for the wrongs of the Communist regime. For the sake of social peace, Havel argued, people should both recognize their own responsibility and forgive others. Under the circumstances, Havel's voice represented reason and morality all at once. Yet at the same time, it was effectively silencing those who would wish to create a detailed record of the recent past.

To forget but not to forgive was the more common strategy in Central and East European countries leaving Communism behind. Together with a vast and varied effort at a recovery of memory long silenced by the regime came the very practical work of eradicating visible traces of the Communist past from the public sphere. Renaming of streets, squares, and whole towns would at times mean a return to the original; often, however, it provided a means simply to replace the now-despised symbolism of the old with references to the alternative historical narrative. In the decades of the regime's rule, towns and cities grew well beyond their previous borders, making it necessary to go well beyond revindication of the past. What was most striking in this deconstruction of memory, in Poland, for example, was how rapidly the exclusion principle had come to apply to non-Communist figures. Polish intellectuals, quick to note the irony of Orwell-in-reverse, started to question the wisdom of displacing the whole of the country's leftist tradition. They were not able to stop local initiatives, though, or the visible urgency of putting anything connected with the idea of socialism behind.

A similar effort to engineer social forgetting could be observed in the once East Germany. There, however, the voices raised against the practice appeared to enjoy more popular support. If all the traces of the country's Communist past were to disappear, the argument went, so would a base for distinctive collective identity. Concern with the inherent inequality between the two parts of Germany would thus perhaps work to prevent any full-scale obliteration of the Communist heritage.[24]

Considering the speed with which much of the "infrastructure" of remembrance was being altered or altogether destroyed by the emergent democracies, the success of the operation may be very much open to question. For social forgetting to take root, more than the most visibly public traces of the past need to disappear. What was made possible by the undertaking, though, was making it virtually impossible to *honor* the now-displaced past. In this respect, the effort in Central and Eastern Europe is not at all exceptional. For just as much as the call to remember often rests on the moral principles of justice, the argument *not* to remember appeals to our sense of historical fairness. More specifically, when we are asked not to remember, we are essentially being asked not to honor or respect; at issue is usually whether a person, a group, or a movement *deserve* remembrance.

The call not to remember is rarely heard until an alternative is voiced. And the strength of such calls seems to depend on the quality of the honoring to take place. Not surprisingly, controversies erupt more sharply when stakes are high. Instructive here is the recent record of the Vatican's declarations of sainthood. The idea that Queen Isabella of Spain, for example, ought to be so recognized sparked tremendous negative response from concerned Catholics and Jews alike, seeing any honor bestowed upon the Inquisition ruler as morally offensive. On a more limited scale, canonization of Father Maximilian Kolbe, a Polish priest who sacrificed his life for that of another prisoner in Auschwitz, came under heavy attack from those familiar with his record as a devoted antisemite. Within the ideologically opposite sphere, parallels may be drawn with the late 1980s efforts, in the Soviet Union, to ensure that Stalin not be honored in any way.

What is objected to in all such cases is both remembering and forgetting, remembering in the glorifying mode and forgetting of the morally repugnant record. Implicit in the objections is a recognition that to grant honorable remembrance is a very effective way of silencing memory of the past. There is also a recognition that the more publicly visible symbols carry greater weight than the historical record provided by scholars.[25]

In the realm of interpersonal relationships, forgetting (and forgiving) others' mistakes is not only a form of common courtesy but often a much needed basis for present and future success. In the life of societies, similar principles tend to apply at the overt level of diplomacy and international politics. Symbolic gestures by leaders, together with the pragmatic realities of economic and other exchange between the United States and Japan, for example, secure the politically "correct" measure of remembering the mutually problematic past. The wide acceptance of the idea that peaceful coexistence among nations requires a certain amount of forgetting becomes evident at times of controversy. At stake then is not the principle, but the definition of the "proper amount"; when then President Ronald Reagan visited Bitburg cemetery, the presence there of graves of the S.S. led many to protest the crossing of a line.

In a world that suffered many conflicts and great wars in this century, the international forgetting is a fact of life. Its relationship to social forgetting within the countries involved remains largely to be explored.

Two forces impacting the vicissitudes of remembrance deserve special attention, I think. The first is that of allowing, supporting, and encouraging the construction and maintenance of morally purified narratives, both ideologically and practically. As mentioned before, the case of Austria would serve as an analytically fertile ground here. The second is the one working in the opposite direction, at least potentially, as when international pressure places demands on a country to engage in full moral accounting for the past. Yet while encouraging social forgetting, locally and on a wider scale, appears to be effective indeed, it is not at all clear that protests issued from abroad translate into altering the patterns of remembrance at home, or even that they result in shifts of image presented to outsiders. Instructive here is the long history of Turkey's denial of Armenian genocide, in the face of mounting pressures from the Americans in particular.

The past of other countries, beyond being implicated directly in the politics of the day, may also at times serve as a rich reservoir of ideological resources (and obstacles) and thus be subject to altogether different demands than those of expediency. For many Western intellectuals, ever since the Russian Revolution, to take a position on the history of the Soviet Union would mean difficult ideological choices. The forgetting of Stalinist crimes, as much as their rediscovery in the 1970s in France, for example, was structured within a complex internal web of political theory and practice and cannot be understood solely by reference to the international scene.[26]

The perspectives adopted on the West's colonial past, on the French Revolution, on the industrialization in England, on the Greek civilization, to name but the most prominent examples, have been historically and may still be today indicative of ideological positions. What is constructed then is less a "reality of the past" but rather a set of tools for politically charged intellectual debates.

The fact that ideological traditions do cross international borders adds an important dimension to our analysis of social forgetting. Very much strengthened is my earlier call for a case-by-case empirical approach, as the complexity of the picture increases. For the most part removed from the direct experience of people doing the remembering, memory now becomes a much more open terrain, open to construction as well as demolition. Distance, literally and historically, when combined with a high degree of ideological relevance, offers great impetus to creative memory work, and especially to mythological production. Forgetting the ideologically troubling past is all too common. It would be analytically wise to bring it under more intense scrutiny.

To suggest, as I do here, that the dynamic of collective amnesia may be prominently implicated in international affairs is to be reminded, once again, of the limited usefulness of purely psychological terms of analysis. It is also to reinforce the point that whether seen as an absence-which-ought-not-to-be or a proper reflection of current societal priorities, any disappeared past can indeed reappear. Political, ideological as well as broadly cultural forces play a role here, and it is with those forces that a better understanding of social forgetting begins.

## Notes

1. For an introductory survey of the analytical perspectives, see *La mémoire et l'oubli*. Special issue of *Communications*, 49 (Paris: Seuil, 1989).
2. See, especially, Anson Rabinbach and Jack Zipes, eds., *Germans & Jews since the Holocaust: The Changing Situation in West Germany* (New York: Holmes & Meier Publishers, 1986).
3. For an informative, comparative case study, see Judith Miller, *One, by One, by One: Facing the Holocaust* (New York: Simon and Schuster, 1990).
4. See, for example, Jonathan Mirsky, "The Party's Secrets," *The New York Review* (March 25, 1993):57-64.
5. For an insightful study of the beginnings of remedial work, see R. W. Davies, *Soviet History in the Gorbachev Revolution* (Bloomington and Indianapolis: Indiana University Press, 1989).
6. See, for example, Lucy S. Dawidowicz, *The Holocaust and the Historians* (Cambridge, Mass.: Harvard University Press, 1981); Gerd Korman, "Silence in the American Textbooks," *Yad Vashem Studies* VII (1970):183-203; Centre de documentation juive contemporaine, *L'enseignement de la Choa. Comment les manuels d'histoire présent-ils l'extermination des Juifs au cours de la deuxième guerre modiale?* (Paris, 1982).
7. The untold story of the Gypsy victims of the Nazi genocide comes close; see Gabrielle Tyrnauer, "Gypsies and the Holocaust: A Bibliography and Introductory Essay," *Montreal Institute for Genocide Studies* (May 1991) 2nd ed.
8. See, especially, Gérard Namer, *Batailles pour la mémoire: La commémoration en France 1944-1982* (Paris: Papyrus, 1983).
9. Exemplifying the challenge well is Michael Schudson, *Watergate in American Memory: How We Remember, Forget and Reconstruct the Past* (New York: Basic Books, 1992).
10. Implicated here are ideas from both the Right and the Left; see Alain Finkielkraut, *L'avenir d'une négation: Réflection sur la question du génocide* (Paris: Seuil, 1982).
11. See, for example, Thomas Sheehan, "A Normal Nazi," *The New York Review* (January 14, 1993):30-35, and the long exchange of letters which followed.
12. Robert Jay Lifton has been one of the most outspoken critics here; see, especially, Robert Jay Lifton, *The Nazi Doctors: Medical Killing and the Psychology of Genocide* (New York: Basic Books, Inc., 1986).

13. See Frank Chalk and Kurt Jonassohn, *The History and Sociology of Genocide: Analyses and Case Studies* (New Haven: Yale University Press, 1990).

14. One of the best and most comprehensive is Henri Rousso, *The Vichy Syndrome: History and Memory in France since 1944*, translated by Arthur Goldhammer (Cambridge, Mass.: Harvard University Press, 1991).

15. The term is Raymond Williams's. More broadly, my approach owes a great deal to an early exposure to his ideas on culture.

16. Mike McConkey, *The Political Culture of the Agrarian Radicals: A Canadian Adventure in Democracy* (unpublished Ph.D. thesis, McGill University, 1990).

17. Most explicitly in Bernard-Henri Lévy, *L'idéologie française* (Paris: Editions Grasset & Fasquelle, 1981).

18. For an American parallel, see Jonathan Boyarin, *Storm from Paradise: The Politics of Jewish Memory* (Minneapolis: University of Minnesota Press, 1992).

19. Ariel Dorfman and Armand Mattelart, *How to Read Donald Duck*, translated by David Kunzle (New York: International General, 1984).

20. For a transcript, see Claude Lanzmann, *Shoah: An Oral History of the Holocaust - The Complete Text of the Film* (New York: Pantheon Books, 1985).

21. For further discussion, in general terms, of the problems facing oral historians, see James Fentress and Chris Wickham, *Social Memory* (Oxford and Cambridge, Mass.: Blackwell, 1992).

22. See Lucjan Dobroszycki, "Restoring Jewish Life in Post-War Poland," *Soviet Jewish Affairs* 2 (1973):58-72. I am indebted to Alina Cala, a Polish ethnographer/historian, for sharing with me the results of her research in the early 1980s. Interviews with peasants in the southeastern regions not only confirmed the prior estimates of how widespread the killings of Jews have been, but also showed that both at the time and decades later, such action was perceived as perfectly "normal." See Alina Cala, *Wizerunek Zyda w polskiej kulturze ludowej* (Warszawa: Wydawnictwa Uniwersytetu Warszawskiego, 1992).

23. For more discussion, see Iwona Irwin-Zarecka, "Problematizing the 'Jewish Problem'," *Polin: A Journal of Polish-Jewish Studies* 4 (1989):281-95.

24. That Rosa Luxemburg became a subject of both a popular movie and public recognition is a telling example here.

25. For a case study of this dynamic, see Norma Field, *In the Realm of a Dying Emperor: A Portrait of Japan at Century's End* (New York: Pantheon Books, 1991).

26. See Bernard Legendre, *Le stalinisme français: Qui a dit quoi? (1944-1956)* (Paris: Seuil, 1980).

# 8

# Memory Projects

The work that goes into the construction and maintenance of collective memory becomes especially visible on projects designed to give presence to the previously absent or silenced past. Looking closer at a few such projects allows us then to understand better the basic dynamics of remembrance. Compressing the otherwise diluted effort (in time and social practice), memory projects call our attention to the fact that there is nothing automatic about entering the public record or being remembered. And while this is not theoretical news, what memory projects do is to bring the idea into the foreground of public discourse with rarely matched clarity. Both through explicit "editorials" and unabashed creation of new symbolic resources, many expose the presence of social and political control over memory to the public-at-large. In that sense, their importance goes beyond the immediate results at hand, as memory projects reclaim more than a past, they reclaim the power to define it.

One of the more intensive and extensive memory projects is that prompted by the feminist critique of patriarchy. Starting with the idea that women had been largely excluded from the historical record and extending this idea to the still-to-be record of contemporary life, feminist writers and scholars set out first to document women's experiences, women's perspectives, and women's roles. Whether the field be art, literature, music, science, or politics, the task is to retrieve what had been lost, to reevaluate what had been present. The scope of this work is naturally quite immense, and the results too varied to be reducible to recordkeeping. Methodological, ideological, and political disputes abound. But what has emerged so far, particularly in North America, is a new set of resources for thinking about the past, both in general and in many specific areas.

Continuously augmented, this new set is still largely the specialist's territory. Used within the movement, and discussed primarily within respective disciplines (though, characteristically, the works often cross academic lines), products of this memory project are still very slowly absorbed within the intellectual canon, let alone the popular one. In a sense, what has been provided by the numerous investigations is the informational base on which collective memory can be restructured. The struggle now is to find ways best to secure the restructuring.

On this issue, too, disagreements abound. For some scholars and activists, the growth and strengthening of "women's studies" within the academia gains priority, for the time being. Others worry about the effects of a "ghettoization" of knowledge such arrangements encourage and risk perpetuating. If new generations are to be capable of seeing human heritage as inclusive of men *and* women, it is not enough, the argument goes, to teach those already accepting the idea. Indeed, it is often pointed out, confining the work to a small sector within university education is close to a guarantee that change be painstakingly slow.[1] On the other hand, the sheer amount of work still to be done in the information gathering mode alone may call for just such a concentration.

The feminist memory project is only a part, of course, of a larger project for change, thus affecting and affected by many an internal debate. Its core *raison d'être*—to retrieve women's history—resonates with the idea that women's experience is different from men's. The results of inquiries, though, can speak to a strict separation of men and women just as they can confirm that the dividing line is a cultural construct. In effect, one can probe the past to strengthen whichever philosophical line one chooses. And while this definitely adds to lively debates, such pliability of the reclaimed past also poses a major challenge to the much needed popularizing of ideas. The newly constructed "realities of the past" risk being embroiled in too complex an ideological battle for the media to handle, and for the public to make sense of.[2]

Another inherent risk in a politically motivated memory project, especially one as closely intertwined with the developing of collective identity, is that of sanitizing the records of the past for the sake of greater inspirational value. Mentioning in passing, for example, that a great advocate of the women's right to abortion, Margaret Sanger, was also in favor of "racial improvement" through eugenics does little for meeting the moral challenge this combination presents.[3] In this respect, though, the disagreements within the movement may work to counterbalance the emphasis on good points; "inspirational value" being itself relative to the professed views allows for the full moral complexity eventually to emerge.[4]

At this stage, the feminist memory project is for the most part still laying the groundwork for remembrance. With a few exceptions,[5] attending to the past has taken the path of inquiry rather than commemoration. Exhibits, art work, drama, and independent film and video productions remain minorities within the predominantly verbal discourse. Symbolic resources are thus skewed, as it were, in the direction of facts and ideas. Even if emotional content is not lacking, emphasis is on knowing about the past, on securing its presence within the informational environment more than the visual one.

Considering this emphasis on the construction of new narratives (and recovery of the ones lost), it is understandable that a major battle ground here be school curricula. Educational practice, more than any other form of public discourse, is called upon to make the products of the feminist memory project widely available. It is still much too early to tell how successful such a strategy can be. The very scope of the restructuring of collective memory that is ultimately aimed for, let alone the opposition to such massive changes, makes this a long-term project indeed. In the short term, though, the already posed challenge to the official canon of tellings, the emphasis on "breaking the silence" as well as that on directly giving a voice to the disenfranchised, have helped—and been helped by—changing the texture of public discourse about the past and present. The battle over school curricula, to take but the most visible example, extends in North America to issues of proper historical credit for the minorities, as do debates on the viability of black or Asian studies. Women's speaking out on abuse within the family has prompted a much wider public acknowledgment of the realities of violence and incest. And the strong current of lesbian concerns joins with the critical recovery of the homosexual experience in the struggle for human rights.

It will be up to historians to trace the numerous linkages here, on the level of ideas as well as institutional practices. What is especially interesting for students of collective memory are the parallels of uneasy accommodation between the particular and the universal concerns. A memory project that is an integral part to strategies of empowerment has to do two things. It has to build up a storehouse of symbolic resources (and inspirational materials) for the group at hand. At the same time, these same resources are deemed generally important and to be included in the official (hegemonic) cannon. The first task calls for memory work that is relatively straightforward—inquiry into the past in search of the "missing pieces." The second task demands editorial work, as it were, which can prove a great deal more problematic. At issue is persuading the majority, and especially the socially powerful, that a restructuring of collective memory should be taking place. Here, appeals to the need for group identity have to be toned down, if not displaced by appeals to universal values—justice, truth, individual rights. Power, which is at the heart of the matter, frequently may acquire the more attractive packaging of enrichment for all.

Power can, of course, take the center stage in a memory project, but this appears much more likely to happen when the work involves many different sectors of the civil society in confrontation with the extant (and to be overthrown) political system. Preservation of the records, especially the records of oppression, now acquires the very direct value of an  instrument in struggle including, but not limited to, retribution. Cruel regimes have a great deal of respect for remembrance, as seen in the elaborate methods used to destroy whatever does not conform to the official line. And people living with those regimes very much share in that respect, knowing as they do that even the smallest act of the "wrong" commemoration can be dangerous.[6] In such tense circumstances, memory projects are still about specific knowing of the past, but there is also the great stress on symbolic (and ideally public) expression of remembrance.

Mothers of the "disappeared" in Argentina understood this dynamic very well indeed; theirs was not only a struggle for preserving the memory of their children, but a direct, and ultimately successful, challenge to the power of the regime. With the policy of *glasnost* in the Soviet Union, the once fully underground efforts to record the state crimes and to commemorate its victims acquired a threatening public presence. There, the unleashed memory projects covered a massive historical territory, well beyond that of martyrology (and responsibility).[7] The struggle, in some cases, was for dignity of those who perished, physically and symbolically. In the case of the organization *Pamyat* (Memory),[8] it has been unabashedly a struggle for power, with all the myth production this can imply. The political stakes are very high, whatever the emphasis.

For it is through a recovery of the past—communal, institutional, national—that the civil society is to emerge.

In Poland, a country where the process began much earlier, and where *glasnost* had been an implicit practice rather than an explicit policy since the mid-1970s, this creative capacity of collective memory was openly recognized by all political actors. Translating into a myriad of small projects, efforts to reconstruct civil society took, once again, the mixed form of documenting the officially to-be-forgotten and symbolic expression of remembrance through public ritual.[9] By the mid-1980s, the regime effectively acquiesced to the presence of alternative "realities of the past," from underground publications to graves of the victims. In 1989, the Communist Party retreated altogether, unable even to pretend legitimacy.

All this is not to say that memory projects alone are responsible for overthrowing powerful regimes. Indeed, it is only once the tight grip of control over public discourse is somewhat loosened that oppositional memory work intensifies and has the potential to succeed. It is to recognize, though, that the energy, if not the risks, involved in the recording and remembering the forbidden past has tremendous rallying force. It is also to recognize that in situations where public debate is not open, reclaiming control over one's history is a major step indeed.

In the cases discussed so far, where a memory project presents a major challenge to the very structure of power built into public discourse, much of the attention of the participants and analysts alike is deservedly turned to the *contents* of new offerings. Facts, figures, dates, all the "hard stuff" of collective memory are the main focus, with the symbolic texture of remembrance often allowed spontaneously to emerge. Public gestures of commemoration, while of great importance as testimony to the struggle are not themselves subject to critical deliberation. Internal debates, which almost inevitably accompany the memory work in progress, tend to center on the interpretation of the newly constructed fragments of the past rather than ways to remember. In that sense, such memory projects are not self-conscious, however much the participants recognize the importance of what they are doing. Actively attending to the past, in other words, need not mean critically attending to remembrance.

Not all memory projects share these qualities. Indeed, most conducted on a smaller scale do not. For what is usually involved in the very concrete undertakings to secure remembrance is the construction, often in the literal sense, of memory markers, where issues of form are as demanding of attention as those of content. Securing remembrance means symbolically representing a given "reality of the past" all the while calling upon the public to pay attention.[10] This can be done with textual means, but words alone may not be adequate. A space, a museum, a monument would be the chosen sites to focus on. And these, by their very nature of a symbolic shorthand, demand careful deliberation on each detail, from the location to material to shape.

Matters of content—and the political implication of its public presence—do not become irrelevant, far from it. But they are now translated, as it were, into minute questions of form. Some of this translation—and the debates that follow—may become public knowledge; the dispute over the Vietnam War Memorial in Washington would be a case in point.[11] When this happens, the framing of remembrance acquires a great deal of additional (explicit) force. At times, effort is made to prevent that, to let the finished product "speak for itself"—and to cover the sharp controversies of the design stage. The Holocaust Memorial Museum, also in Washington, where planning took several years and several emotionally charged turns would exemplify the latter.[12]

The high public visibility, as well as the complexity of the events themselves, account for much of the self-conscious attention to detail here. But even on memory projects that are not as problematic, yet still focused on securing remembrance, great care may be taken in the selecting and framing of materials at hand. Consideration is given to what we may broadly term "pedagogical" value, especially when the final product is to be actually used in educational practice.[13] To evoke remembrance among people who know little and feel even less about an event *is* a challenge. One of the ways in which this challenge can be met—often tried in schools or small communities—is to involve everyone in the project. Asking children to gather information—or adults to reminisce—while providing critical guidance and commentary brings the events emotionally closer, thus augmenting the potential for remembrance beyond learning lessons. Incorporating local history in projects dealing with such big entities as World War II or Vietnam allows for the need for personal relevance of the past if it is to be remembered.

Drawing in of nonspecialists, if at times a deliberate strategy adopted by the specialists, may occur a lot earlier and more directly. Indeed, it is often with nonspecialists that memory projects begin; it was the Vietnam veterans themselves who initiated work on what would become The Wall, to take but one example. In this respect, memory projects are quite unique within the general area of production of collective memory—they welcome participation from ordinary people, at least in principle. The elements of personal relevance, personal interest (and, frequently, personal memory) acquire positive value, in notable contrast to work by historians or even journalists. The securing of public remembrance cannot, however, be a private matter, on a small or a large scale. Expert knowledge, expert artistry are not sufficient either; indeed, at times they are not applied at all. What is required is public support, in the very concrete sense of funding and in the broader terms of rules governing public discourse and public space. Individual initiative and work can carry a memory project in its first stages, but without some institutional back-up, the results could not become available beyond a small circle of those directly involved.[14]

The need for public support can extend participation in a memory project rather widely, not in the direct sense of working together, but in the equally consequential terms of sponsorship and the power of critique it entails. Projects that require considerable expenditures and/or access to the media face a particularly acute demand to justify their own existence to potential supporters, and then to the public at large. Oppositional memories are put at an immediate disadvantage here, both ideologically and practically.[15] But projects that do find willing sponsors readily are also not problem free. Political loyalties, commercial considerations, desire to appeal to wider audience, all can result in effective self-censorship on the part of memory workers.

What the demand for garnering public acceptance strengthens is the already considerable explicitness of the very process of framing remembrance. Because memory projects operate on new and often controversial terrain, and because the remembrance they aim to secure is rarely "natural" for the community at hand, the work involved contains building up of a rationale for itself.[16] On a memory project I studied closely in the early 1980s—Poland's extensive invitation for the Jew to inhabit the country's heritage—where remembering was indeed running counter to the long history of ignorance and indifference, the emphasis on the reasons for remembrance for a long time equalled that of the actual construction of it. And while this may be an extreme case, a particularly strong challenge to the established patterns of collective memory, the very need for self-justification is by no means unique. North American debates about school curricula, we mentioned earlier, are also primarily about rationale for change and secondarily about the logistics. In the context of Central and Eastern Europe, the work of the recovery of memory proceeds amidst disputes about the social and political consequences; not everyone agrees even on the basic principle that freedom of historical inquiry is a key component of a democratic process. When a group of citizens in a small town in Germany decides to document the town's history, including the Nazi period, they cannot just call upon local pride; the hard work of persuasive justification begins.

The fact that memory projects remind us not to take remembrance for granted brings them analytically close to conflicts where a given historical "truth" is being contested. In both instances, the otherwise quiet presence of the past is being disturbed, as it were, for all to see. Yet while confrontations over the content provide us with implicit clues about the role of collective memory, the rationales heard from project workers offer the invaluable direct testimony to the actors' own understanding. An analyst cannot, of course, treat such testimony at face value; precisely because public support is so often at stake, an element of "packaging" would be importantly present. In that sense, what project workers tell us is also what they perceive to be the justifiable reason for their efforts, thus shedding light on the wider societal dynamics of remembrance. In Canada, for example, numerous proposals to document (and teach) ethnic history are "sold" to government funding agencies in the name of multiculturalism, an increasingly accepted proposition. Thirty years ago, the same idea would have had to be presented in terms of integration and assimilation to garner support. Project workers, then and now, might be doing exactly the same thing; societal climate changed.

The articulation of memory's significance by those working on its construction must also be analytically detached from the meanings acquired by the product. However explicit is the framing of remembrance at the point of origin, as it were, there are no guarantees that a text, a monument, an exhibit would be "read" as intended, even within the immediate constituency of the project.[17] Over time, too, the "editorial" statements tend to move far into the background of the memory markers themselves, further facilitating a multiplicity of interpretations. In the end, the importance of the newly constructed "infrastructure" for remembrance may be in its very existence, allowing for different uses to emerge, compete, conflict.

Memory projects are thus best to be studied as they happen, for this is when we are given the rare opportunity to observe the framing process. Once in place, products of such concerted efforts to affect the structure of collective memory come to coexist with many other symbolic resources, which would have their own histories. Even though, by their very nature, memory projects provide resources that had not been available before, filling in the gaps, as it were, it would be a mistake to see them as operating in a symbolic vacuum. Indeed, the absence within collective memory they seek to counteract can be itself a powerful grid for interpreting the past. In other cases, reclaiming control over history works to displace the previously established canon of tellings, a still more concrete structure of remembrance. Most significantly, perhaps, the very realm of the new symbolic resources may extend well beyond the project's territory. Once the public's attention is directed towards a given aspect of the past, and once certain key works are completed by the project's members, it is often like a signal to others that a topic is "in." From the point of view of potential restructuring of collective memory, this undoubtedly spells success. On the other hand, with the much broader participation in the construction work, the original goals of a project, its clear direction and statements of purpose may no longer apply to all of the production in place.[18] Especially on large and long-term memory projects, it then becomes difficult to separate the deliberate from the incidental.

Beyond this element of an unplanned growth, many memory projects have an in-built mechanism for including works not originally created on the project itself, thus for reframing of extant resources. Indeed, though we may be giving most credit to the production of the new, bringing back the old under a different tag of relevance, as it were, is often equally important.[19] Renaming of a public square, renovating a house of prayer turned to a warehouse, displaying once hidden photographs—these are but few of the forms taken by reworking of the "old stuff." To build meaningful linkages with the past might be virtually impossible without some of this reincorporation taking place, however difficult it is at times.

The need to use materials created in quite different historical (and symbolic) context may lead to problems, though. When the Royal

Ontario Museum in Toronto put together an exhibition devoted to the history of Canadian missionary work in Africa, local black activists staged weeks of long protests at the door, accusing the curators of racism. At issue, in particular, were several photographs, shot by the missionaries and now on display together with the artifacts they had brought home. For black activists, these pictures of the "primitive Africans" were just that; museum officials argued, in turn, that the photographs accurately depicted the attitudes of the time. The dispute reached the mass media, where it became linked with other ongoing controversies, not so much about the sophistication of audiences (which was appealed to by the museum advocates), but about the "property rights" to meaning production. At issue now would be the propriety of majority cultural institutions and artists to talk about the experience of blacks, Native Canadians . . . and women. Mutually exclusive claims to the past were staked as well. Appropriating the history of the Other in the name of Canada's diversity proved highly offensive to the Other, or more specifically, to writers and artists struggling to be heard in their authentic voices.[20]

Not resolved, not resolvable, what this dispute brought into the foreground is a key dilemma for memory projects aiming far beyond the symbolic vocabulary of the target audience. When the task is to include the Other among the referents of collective remembrance, how is one to balance demands for authenticity with the threat of Otherness remaining on the outside? And, who should be doing the memory work—those once excluded, or those once excluding?

As we have seen, the issues are far from settled on the feminist project, where the call for inclusion came from the Other. Settlement is also not likely in the Canadian case, where the initiative to reflect the country's multicultural fabric in the tellings about the past is more evenly split between old elites and applicant Others.

It is instructive, in this context, to look at a case where the questions have been answered, if somewhat by default, in favor of the exotic. In Poland, where the recovery of the Jewish heritage has been virtually exclusively an undertaking by the Polish hosts, the Jew proved most appealing when most foreign. Among the tremendous variety of cultural productions devoted to things Jewish, the ones finding the broadest audience and most popular appeal are renditions of very Jewish (and mysterious) Jewishness. Relying largely on imports—works by I. B. Singer, for example[21]—does not guarantee authenticity in reading, but it does introduce a whole new and exotic lexicon. The idea of enrichment thus appears to translate well into remembrance of the Other as a colorful figure, interesting because of his Otherness. At the same time, though, the voice of the Jew is heard highly selectively, as any expression of anger or criticism of the hosts would be toned down, if not rejected altogether. In that way, the "Jewish memory project" in Poland remains within the established pattern of a presentation of self while presenting the Other.

As North Americans struggle with their (increasingly recognized) cultural diversity, we can expect several more rediscovery-of-heritage projects to enter the public agenda. At this point, it is not at all clear whether preserving the difference of the Other(s) would win over a search for common historical threads. For students of collective memory, this is a fertile ground indeed for investigating what the past is meant to do, and what it actually does.

## Notes

1.  Another broader issue enters the debate as well—that of the nature of feminist scholarship and pedagogy, or the degree of change called for.
2.  To take but one example: in Ontario, the 1992 proposed changes in employment legislation to secure equity for women brought forth only a very limited public discussion. The issue *is* important, but few journalists are equipped to explain what exactly is at stake.
3.  In one of the standard texts, Josephine Donovan, *Feminist Theory: The Intellectual Traditions of American Feminism* (New York: Ungar, 1986), 52, the reference is only to a "limited population growth."
4.  Claudia Koonz, *Mothers in the Fatherland: Women, the Family and Nazi Politics* (New York: St. Martin's Press, 1987) is exemplary in this regard.
    I am grateful to Claudia Koonz for providing me with reviews of her book as well as her insights on this point.
5.  On December 6, 1989, Marc Lepine gunned down fourteen female engineering students at the Université de Montréal, explicitly aiming at "feminists." Now referred to as the "Montreal massacre," the event is widely commemorated in Canada with vigils, marches, and other events.
6.  See, for example, Fang Lizhi, "The Chinese Amnesia," *The New York Review* (September 27, 1990):30-31.
7.  For a useful summary, see David Remnick, "Dead Souls," *The New York Review* (December 19, 1991):72-81.
8.  *Pamyat*, with its advocacy for honoring Stalin and strong currents of antisemitism, had a large degree of (implicit) support from the opponents of the reforms.
9.  See, especially, Bronislaw Baczko, *Les Imaginaires sociaux. Mémoirs et espoirs collectifs* (Paris: Payot, 1984).
10. For a rich analysis of this process, see Karal Ann Marling and John Wetenhall, *Iwo Jima: Monuments, Memories, and the American Hero* (Cambridge, Mass.: Harvard University Press, 1991).

11. See *Monumental Histories*. A special issue of *Representations* 35, Summer 1991.
12. See Judith Miller, *One, by One, by One: Facing the Holocaust* (New York: Simon and Schuster, 1990).
13. See, especially, Ivan Karp and Steven D. Lavine, eds., *Exhibiting Cultures: The Poetics and Politics of Museum Display* (Washington, D.C.: Smithsonian Institution Press, 1991).
14. See, especially, Michael Kammen, *Mystic Chords of Memory. The Transformation of Tradition in American Culture* (New York: Alfred A. Knopf, 1991).
15. See *Between Memory and History*, edited by Marie-Noëlle Bourquet, Lucette Valensi and Nathan Wachtel, *History and Anthropology* 2, 2 (October 1986).
16. For interesting examples, mostly emphasizing the goal of "healing," see Thomas Butler, ed., *Memory: History, Culture and the Mind* (Oxford and New York: Basil Blackwell, 1989).
17. For an excellent case study, see James E. Young, "The Biography of a Memorial Icon: Nathan Rapaport's Warsaw Ghetto Monument," *Representations* 26 (Spring 1989):69–107.
18. For example, even though the recovery of Poland's Jewish heritage began on the note of cultural pluralism, the work actually produced over the last ten years is heavily skewed towards memory of the Holocaust in general, and personal testimony in particular.
19. See, especially, David Lowenthal, *The Past is a Foreign Country* (Cambridge: Cambridge University Press, 1985).
20. This particular debate in 1990 coincided with attempts to redraw the rules for funding cultural projects by Canada Council (a federal agency); the issue remains on the media agenda.
21. With the now privatised publishing industry, keeping track of bestsellers has become a common practice. Singer's works have been consistently in the top 10 (on the lists compiled by *Polityka*).

# 9

# Truth Claims

Among many social scientists today, it is not altogether fashionable to speak of "truth." The underlying theme, after all, in so much of inquiry is that of construction—of facts, ideas, images, and values. This inquiry into the dynamics of collective memory is, in many ways, equally concerned with how "the past" comes to be for us what it is. And yet, precisely because common sense tells us that what did not happen cannot be remembered (though it can be talked about otherwise), there are no easy analytical escapes from dealing with truth. Indeed, no matter how much equality we may grant—in principle—to different interpretations of the same events, there is always a point at which both scholars and ordinary folk start to cry foul. Academic reviews and popular media may pay homage to the philosophical doubts as to the status of reality, but in their practices, and especially in their arguments about quality, the premise of knowable truth persists. Collective memory in particular may be increasingly recognized as both an all too selective and mediated version of the past (often when contrasted with findings of historical research), but that does not absolve it from judgments of accuracy. The essentially mythical structure of remembrance, the often all-too-obvious ideological bents, the emotional charge of symbols and disputes, in short, the expected departures from objective (and dry) facts do not make collective memory into a terrain of pure fiction. What they do do is necessitate a closer look at their own truth claims. For in order to understand how collective memory works, we must appreciate how it is framed in relation to its base—collective experience.

Memory work, the work of giving order and meaning to the past, is not an analytically homogeneous process. At times, in the inquiries by investigative reporters, memory work may follow the principles of scientific inquiry. At other times, as when ordinary and not-so-ordinary people write up their biographies, the work involved is that of storytelling. The truth to life of the television series *Roots* is of mythological quality. The emotional power of the Vietnam War Memorial is a work of art. And the crowds' cheering at the taking down of monuments to Communist heroes in Poland is an apt symbol of that country's rejection of the imposed vision of history.

To students of collective memory that very diversity within its construction *is* a challenge. It may not always be recognized as such, since the researchers tend to focus on internally consistent "chunks" of the diversified whole of remembrance, but it becomes immediately apparent when the emphasis shifts to "chunks" of experience. To understand how the West Germans have coped with their "unmasterable past," one cannot (ideally) ignore the movies nor the stores selling Nazi memorabilia when studying school curricula.[1] When I studied the invitation extended to the Jew to inhabit Poland's memory, the only way to make sensible sense of it was to look at exhibitions as well as press polemics, at new books as well as the restored old buildings, at the memorial ceremonies as well as the production of *Fiddler on the Roof*. The serious, the mundane, the sacred, the dramatic, the exotic, and yes, the commercial—these are all facets of remembrance. And before inquiring into *what* they tell us about the past (and the present), it is helpful to recognize their distinct ways of framing-while-communicating ideas and feelings.

At issue here are primarily the differences in "readings" engendered by particular forms of memory work.[2] Allowing for all the other factors which would influence how a person responds to a cluster of meanings—personal experience, knowledge, values, ideals—there remain often sharp differences in the potential response to those meanings inherent in their mode of presentation. Indeed, the very scope of the meanings presented depends largely on their locale, be it a parade or an academic treaty.

To say this is not to restate McLuhan's "the medium is the message," for in looking at collective memory, contents matter more than the forms. It is to recognize that the analysis of public discourse in general must allow for the mixing of standards and standard procedures applied to the production of meaning. Whether we like it or not, comparing apples and oranges is often a necessity when tracing cultural trends. The task here is to clarify what kinds of apples and what kinds of oranges are we throwing in together when speaking of collective memory.

The fact, remarked on earlier, that people do get upset when remembrance of the past is not faithful to that past (as they see it) may serve as a useful point of departure. Clearly, the negative reaction among some Vietnam War veterans to the plan of only listing the dead on The Wall is not quite the same as Habermas's outrage at the historians' attempt to relativize Nazi crimes. At the heart of both, though, is the now out-of-fashion idea of the "essence" of the historical reality. Practically all memory work, from the sophisticated writings by academics to the simple gesture of laying flowers at the likely, but unidentified, site of our loved ones' death is judged, however implicitly, as to its "fit" with the past experience.[3]

When memory work takes on an oppositional thrust, such as when the past is recovered or revised against the established canons, that work's very *raison d'être* lies in its claims to a better, more complete or more honest truth. When a country's official memory runs counter to the memory shared by many of its people (the case in Eastern Europe during the postwar decades), truth becomes less of an analytical category and more of a rallying point for the struggle for freedom. In both of these cases, at the center of claimed or reclaimed truth about the past are hard historical facts—events, people, their actions, their writings. In other words, in large-scale efforts to secure remembrance of once forgotten or once-to-be forgotten elements of collective experience, the operational meaning of truth is that of our common sense notion of "this really happened."

Among the different people who engage in memory work, historians are often granted a special status as those with the strongest claims to the truth of "this really happened" kind. Despite the long tradition of debates within historiography, and the by now considerable evidence to the contrary from sociologists of science, ordinary people in democratic societies do not ordinarily question the historian's authority to proclaim truth. Only when confronted with a blatant misuse of that authority— usually, though, framed as something which happens in undemocratic societies—are nonspecialists ready to become suspicious. (The situation is, of course, radically different for those living in places where history is ruled by ideological fiat.) For all the strength of the feminist critique of established history, the repair work being undertaken is again a province of historians. Methodological disputes as well as epistemological challenges that may pervade academic writings do not easily enter public discourse proper. The popular perception of historical scholars as "experts" cannot be discounted just because we as academics may know better. In this day and age of mass media especially, where reliance on expert knowledge both legitimates the contents of television productions and strengthens the very legitimacy of the experts, students of collective memory would be well advised to overcome their own doubts and take these truth claims seriously.

The role of historians as advisors to media producers or to commissions in charge of public commemorative works and events, when coupled with the growing interest in nonfiction that gives at least some scholars an unprecedented amount of public exposure, provide for an extensive contribution of historical research to the construction of collective memory.[4] Where that contribution is most crucial, however, is within the educational system proper. Once again, allowing for the fact that many children and young adults may not have taken history courses or may have little interest in them, the contents of school curricula remain the key transmission device for expert historical knowledge. And if the study of literature can reveal more about the past than the dry descriptions of facts, the students learn early to appreciate the difference between subjective account and objective truth, or that historians provide the latter. The very format of textbooks, including those used at the university level, sends a clear message of facticity. Pupils may be encouraged to reflect or assess different explanations, but in the end, they should all know "what really happened."

How important the school is within the whole socialization package as far as making sense of the past is concerned is a matter for empirical investigation. It is indeed regrettable that otherwise informative studies of the curricula, most often concerned with their "inadequate treatment of . . . , " pay so little attention to the context in which the schools function. Recognizing that our understanding of the actual impact of history lessons is not adequate, I would suggest, though, that their unique position to provide young people with authorized truths about the past makes their study a crucial element of inquiries about collective memory.

Just as the actual importance of history textbooks is a matter for investigation, so is the broader question of the role played by historians in the construction of their country's sense of the past. Beyond the easily apparent differences between the respect for historians in a democratic society and the suspicions they engender as guardians of official doctrines, there are also the more subtle distinctions informed by cultural attitudes. In a country like France, where intellectual debates are not restricted to academics and where reading is still a highly regarded activity, printed discussion of what might otherwise appear as obscure points of an historical record gains both a wider audience and greater resonance than in the United States, for example.[5] Historians in Germany, traditionally regarded as providers of national pride, and still struggling with such high orders, receive a hearing among their people that reflects that.[6] In the countries of Eastern Europe, where at the beginning of the decade so many historical works were being rejected and their authors issued public summons of accountability, the future of the profession may depend on its ability to reclaim a "pure" scientific status.[7] In short, what is expected of historians at a given time in a given place may well define their impact on public discourse at large.

Finally, the authority of the historians' claims to truth is very much dependent on the proximity of the collective experience itself. Recent history, after all, is not just a subject of study; it is a part of individual biographies as well. If ordinary people are rarely equipped to challenge the expert views of the Roman Empire, they are both perfectly capable and often highly motivated to question the wisdom of academic definition of their own past. The potential for disagreement can account not only for active counterproduction of remembrance, but is also at source of the withdrawing of credit from professional truth-makers.

And yet, when that happens, when historians are not trusted as purveyors of collective past, the very standard of historical truth is, if anything, reinforced. For when people dispute the definitions of "what really happened" based on their own knowledge of the events, they are empiricists par excellence.[8] (I am, I should stress, referring here to collectively posed challenges, not to individual's rejection of authorized truth.) In other words, whether a particular account of the past produced by historians is countered by other historians or by ordinary people who "were there," the right to enter collective memory is equally based on the claim to objective truth.

When we add journalists and a whole variety of nonhistorically trained intellectuals to the already substantial contingent of professional and lay defenders of historical truth, the work of remembrance may indeed appear as modeled on, if not actually ruled by scientific procedures. Yet if we think of collective memory as providing us with resources for making sense of the past, establishing the base line of "what really happened" is only that, establishing the base line. To make sense is to give meaning to the facts and figures, to assign significance to some events and people over others, to see patterns over time, to define deviations. Making sense of a specific experience is also a process of evaluation, primarily in moral terms, of its place in the universal human drama. Finally, it is a process of emotional classification, as it were, of attaching feelings from within a wide range of those involved in remembrance not only to ideas about the past, but most importantly, to places, objects, and images which serve as memory markers.[9]

A powerful monument such as the Vietnam War Memorial in Washington does not "tell a story" of the war; what it does do exceptionally well is to evoke feelings, and to offer a site for often very personal reckoning with a shared trauma. Its claim to truth—which was disputed—rests on its ability to symbolize the essence of complex historical reality. Openly framing remembrance, The Wall gives mourning for the young who died precedence over honoring the fight itself; its very (belated) presence and its locale add to the sense it is asking Americans to make of their country's involvement in Vietnam.

Collective memory would be much impoverished if it could not reside in physically distinct spaces—cemeteries, memorials, monuments, but also buildings and structures from the times long gone. Indeed, the care so often taken by countries and communities to preserve as well as construct such memory markers points to a widely shared recognition that our link with the past has to be supported and maintained in ways which give it permanency. These memory markers, though, are also special, at times approaching the status of sacred places.[10] Set apart from the flow of everyday life, memorial structures in particular are set up for the enactment of rituals, both private and collective. Whether a prayer, laying of flowers or minute of silence, the burning of candles or an elaborate parade, gestures of remembrance might look awkward indeed outside of these special places. Often associated with special occasions as well, the acts of commemorating the past symbolize that past just as much as they symbolize our sense of obligation. Through their very presence, memory markers call upon us. And through their particular forms, they frame the symbolic texture of our remembering.[11]

Unlike historical accounts of what happened, which ask us to learn and to understand, physical memory markers demand attention, action and feeling. They mark particular collective experiences as important, all the while crystallizing the particulars of the past into symbols. Sometimes, these symbols serve as closures in that they come to possess a definitive meaning. At other times, the range of possible readings is much wider, if never completely open. However we may judge such symbols in aesthetic terms, they work as art does. And their claims to truth are very much like those staked by art—of representing the true meaning of human experience.

Monuments cannot lie, of course, in the same ways that historians can. Yet if repair work is now undertaken in Auschwitz to render the camp museum more truthful to the realities of Jewish extermination, it is indeed in recognition that the symbolic absence of Jews was a lie. It is also in recognition of the primary importance of memory markers as sites soliciting remembrance and not just making it possible. In other words, among all the varied forms of public discourse about the past, it is the memory markers that most actively engage remembrance.

If historians' works and physical memory markers are taken as two extreme ends of a continuum, much of what informs and forms our sense of the past can be found inbetween. Public storytelling of the contemporary variety through television and film, novels, poems, biographies, autobiographies, theater productions, and commemoration ceremonies—all may mix, in a variety of ways, claims to speak of "what really happened" with claims to capture the true meaning of the past.[12]

The very presence of an event or a person among matters publicly discussed is often the first step towards entering collective memory; after all, media coverage of today rapidly becomes a form of instantaneous memory construction for tomorrow's sake. And even if with the passage of time, not all and not even most of important stories of yesterday are actually remembered, the degree of popular exposure being no guarantee for posterity, the very principles behind that exposure can tell us a great deal about the dynamics of remembrance as well. For the framing of stories as dramatic, newsworthy, significant or just plain interesting applies to the present as well as the past; indeed, in the increasingly crowded market of ideas and images, the demands placed on the "old stuff" to justify its relevance to contemporary audiences are high. If historians can often pursue subjects because, like Mt. Everest, they are there, a film producer searching for funds to support yet another project on Vietnam has no such leeway. On the other hand, if the restoration of a synagogue in the east part of Berlin merits to be done simply to secure remembrance, the complexity of the narrative in Lanzmann's *Shoah* filmed for the very same reason, immediately raises the issue of contents.

Claiming our attention *and* claiming to be a faithful rendition of the past, memory works in this large area combining popular culture and art mix varied narrative strategies, ideas, and emotions. Considering the great diversity of forms found here, it would be unwise to proceed further with any generalizations. It is possible, though, to look closer and more systematically at the predominantly few strategies used to claim a "fit" with past experience.

Let us begin with the type of memory work that relies heavily on the claims to factual truth, this time, however, of a subjective kind—eyewitness accounts. From records compiled at the time of the events to autobiographical writings composed decades later, the "raw" quality of the narratives is what gives them strength. For collective memory to rely on such personal memories is an unusual occurrence, though. The expected partiality (in both meanings of the term) of such accounts makes them suspect to those searching for objective truth; the often ordinary background of the people writing them lessens the interest their stories might generate beyond their small communities of memory.

These two rules, working jointly against individual construction of collective memory, do become suspended, as it were, with regard to extraordinary experiences. Most notably, in this century, the reception of writings from the Holocaust and writings by the survivors represents a case of bracketing intellectual doubt in favor of the obligation to bear witness. Other projects in oral history, while not faced with the same traumatic covenant to record the experience of ordinary people, follow a similar trust in the value of individual witness.[13] At times originated by researchers and oftentimes edited for publication, the testimonies by people who "were there" still retain their key appeal—speaking to us in voices so close to our own. Their claims to truth are those of authenticity.

Authenticity is also a claim, if not a mark of many artistic representations of the past. And if having been there is not technically a requirement for creating a true rendition of the experience, the authority of an artist is definitely greater when there exists a biographical connection. Contrary to historians, who rarely receive extra credit if any credit at all[14] for describing events they actually witnessed, novelists, poets, painters or filmmakers who draw on their own memories tend to gain in credibility, at times irrespective of their aesthetic accomplishments.[15] Whether recounting actual events or fictionalizing the account better to capture their meaning, the artist-as-witness is perhaps the most effective of all memory workers. The unique combination of the art's power to evoke feelings, to build empathy, with the "empirical" claim to authenticity frames remembrance in the greatest intellectual *and* emotional depth, as it were. And when such combination is used, as it often is, to speak of the ultimate good and evil, the call upon us to remember is complete.

It is not an accident that the artistic bearing of witness has become so prominent in our century, and especially in its latter half. Beyond the developments internal to visual arts and literature, history itself (im)posed tremendous challenges on memory work. The world wars, the *gulag*, the "Final Solution," the bombing of Hiroshima and Nagasaki, Vietnam, Cambodia—this is an unprecedented series of traumas to absorb. What is more, these traumas all implicate, to a greater or lesser extent, a host of peoples. Indeed, at times these are traumas implicating the very ideas of humanity and civilization. To weave such experiences into the fabric of collective memory is both more difficult and more compelling of a task than ever before.

Of all the great traumas of the twentieth century, none more than the Holocaust challenged our ability to understand and to remember. And just as memories of ordinary people receive a special recognition here, so the other rules of historical credibility shift away from the usual standards, allowing the artist-as-witness to claim an unprecedented degree of authority. As much as some historians call for normalizing the scholarship in this area, others still share with the nonspecialists a certain humility in face of experience that can never be fully comprehended (see chapter 2). Survivors and only survivors can judge the authenticity of accounts. Among them, artists are in a privileged position only in that they can also convey what such authenticity implies in ways which are intellectually and aesthetically rigorous.

Tracing the public itinerary of some of the best known artist-survivors, it becomes apparent that with time "bearing witness" translates into active guardianship of truth; it is as if the criteria of authenticity which first emerged from the challenge of recording one's experience gradually gain in authority as the ultimate standards for assessing memory work in general. Elie Wiesel, Saul Friedländer, a Polish Jewish writer Henryk Grynberg—all have not only described what happened to them and their loved ones, but went on to defend the memory of the Holocaust from abuse and distortion. And if they are joined in the latter task by a wide array of memory workers who are not survivors, it is still to them that we listen most respectfully.

Is it possible for artists who did not live through the traumatic experience they depict to command the same authority? Yes, but it is also a great deal more difficult. Unlike the ordinary human drama, descent into *Hell* is not a subject or material one works with for the sake of *Art*.[16] And even with the best of intentions and the greatest of talent, artists remain open to charges of inauthenticity. Theirs, after all, is neither the authority of scholarship nor that of direct experience. At times, it is the power of artistic vision that in and of itself serves as a claim to truth; Coppola's *Apocalypse Now*, drawing on Conrad's *Heart of Darkness*, exemplifies this approach. At other times, the artist becomes essentially a transmitter for voices of witnesses, however much his vision impacts on the whole, as in Lanzmann's *Shoah*. Most frequently, perhaps, there is a mixture of fictional order and factual elements working to create a credible sense of the past. But credible for whom?

If the success of the television series *Holocaust* can teach us anything, it is that the lack of historical authenticity, as defined by survivors and academic experts, has little if any impact on how the audiences judge the work's credibility.[17] And while this is a major issue for all concerned with preserving the memory of the Holocaust, students of remembrance are perhaps better advised to accept the situation and proceed from there, proceed with questions about how certain stories rather than others come to form ideas and images of the past.

The authority of the storyteller, as we have seen, provides only a partial answer here. The essential component of the answer, it seems, is the story itself. A "good story," in the parlance of television producers, has a much better chance of entering collective memory—in this age of television productions—than a narrative devoid of drama. And a "good story" is usually the one where the protagonists are at once universally human and historically concrete, where their actions can be understood without the need to delve too deeply into contextual complexity. What this implies is a certain mythical consistency within the offerings of popular storytellers. Whether the subject is American black history or the extraordinary life of Raoul Wallenberg, World War II or the saga of the Kennedys, the basic structure of the story remains remarkably similar. Watched by millions, television miniseries such as *Roots* or *War and Remembrance* draw on a small set of mythic principles, themes that resonate with well-established ways in which our culture helps us to make sense of ourselves and our world.[18] At the same time, these are narratives that often explicitly claim to be historically accurate, even or especially if the story as such is fiction. This is a powerful combination indeed, of the direct empirical base and the appealing packaging.

Being both a mass medium and one which coexists with the very ordinary doings of our daily lives, television rarely frames its programming as a special time for remembrance. Most often, stories about the past are presented as interesting and worth knowing about, a form of education-through-entertainment. And the response from viewers indeed indicates that for many people, television offers the main, if not the only information they have about a great number of historical events. The framing process here is at its most basic, then: exposure.

Beyond telling good stories, television, however, has the capacity to frame remembrance in a much more direct fashion. In its news and current affairs programming—a source of choice for the majority of North Americans when trying to keep up with what happens in the world—a considerable amount of air time is devoted to constructing patterns into which one should fit today's occurrences. And, with considerable regularity, events from the past are recalled for their own sake as well in a virtually infinite series of anniversaries. In 1988, it was 1968 which was "making the rounds" across news outlets. In 1989, the fiftieth anniversary of the outbreak of World War II prompted a massive coverage for war-related topics. In 1989 as well, the end of a decade became an occasion for various forms of "looking back," whereby a multitude of events would be ordered and prioritized.

Whether used to contextualize a current news item, or on its own terms, the past here acquires a very definite structure of relevance. Time for the presentation is severely limited. Good visuals often set the direction for the verbal commentary. The result is a highly selective (but not random) "primer" on history.

As with school curricula, the actual impact of such television-made history lessons is a matter for empirical investigation.[19] It is also an open question as to what extent television (and newsprint media) would be recognized by the public as a purveyor of objective truth. The role television plays in different countries depends on a number of factors, from political to economic to cultural. Definitions of a "good story" also vary. Having said that, I do think that a better understanding of how television frames remembrance is the first order of priority for students of the present and future of memory construction.

In as much as television, at least in North America, has overtaken other producers of public discourse in the sheer numbers of people being reached, and, as some critics would argue,[20] changed the very quality of that public discourse, it is still within the older forms of storytelling that we find essential clues to how collective memory is constructed. Television did not invent the mythic structure of narratives, it borrows them from drama, literature and its already indebted cousin, film. Television also did not invent the rule that pictures are worth more than a thousand words; photography is now more than 150 years old, and it, in turn, has borrowed from painting. The claims to balance and objectivity in television reporting developed on a model of newsprint journalism, as did those to influence on public opinion. And the sense of what constitutes a "good story" about the past is the one shared by virtually all popular media, including that which is the oldest—the oral tradition of storytelling. In short, to inquire into *how* television frames remembrance calls for using a host of critical approaches. At the same time, when one is focusing, as we are now, on the capacity of memory work to claim historical accuracy, it must be recognized that television productions enjoy a highly privileged position. Apart from the overtly fictional treatment of the past, television presents us with reality-based drama, docudrama and document where the strength of writing, visuals, and faithfulness to detail all combine. It is as if television in its many borrowings favored those which make "this is how it happened" sound true.[21]

Among the other media, only documentary film has similar capabilities. Documentary films, though, are rarely successful enough to warrant wide distribution. Still, some become a standard element within the educational system, thus gaining a great deal of additional legitimacy. Some, even if initially shown to small audiences, become much discussed events; Ophuls's *The Sorrow and the Pity* and Lanzmann's *Shoah* exemplify the potential resonance of controversial memory works.[22] The key word here is "controversial," for in contrast to television productions (at least in commercially run systems), documentary films can and often do adopt a stance bound to offend. Their claims to historical truth are then bound to be critically scrutinized on a par with those made by historians.[23] In aiming to remind and to teach, while rarely if ever to entertain, these documentary films combine in an almost perfect balance the two distinct frames of remembrance—an account of the past and a marker, a locale.

Films like *Shoah* or *The Sorrow and the Pity* do more than that, though. For they are also, in their different ways, meditations on the very process of remembering. The certain self-consciousness about memory work one is doing, which they share with films using purely fictional elements such as *Heimat* or Syberberg's *Our Hitler*, brings them onto a much wider terrain of memory *works* par excellence. Poets, writers, visual artists, through their art give meaning to the past while calling our attention to the act of remembering. In contrast to accounts and stories about the past where that past is at the center stage, we are now asked to reflect about ourselves, our own ability and willingness to look back. Whether directly interwoven within the contents of a poem or a novel, or achieved through more formal means, this demand for reflection frames remembrance as fragile, problematic *and* needed. Rather than telling us that the past is knowable and known, it is pointing first to the artist and then to us as people who must work to create it.

Considering what I have said earlier about our common sense inclination to treat the past as something "there" not to be tampered with, memory work that calls attention to the work involved in remembrance may appear as an overly intellectual, alien type. Sometimes it is. Most often, though, as work explicitly undertaken to provide a bridge between the past, the present, and the future, its focus on difficulty as well as necessity of remembering is an accurate reflection of our modern condition. It is not a coincidence that so much of the self-reflective memory work represents an effort to approach the Holocaust, the trauma of ultimate challenge. Whether literally or metaphorically created by the children of survivors, pictures of the past gain authenticity here only by reference to memory itself. In other words, when confronted with a legacy so painful to accept and yet impossible to shed, when struggling with all the ambiguities of remembrance, claiming to speak of historical truth is not enough. The search for meaning of the trauma must remain in the foreground, open to our view, as it were, and opening, in turn, the possibility of empathy through remembering.[24]

Memory work reflecting on itself is not, of course, limited to the legacy of the Holocaust. A great deal of autobiographical materials, written as well as filmic, share in the recognition of remembrance as tenuous, problematic, yet necessary. Yet if we may readily accept doubts about "the" meaning of events voiced by individuals, it is only when we collectively have difficulty in remembering that we grant the status of truth to accounts emphasizing questions and doubts.[25]

If works of artistic representation of the past generally call for certain feelings towards that past, the self-reflective ones make a much more direct statement in guiding our ways of remembering. In that sense, they come close to the effect of special presence engendered by monuments as well as commemorative rituals. No longer just a source of ideas, images, and sentiments about the past, with memory at the very center of the work, however tenuously proscribed, all these memory works ask us to remember.

What emerges, then, from this broad examination of the building blocks used in the construction of collective memory is a continuum between knowing and acting, where our sentiments towards the past move from those of absorbing its meaning to those involved in active remembering. At one end, entry into memory is guarded by principles of scientific investigation; at the other, it is secured by powers of performance. And inbetween lies a vast area of storytelling claiming our attention by virtue of the quality and the significance of the story itself.

The ideal of "truth" with which we began this inquiry, the sense that memory should be faithful to the actual past *felt* especially by those fighting with distortions, is also a combination of cognitive, emotional, and moral imperatives. What enters collective memory must of necessity represent only a fraction of "what really happened." Yet claims to factual accuracy carry only limited authority in the selection process. The fragments of the past that acquire permanent public presence are those judged worthy of remembering, as well as worthy of knowing about.

## Notes

1. See, especially, Saul Friedländer, *Reflections of Nazism: An Essay on Kitsch and Death*, translated from French by Thomas Weyr (New York: Harper and Row, 1984).

2. A good starting point here is Erving Goffman, *Forms of Talk* (Philadelphia: University of Pennsylvania Press, 1981).

3. For a fascinating look at how "essence" can win over "truth," see Karal Ann Marling and John Wetenhall, *Iwo Jima: Monuments, Memories, and the American Hero* (Cambridge, Mass.: Harvard University Press, 1991).

4. For self-reflection, see David Thelen, ed., *Memory and American History* (Bloomington and Indianapolis: Indiana University Press, 1990).

5. See, especially, Henri Rousso, *The Vichy Syndrome. History and Memory in France since 1944*, translated by Arthur Goldhammer (Cambridge, Mass.: Harvard University Press, 1991).

6. See Charles S. Meier, *The Unmasterable Past: History, Holocaust, and German National Identity* (Cambridge, Mass.: Harvard University Press, 1988).

7. For a study of the transition point, see R. W. Davies, *Soviet History in the Gorbachev Revolution* (Bloomington and Indianapolis: Indiana University Press, 1989).

8. See, especially, Barbie Zelizer, *Covering the Body: The Kennedy Assassination, the Media, and the Shaping of Collective Memory* (Chicago: University of Chicago Press, 1992).

9. For a more general discussion of the interplay between ideas and sentiments, see Bruce Lincoln, *Discourse and the Construction of Society: Comparative Studies of Myth, Ritual, and Classification* (New York and Oxford: Oxford University Press, 1989).

10. See Betty Rogers Rubenstein, "The Shape of Memory: Some Problems in Modern Memorial Art," in *Remembering for the Future: Jews and Christians During and After the Holocaust* (Oxford: Pergamon Press, 1988), 1790-98.

11. See, for example, James Young, "The Texture of Memory: Holocaust Memorials and Meaning," in *Remembering for the Future: Jews and Christians During and After the Holocaust* (Oxford: Pergamon Press, 1988), 1799-1812.

12. For an excellent analysis extending the work of transmitting memory beyond public storytelling, see Michael Schudson, *Watergate in American Memory: How We Remember, Forget and Reconstruct the Past* (New York: Basic Books, 1992).

13. See, for example, Neil M. Cowan and Ruth Schwartz Cowan, *Our Parents' Lives: The Americanization of Eastern European Jews* (New York: Basic Books, Inc., 1989).

14. Yisrael Gutman, *The Jews of Warsaw, 1939-1943: Ghetto, Underground, Revolt*, trans. from the Hebrew by Ina Friedman (Bloomington: Indiana University Press, 1982) is a striking example—with the author remaining silent about his own experiential knowledge of the events he describes, though, it could be argued, it is that knowledge which matters most.

15. Jerzy Kosinski's *The Painted Bird* illustrates this dynamic. As a child Holocaust survivor, the writer would be granted credit for imagery approaching a pornography of horror in ways difficult to conceive if a non-survivor was involved.

16. For example, the failure (despite their commercial success) of both the novel and the film *Sophie's Choice* stems largely from treating Auschwitz on a par with erotic fantasies.
    See, especially, Alan L. Berger, "La Shoa dans la littérature américaine: témoins, non-témoins et faux-témoins," *Pardès* 9-10(1989):73-93.

17. See Judith E. Doneson, *The Holocaust in American Film* (Philadelphia: The Jewish Publication Society, 1987).

18. For a comparative/historical perspective, see, especially, James Fentress, and Chris Wickham, *Social Memory* (Oxford and Cambridge, Mass.: Blackwell, 1992).

19. See, for example, Kurt Lang and Gladys Engel Lang, "Collective Memory and the News," *Communication* 11(1989):123–39.

20. For one of the sharpest critiques, see Neil Postman, *Amusing Ourselves to Death: Public Discourse in the Age of Television* (New York: Viking Penguin Books, 1986).

21. With the introduction, in 1993, of television movies which went into production while the events were still unfolding (on the bombing of the World Trade Center and the standoff in Waco, Texas), we seem to have crossed an important line.

22. For further discussion, see Henri Rousso, *The Vichy Syndrome: History and Memory in France since 1944*, translated by Arthur Goldhammer (Cambridge, Mass.: Harvard University Press, 1991).

23. I am grateful to Terry Copp for providing me with the transcripts of the Canadian Senate 1992 hearings into the merits of the CBC *The Valour and the Horror*, the much debated production about Canada's participation in World War II.

24. A most telling example of this genre must be the comic book, Art Spiegelman, *Maus: A Survivor's Tale* (New York: Pantheon Books, 1991).

25. See, especially, Lawrence L. Langer, *Holocaust Testimonies: The Ruins of Memory* (New Haven and London: Yale University Press, 1991).

# 10

# Instant Memory

Against the cluttered flow of everyday life—and the even more cluttered information environment—certain moments stand out, defined as deserving to be remembered. These are the events that enter private and public records on the spot, increasingly with the help of audiovisual technology. The "instant memory" so produced need not endure, as a change in context renders the original into a different experience altogether. On the other hand, the passage of time itself may make the "as it happened" record more precious, more important as a direct testimony. Whatever the ultimate fate of "instant memory," its construction deserves our analytical attention. For it is one of the prime sites to observe the interplay between the quality of experience itself, the production of a record, and remembrance. It is also where claims to truth receive most credit.

A few days ago, my son celebrated his fifth birthday. This time, we decided on a big party for his and our friends, complete with favors, hats, balloons, and the cake. All went well; everyone enjoyed the picnic and I also managed to capture some of these special moments on video. Pictures, too, were taken during the blowing out of the birthday candles. And, in a week or so, I should be able to write a little memory note about this and other events of the last few months, as I have been doing since Joshua was born.

That whole day, from the morning presents to the unusually late goodnight, was meant to be memorable. The festivities, while not staged for the camera, invited filming in a way that an ordinary day does not. At the same time, my experience with writing those memory notes is such that they, more than any visual record, can best convey the joys and trials of Joshua's growing up. Reading one after some months frequently brings back not just the moments, but the whole texture (and chronology) of the rapid development, otherwise easily lost in the midst of the new.

There are some key lessons in this family tale. First, that trying to secure remembrance takes work, but it is work of two different kinds. There is the emotional and practical investment in creating a special time, separated from the ordinary living, a time that would have memorable enough qualities to "register" in our minds. Many occasions may be socially designated to serve the purpose: birthdays, weddings, graduations. Others can be crafted by the individuals themselves as they define markers in their lives. The moments can be quite small in the overall scheme of things—or quite big—but they all share that distinct intensity of awareness, the felt desire to remember, that moves the experience immediately beyond the moment itself.

The other type of work is of a still more practical nature, as it involves often an elaborate technical means to create a record. Special occasions may hold a privileged position here, in that they almost automatically become recorded. In some cases, indeed, it is difficult to disengage the experience and the record; one need only reflect on the enormous care and expense granted to wedding photography (and video). But the not-so-special times may prompt the recording work as well, especially when we know they would not be possible to repeat. Children, by the very nature of their not staying children, receive particular attention. Holidays away from home, let alone expensive trips to exotic locations, would be another prime time for picture-taking and diary-writing, as well as souvenir-buying. For some people, of course, the very act of living is worthy of preservation in its forever changing form, through writing or pictures.

All these mnemonic devices are used in recognition of the frailty of human memory. But their role is rarely, if ever, limited to that of reproduction. Even the most sophisticated technology of film and video, allowing for direct documenting of events as they happen, is highly selective in focus and thus transformative of meaning. Writing, though sometimes used for purely factual recordkeeping, is ever more selective just as it is capable of assigning the meaning to the experience being described. An audiotape stands somewhere in between, since it can be used to record as well as to narrate. The medium of "instant memory" matters, even when it is only used as an aid to our cognitive capacities.[1]

(As we will discuss later, its significance grows exponentially when it is applied on its own.)

The active tending to the present so that it be remembered does affect the experience itself, but such effect can only endure (and rarely completely does) for the participants. The introduction of recording techniques, on the other hand, has, at least potentially, long lasting consequences reaching well beyond the actors themselves. Once the record is made, it can move around, as it were, both in time and in space. Old family photographs, though generally kept within the family, can become part of a museum exhibit. Diaries, private as they are, may decades or centuries later be used by historians. Home movies, too, are likely to become valuable resources for future accounts of life in American suburbs, for example. In short, "instant memory," once moved outside the individual mind, can and often does become public property, providing us with some essential raw material for constructing "realities of the past." And as historians continue to enlarge the scope of history to include the ordinariness of life, we might indeed expect more of such transfers from the private to the public sphere to occur.

So far, our family tale led us in the understandably skewed direction of remembering the joyful, the pleasant, the special. But if indeed our urge to create "instant memory" applies mostly on such bright terrain, the definition of "special" may at times acquire an opposite, sombre, or altogether tragic tone. Numerous reports we have from the Holocaust testify, both by their presence and in explicit ways, to the deeply felt obligation to record the traumatic experiences.[2] In the Warsaw ghetto, efforts to gather (and hide) materials for posterity were indeed organized as a key part of the resistance. Doctors, faced with hunger-related disease and dying on an unprecedented scale, wrote down what they perceived as invaluable scientific data—the horrific detail of the limits of human endurance. Several people, both public figures and not, kept diaries, under the most demanding of circumstances. And several survivors saw their very survival in terms of a sacred duty to remember those who died.

The commandment "to record" was itself a sacred one, rooted in the Jewish tradition. Fraught with dangers, it was also a direct response to the Nazis' concerted effort to erase all possible traces of their crimes, and to erase the memory of the whole people. There was then a real sense (and as the future has shown, a justifiable fear) that unless a record be made, the experience of camps and ghettos would move into oblivion.

At the time, many a report was indeed not believed, only strengthening the conviction that witness be given.[3] Those reports that were destined for the outside world were, of course, also a desperate cry for help. But a great deal more of the bearing of witness was done without such hope for immediate results, indeed, with often only a slight hope that the record would itself survive. The duty to memory—to universal memory—prevailed.

Survivors themselves cannot forget. They can choose silence, but they cannot forget. In that, they are joined by others who have been through personal or collective traumas—people who are forced to remember. The experience was not of their making, but it cannot be unmade, it cannot, with the best of efforts, be left unattended. It can, however, remain enclosed within the individual's memory. Here, it takes work to make such memory enter even the very private record, let alone the public one. Moments that are not memorable but rather impossible-to-forget place their own special demands on remembrance. The sense of sacred duty felt by many Jews during the Holocaust provided for a strong counter-force to the urge to forget. In other cases, different principles need to be evoked for people to share and record their trauma. A victim of child abuse, for example, who years later sets out to write about the experience, may be motivated by the desire to help others. A Vietnam war veteran who talks to college students feels he, too, can help, both to educate and to secure remembrance.

Because of the emotional intensity, and the pain associated with such traumatic memories, it is often that we conceive of the dynamics of remembrance involved here in psychological (or therapeutic) terms. And yet, the sharing of those memories cannot be detached, at whatever level of analysis, from its social context. Even within the family, attending to a traumatic past is not a purely individual matter. For example, Holocaust survivors who came to North America often sheltered their children in silence, while those who stayed in Poland were much more likely to talk. Why? In part, at least, because in Poland, where virtually every family suffered tragic losses during the Nazi (and Soviet) occupation, the Jews' experience was included in collective mourning.[4] In North America, by contrast, survivors were an isolated group. For Vietnam veterans publicly to come forward, especially still during the war, required a support system originated by those opposing the American involvement.[5] For abuse victims to go on national television with their stories would not be possible without a generally receptive and concerned climate of opinion (at least, media opinion).

What makes the transition from "instant memory" to remembrance different—and often difficult—in the case of traumas is that the existence of records is more the exception than the rule. The creation of records is then mostly a work of reconstruction, from a time distance, with all the mnemonic problems that this implies. After forty years, "bearing witness" becomes suspect, and not only in legal terms. Historians in particular turn back to records compiled at the time, however inadequate these may be. In that sense, the framing of remembrance reverts to its retrieval mode.

If, in this discussion of "instant memory," I have devoted so much attention to individual experience, it is because the actors' participation is very much at the core of this phenomenon. It is time, though, to turn to its ever-widening peripheries, where memory is not only instantly produced but immediately collective in nature: the intervention by the media. Here, the very clear line separating memorable moments we actively create and those never-to-be-forgotten moments we are compelled to live through becomes a blurred one, emotionally and analytically. The mediated experience is not our own, the vicarious participation can neither be as pleasant or as tragic as the real one.[6] Attending to the present so it be remembered, when all of attending to the present by definition involves creating a record, does not have the same special qualities any more, either. And yet, as tempting as it might be to treat all of the media production, but especially the news and current affairs part, as the "first draft" of collective memory, this is not analytically productive. Yes, the media provide us with a vast reservoir of raw material for later construction of the "realities of the past," in this capacity acting as a giant sifter and selector.[7] But the framing of "instant memory" takes a stronger form as well, and that is one of social definition of worthiness vis-à-vis remembrance. "Instant memory" belongs to the terrain of newsworthy events, but it is that fairly limited realm we are asked to preserve, individually as well as collectively. Whether we actually do is another matter altogether, as the shifting social and political context can deprive the once memorable moments of much of their original force. At the time, though, that "instant memory" is being produced, we are told, often explicitly, that this moment (and increasingly, this image) is to endure.

One of the most media celebrated occasions in recent history was the first man's landing on the moon. Very directly, those watching the television sets, were told they are witness to history in the making. Images of that landing, together with the famous "one small step for man and one giant step for mankind" appeared destined to endure not just in American memory, but universally. Twenty years later, as the media commemorated the event, it became clear that even for those actually witness to it, let alone the next generation, landing on the moon was no longer such a pivotal event. The hope and exhilaration of the original was gone, if only because people's lives proved ultimately unaffected by it.

In 1989, a very similar media boom surrounded the breaching of the Berlin Wall. While here, we may be perhaps more confident that the historical value of this event would endure, *how* it will be remembered twenty years later is only for the future to tell.

Both of these events, it might be argued, were memorable in their own right, with the media coverage only enhancing their visual qualities. It would also be rather absurd to claim that the assassination of President Kennedy, for example, would have been quickly forgotten were it not for the pictures. But if several events indeed fit the model of the media seizing on the widely perceived "historical moments," of media-as-mediators of memory, quite a number do not. First, there are times when the very definition of historical significance—and thus the scope and direction of coverage—is media produced. Constitutional debates in Canada, culminating in the fall of 1992, were for a few years framed by the media as a key development in the life of the country, to be remembered as such. Meanwhile, opinion polls, even at the crisis point, showed a remarkable degree of public ignorance and indifference. Journalists' assessment of the memorable significance was definitely at odds here with the interest of ordinary Canadians.

At the other end of the spectrum, the very presence of television coverage in particular *can* make a tremendous difference. For most North Americans, the student protest in China ending with the Tiananmen Square massacre, became an "instant memory" mainly because the Western reporters were allowed to send many powerful images out. At issue here is not only the ability to command media—and public—attention, but more importantly, the scaling of the events to human size. A picture gives the all-too-complex reality a face. It offers the crucial emotional bridge between the distant events and our private world.

What is perhaps most remarkable in this case of "instant memory" production is how extensive the realm of collective remembrance was made to be. In a true "global village" fashion, North Americans were asked to bring the tragedy in China within their own sphere of relevance. Unlike developments in Eastern Europe, heralded as the end of the Cold War and thus of direct (while explicated) significance to people in the West, events in China carried, in their final stages, a much more mixed message. With little hope for change, Tiananmen Square thus acquired an universal meaning of resistance to oppression, of a struggle for democracy, becoming an identifiable if an already abstract icon.

The presence of cameras during the protest in China had also direct (if short-lived) political implications. Providing a record of the events meant, in this case, providing documentary evidence of repressive violence, evidence used to counter the official Chinese voices of denial. Knowing that the world would know made the students' actions bolder, words stronger. Here, "instant memory" came to serve as a protective shield, however ultimately ineffective.

Recognizing the power of visual record *as* record, its power to belie propaganda statements by the authorities, has not been unique to China. First photography, and then increasingly the video technology, have been used by dissident forces in countries such as Poland to produce documentary evidence of state oppression. Taken illegally, the pictures may be of very uneven quality, but this too adds to their value—that of "truth." Their distribution, both within the country and to news outlets in the West, initially served mainly defensive purposes. In time, though, the record becomes the base for remembrance proper. During the first few months of legal Solidarity, for example, photographs taken of the workers' protest in 1970 became part of a widely attended exhibit commemorating the struggle. When Poland's foremost film director, Andrzej Wajda, made a movie, *Man of Iron*, about the birth of Solidarity shortly after the events occurred, he prominently included images modelled on those produced by amateur photographers at the time. The artist creating "instant memory" after the fact worked to preserve the original in full recognition of its strength.

In 1988, Polish workers in Gdansk again went on strike, demanding that Solidarity become legalized. This time, an independent filmmaker, Piotr Bikont, joined them in what proved a political breakthrough. The long documentary he produced combines the highly professional qualities of artistic presentation with the raw nature of material, including an unplanned scuffle of the director with state security forces. "Instant memory" at its most powerful, it is both a record and a form of monument to the courage of the workers.[8]

What we can observe here is one of the basic principles of producing "instant memory"—its ultimate claim to truth as a record.[9] Whether artistically treated in fictional or documentary modes, the constructed "reality of the past" supports itself with the as-it-happened imagery. All the while framing the experience itself, memory workers assume an unobtrusive presence. From the viewer's perspective, the record *is* a record, even when it actually does a great deal more than securing remembrance.

Among seasoned media critics, the idea that "instant memory" would be a true record of the events is analytically preposterous. Yet for the audience at large, it is precisely such documentary value of material gathered on the spot that claims attention—and, potentially, remembrance. The bearing of witness that used to be restricted to direct participants has now been technologically transformed into being a witness. A video camera is not simply a more sophisticated recording device, it is a means allowing nonparticipants to feel as if they were there. And although we know that such vicarious participation cannot match the "real thing" in emotional intensity, it is still qualitatively very different from the experience of reading about or listening to or looking at a photograph of. . . . Not complete, of course, since both touch and smell are missing, the being-there-via-the-camera claims the largest perceptual territory nevertheless. And in doing so, it can most convincingly stake claims to true representation.

Added to this potential of audiovisual technology to produce a "true record" of events should be now the explicit (and implicit) claims by its practitioners that such indeed is their role.[10] The various structural devices of television coverage—from the backdrop of actual locale used for reporters' narration to editorial preference for "going live"—work well to create the appearance of being there, together with that of camera's neutrality. The complexity of production and the multistage assignment of meaning to the recorded events are hidden from view of all but the analytically inclined. The sophistication of means is to translate into simplicity and plausibility of results.

Such strong claims to faithfulness to reality should give the audiovisual "instant memory" a highly privileged position vis-à-vis other forms of recording events. Judging how important *control* over the technology has become—by the priority granted to taking over television stations during the political upheaval in Eastern and Central Europe, for example—this may indeed be the case. At issue, though, is not only the quality of record, but prominently its public distribution. The "reality of the past" constructed (in the present) through being there with a camera is immediately accessible to a great many people. As a resource, as a base for remembrance, the broadcast "instant memory" would appear to have no equals.

Yet once we shift our observation point away from societies where a struggle for public truth is taken most seriously, an altogether different picture begins to emerge. In North America, where saturation with television is most pronounced, this very omnipresence of a mediated "being there" may be working against rather than for collective memory.[11] When the importance of securing a record gives way to largely commercial considerations of attracting an audience, the terrain for "instant memory" at first appears to expand vastly. Yet as we observed earlier, the appearance is deceptive in that much of what is newsworthy is not defined as worthy of remembrance. Indeed, for an event reported on to be framed as memorable takes a good deal of special work. The interruption of regular coverage, staying with the "story" for a long time, reproduction of images in newspapers and magazines, editorial comment—these are common techniques for defining events as especially significant, and thus, at least potentially, memorable. The selection of those events, though, follows the rules of the commercial medium and not necessarily those of communal remembrance.

Television is a highly competitive business. Of the many implications of this, one is of particular interest here—and that is the perpetual quest for novelty and drama the system produces. Television news, current affairs programs, docudramas, and features unabashedly chase after "big stories" of the day, allowing room for delving into the past, of course, but rapidly shifting priorities nevertheless. It is this shifting of priorities, the framing of events as important today and unimportant, if not inexistent, tomorrow that is a cause for some concern. Writing these lines during the second week of the war in the Persian Gulf, I am reminded daily of television's capacity and willingness to forget. The public was reminded as well, when a Lithuanian government official appealed directly to the media to keep his people's "story" on the air. The fact that during the first day of the war, not a single moment of then continuous news coverage (on ABC) was devoted to Soviet actions in the Baltic Republics is only one of the more poignant examples of this in-and-out-of-the-headlines practice. AIDS activists who stormed the CBS newsroom, demanding some attention to *their* cause a few days later were all too aware of the consequences of disappearance from the public agenda. Voices of alarm from those concerned with the deteriorating conditions in Africa, heard for more than a year of media preoccupation with Europe, intensified as well. In Canada, the government that introduced a highly unpopular tax just two weeks prior to the outbreak of the war had no complaints, of course.

The principles of such first selection are not easy to define analytically. One cannot assume, for example, that an underlying ideology would be responsible for the narratives' inclusions and exclusions—in a way we often can within academic or polemical print discourse. For commercial television, "good stories" may be those judged most relevant to the public, or those with the best visuals, or those valuable for their unique point of view, or simply those well told. On any given day, unless an event becomes subject to special, extensive coverage, the sheer time limits of news broadcast result in further choices that may have little if anything to do with the qualities of the stories themselves. Back in June of 1989, for example, while events at Tiananmen Square unfolded, capturing the attention of American networks, the day of the first democratic elections in the Soviet Bloc (in Poland) coincided with the day that Ayatollah Khomeini died in Iran. What, on another, "slow" day, could have been a big story—it was, from an historical point of view—became two lines devoted to election results.

There is another problem, too. As we have seen, international coverage is a prominent part of television-produced "instant memory." When such coverage is accorded to politically important developments, even in remote parts of the world, it might be argued that the audience would perhaps grant them some relevance. When the coverage turns to natural and manmade disaster, such as Ethiopian famine, we know that some people are moved to help while others may store the imagery under the general heading of "human condition." It would be very difficult to claim, though, that events rendered "memorable" on a *global* scale have priority of entry into localized collective memory. Indeed, the very bridging of geographic and cultural distances that so much defines the medium of television can work against its capability to affect remembrance. The power of the imagery of Solidarity lies with its rootedness in actual experience of large numbers of people in Poland. The same imagery, when transposed onto North American television screens is no longer so rooted—or so powerful. If it is stored, it is literally stored among television tapes to be used when subsequent developments warrant it. In that way, it remains a resource for remembrance, but only within the limited realm of television news. Not having a genuine connection with communal life and concerns, the important events from afar can claim our attention, they can only rarely claim the emotional investment in remembrance.

Here we come to perhaps a central consideration for analyzing "instant memory"—the role of sentiment. As we have seen, individuals attend to moments that are special, whether through joy or sorrow, special in their emotional intensity.

On a social scale, the tending to the present so it be remembered may become more intellectualized, in a sense that the frame of "historically significant" rests at least in part on ideas, often inscribed ideas about the world. Yet producing "instant memory" is not a cognitive exercise, the urge to record and to remember remains imbued with strong feelings. (We recognize that when we ask historians not to work with current material, or at least to distance themselves from it.) Strongest among the participants and witnesses to the events, this emotional investment can be conveyed to others with the use of a camera, it can be enhanced with the skilful editing and music but it cannot be created *ex nihilo*. For the viewing audience to respond to the imagery *as* "instant memory," there has to exist a connection with their private emotional world, their own sphere of relevance.[12] When such link takes the form of "sharing in humanity," remembrance becomes tenuous, unless some additional framing work is done to make this particular instance of universal experience special.

Television producers inadvertently acknowledge this persistent need for an emotional connection when, in covering distant events, they zero in on imagery which can give them a "human face." (They also openly attest to the principle when discussing the requirements for a successful historical docudrama.) Often, it means reaching to eyewitnesses for their still charged stories, allowing the camera to register the rawest of feelings, or at least feelings that would be least transformed by the journalistic presence. Considerable efforts notwithstanding, though, "instant memory" of global dimensions remains on the margins of communal remembrance.

What emerges so far is a mixed assessment of the medium's effectiveness in the production of "instant memory." On the one hand, as a medium of witness, television has no equals (so far), both in terms of the record produced and its public availability. On the other hand, when it offers "instant memory" of events well beyond the audience's realm of concern—as it increasingly does, not only in North America—it is *not* providing people with important resources for constructing their "realities of the past." Without the larger and historically concrete frame to fit them into, without a direct emotional connection, the imagery assigned global significance is of passing interest. Passing interest cannot sustain remembrance.

A great deal of television programming is of passing interest. This too means that however special the "memorable moments" are made to be, they exist within an environment not conducive to attentive depths. And, the frequently used strategy to forge emotional ties with the people on the screen is something that television may do best, but also something it does routinely (witness the attachment to soap opera characters, for example). On both counts, attending to the present so it be remembered suffers from meaning devaluation, as it were.

Another key factor to consider while reflecting on the role of television-produced "instant memories" is their claim to societal representation. As many critics have pointed out, the perspective adopted in much of television programming does not reflect the diversity found in society itself. Commercial considerations alone do not allow for controversial, conflicting, minority viewpoints.[13] A set of unspoken assumptions about what "United States" or "Canada" or "France" signifies can indeed be seen as guiding the selection of events deemed memorable, the choice of witnesses, the structuring of narratives. While control over the medium may be becoming both less nationally centralized and more globally interconnected, it is definitely not passing into "the hands of the people." What this implies is that even within the realm of events directly relevant to the audience, considerable numbers of people would find the television framing of "instant memory" seriously wanting vis-à-vis their own experience, and would be unlikely to identify with the meaning assigned to it, or would find that what is memorable to them was altogether excluded from the record.

As we have said, the kind of present reality that individuals attend to for purposes of remembrance is usually of special emotional intensity. It is a present that matters a great deal. If people may be routinely willing to accept viewpoints very different from their own for the sake of entertainment or even information, they are much less willing to discard their own feelings when memory is at stake. An especially clear illustration of this differential of tolerance may be found in the response to television among viewers in then still Communist Poland.

During the early 1980s, when television was very much compromised by its support in the rule of martial law, when most prominent actors and journalists boycotted the medium (and those who did not received scorn from the public), when, in short, the stark realities of power were most visible, people did not stop watching. Indeed, judging by the emptied streets, they watched television more than before. With a lot of foreign films and repeats from better times, programming proved a good enough diversion. At the same time, though, the concerted effort to frame the imposition of the martial law as a nation-saving event failed formidably. And while the counter-memory work would only involve a minority of opposition activists, using underground presses and secret seminars, the refusal to accept the official line was very widespread. People cared that their children not remember Solidarity as a destructive force; cared enough to continuously tell stories rather than just turn off their television sets.

The ability to frame public "instant memory" with electronic media *is* a prized political possession. Yet we must also recognize that when their experience greatly matters to people, when they themselves wish to preserve it, they can and they will produce a record, be it only in the form of stories. Immediately felt and directly relevant, such records resist the definitions imposed from outside extremely well. Stakes are often high, for collective identity and dignity are likely to be involved. Disenfranchised groups, who do not find their views within the media offerings, do not dissolve as a result. Collectively constructed "instant memory" gains a great deal of persuasive power from technologically produced imagery, but it is not dependent on it. What it is dependent on, and what television alone cannot supply, is the emotional investment in the present.

## Notes

1. For further discussion, see Edward S. Casey, *Remembering: A Phenomenological Study* (Bloomington and Indianapolis: Indiana University Press, 1987).
2. See, especially, Shimon Huberband, *Kiddush Hashem: Jewish Religious and Cultural Life in Poland During the Holocaust,* translated from Yiddish by David E. Fishman (New York: Yeshiva University Press, 1987) and David G. Roskies, *Against the Apocalypse: Responses to Catastrophe in Modern Jewish Culture* (Massachusetts: Harvard University Press, 1984).
3. For an extensive analysis of the "credibility problem," see Deborah E. Lipstadt, *Beyond Belief: The American Press and the Coming of the Holocaust 1933-1945* (New York: The Free Press, 1986).
.4 While this meant that individual survivors would feel more "comfortable" (not an apt term here), it also worked against perceiving the Holocaust as unique.
5. See Robert Jay Lifton, *Home from the War* (New York: Basic Books, 1973).
6. For a comparative perspective, see Daniel Dayan and Elihu Katz, *Media Events: The Live Broadcasting of History* (Cambridge, Mass.: Harvard University Press, 1992).
7. Linda Dittmar and Gene Michaud, eds., *From Hanoi to Hollywood. The Vietnam War in American Film* (New Brunswick and London: Rutgers University Press, 1990) makes a strong but context-specific case for carefully attending to the initial television coverage in particular.
8. Interview with Piotr Bikont, after the screening at Bard College, May 17, 1990.
9. The fate of the video recording of the beating of Rodney King illustrates this dynamic in particularly poignant ways, from the initial reactions to its screening on television to the reliance on it in court proceedings.
    It will be interesting to observe the impact of the recently developed "digital photography" on this faith in recorded images; the technology allows for an unprecedented degree of creative freedom, while preserving the appearances.
10. For a detailed analysis, see Barbie Zelizer, *Covering the Body: The Kennedy Assassination, the Media, and the Shaping of Collective Memory* (Chicago: University of Chicago Press, 1992).
11. For a provocative reflection, see Brian Fawcett, *Cambodia: A Book for People Who Find Television too Slow* (Vancouver: Talonbooks, 1986).
12. Karal Ann Marling and John Wetenhall, *Iwo Jima: Monuments, Memories, and the American Hero* (Cambridge, Mass.: Harvard University Press, 1991) offers rich material on this point.
13. For further discussion and wider scope, see George Lipsitz, *Time Passages: Collective Memory and American Popular Culture* (Minneapolis: University of Minnesota Press, 1990).

# 11

# Intermediaries

A teacher tells his class that the poem they are about to read is a definitive statement on how soldiers felt in the trenches during World War I; a museum guide first directs the visitors to the display of official records; a television producer decides that the program on Native Canadian land claims should run as part of the educational series on Canadian history; a publisher times the release of two books on Iraq to coincide with the impending military invasion. Strictly speaking, no memory work has been performed here, no *original* resources for remembering the past have been produced. And yet, there is no doubt that the choices made at such intermediary levels matter, both in terms of what enters into collective memory and how. Indeed, it might be argued that the task of constructing "realities of the past" is ultimately that of editorial framing of raw materials, of giving sense and structure to physical traces, records, tellings.

Such memory work at arm's length greatly enriches the possibilities in terms of assigning meaning to the past. It also presents us with some unique analytical challenges. Precisely because so much can be done by the intermediaries, focusing on "texts" alone may be a self-defeating strategy, especially when studying the works' claims to truth and authenticity. The meaning internal to the work, too, can become so transformed by the time the "text" reaches the public that an altogether different one emerges. The temptation then is to focus on the final product, but if we do, our understanding of the dynamics of collective memory becomes rather impoverished. Introducing more complexity into an already demanding analytical process is not something to be done lightly. Heuristic returns must be quite high to justify the extra effort. In this chapter, I will be suggesting areas where this is indeed the case, or where memory intermediaries deserve to take the center stage.

It might be best to begin with the recognition that securing public presence for the past is almost always a collective endeavor, involving various types of intermediary work. There is a certain division of labor in place, with some people taking on the highly creative tasks of producing a "text"—be it a book, a film or a museum exhibit—while others are concerned with marketing and distribution. And since so much of the work relies on original materials—artifacts, records, old photographs, writings from the times—we have an additional layer here of the creation of these raw pieces. At the other end of the symbolic chain, as it were, there are critics, opinion makers, and educators offering their interpretation, their frame for the text at hand. And all this happens before an individual "reads" it.

It is very much to be expected that there occur several shifts in meaning. What is of interest to students of collective memory is the pattern, if any, for the emergence of a "victorious frame." At the very least, we would like to know more about the struggle itself—as there often is one—between different ways of framing what and how is to be remembered.

In 1990, the Royal Ontario Museum in Toronto put together an exhibition entitled "Into the Heart of Africa," using many of the artifacts and photographs brought back to Canada by the nineteenth-century missionaries.[1] The structure of the exhibit, and especially the long explications accompanying the display, reflected its curator's intention for the "tale" to be that of exploitation and racism. Trained in anthropology and informed by highly sophisticated, postmodern sensitivity, the curator was very much taken aback when members of the local black community accused the exhibit and the museum of racism. A flurry of commentaries followed in the press, and while "Into the Heart of Africa" was allowed to complete its run, all the planned travel arrangements were cancelled. After long and protracted negotiations, the museum issued a carefully worded apology for inadvertently hurting community feelings. While officially settled, the controversy did not die, with views on the issue sharply dividing people on both sides of the racial line.

What most upset the critics in this case were the photographs, with their depiction of African "primitives." The written commentary reframing the images did not go unnoticed, but was said to be a highly ineffective way to change perceptions of an average museum visitor, and especially those of school children routinely ignoring long, complex explanations. When defenders of the exhibit added in their sophisticated comments, the argument took an anti-elitist turn. If the reframing effort could only be successful for a few, bred on postmodernism, that only added insult to injury. At issue was clearly more than curating methodologies.

For students of memory, controversies such as this offer a special opportunity, as they bring to the foreground the work behind the final product, with all the radical shifts in meaning along the way. What was attempted with "Into the Heart of Africa" is not an isolated incident, either. Present sensibilities on issues such as racism or sexism lead to many an effort to reread texts from the past, to use literature in particular as "evidence" of historical wrongs. These efforts too meet with resistance, though ordinarily not from the victim groups. The outrage over the exhibit may be an indication that images are more resilient to reframing, or at least that a complex commentary is a weak companion to visual persuasion. Photographs speak to us about the reality they capture; it takes an altogether different, usually analytically inspired, sensitivity to ask them to speak about the photographers. And even if we are listening for those authorial clues, the image itself retains its powerful voice all along.

Some years ago, I was browsing through big coffee-table books while visiting with friends in California. I came across a splendidly edited album of photographs of African tribesmen in their ritual body attires. About halfway through, I flipped to the front page—these pictures were taken by Leni Riefenstahl, Hitler's court filmmaker. What ensued was a long and at times heated discussion with my friends, who knew two of Riefenstahl's films—and who saw nothing wrong in admiring her current work. As troubled as I was by the moral implications involved, I too had to admit that the images were powerful—and beautiful—in their own right. Even recognizing that the choice of the subject could well be a logical extension of the Nazi fascination with race had little effect in the end.

Such symbolic independence of images can work the other way, too. In 1986, a writer/photographer team published (in the U.S.) *Remnants: The Last Jews of Poland*, a well-meaning testimony to the disappearing culture.[2] On their own, the stories were highly sympathetic to the people they were about, if all too sensitive to the difficulties inherent in non-Jews undertaking the task. The pictures, though, some one hundred of them, told a different tale altogether. They made for a display of exotic specimens, curious creatures as if already dead. The only warmth left was that of a nostalgic glow usually reserved for objects.

It is possible I reacted too harshly to these particular images; after all, I could have been easily included. But the fact remains that they, rather than the text, carried more weight here; the attitude to Poland's Jews, they both reflected and encouraged, also proved to fit very well indeed into the then new patterns of remembrance. What troubled me, in this case, was that this attitude be invisible, that it would seem natural to those looking at the pictures, all my critical efforts notwithstanding.

Yet if the perspective on the world, embodied in a photograph, appears to resist reframing efforts, the same cannot be said about our ways of seeing the photograph itself. The very presence of photographs within a museum exhibit defines them as elements of historical record; the confusion in Toronto was about what exactly the pictures were the record of, not about their documentary value as such. When photographs are exhibited in an art gallery, we are asked to see them as works of art instead. As many debates testify, when such status is given to erotic images, the frame is all too open to demolition. Photographs in books may acquire a number of different definitions—as art, as document, as illustration, as glimpses into the private sphere, as shorthand for complex realities. Publishing pictures "from the family album" gives them new importance while retaining the old definition.

For students of collective memory, clearly not all of such framing practices are equally relevant. What would interest us the most is the work involved in transforming private into public remembrance, the assigning of documentary value to individual images while placing them in a larger context of recounting the past. The putting together of a book (or exhibit) on municipal history, the use of original stills in films, or in mixed-media educational tools—these are all instances of memory intermediaries acquiring a priority role in the framing sequence. As we learned, such editorial effort need not effectively change the meaning of the photographs; it does, though, bring the imagery to particular, memory-directed attention.

More generally, it is the work of those who define existing "texts" as important to our sense of history and then proceed to use them in a coherent story that calls for further reflection here. To understand how collective memory is constructed, we naturally tend to focus on writing or image-making deliberately invoking the past. Yet while justified, such strategy poses risks of ignoring a rather large territory where the past itself serves as a reservoir, to be freely rummaged through for memory markers.[3] In the process, "texts" that were never intended to be a historical record become just that. Unlike photographs, which are memory markers at conception, as it were, these are all framed as such after the fact. And since their original meaning is often no longer readily available to us, it is up to the memory editors to restore it, alter it or perhaps make it up altogether.

At its most immediate, rummaging through the past can produce a form of "textual" history—whether of armaments, early movies or calendars. The objects or pictures speak of their own development over time; they function indirectly as a record of culture. Familiar to museum visitors, such a specialized display of (mostly) technical achievements tends to frame the past generally as stages of progress. Even when nonlinear in design, that is when only one specific period is the focus, such looking back relies on our vantage point in the present—a vantage point that rarely allows for any sense of inferiority.

Material objects, including dwellings, can be framed in an altogether different fashion as well. No longer confined to one or two categories, their selection aims at reconstructing, as best as possible, a certain way of life. Rather than speak of their own development, artifacts, and buildings are asked to tell a tale of their once owners and inhabitants. Frequently, the display is not complete until human figures are present, whether literally or through make-believe. Here, the explicit aim is unashamedly voyeuristic—we are taken on a journey back in time, looking in on the "real people."[4]

Whether it is a pioneer village or an aristocratic palace, the effort to recreate a way of life almost inevitably makes it seem cleaner, more orderly, prettier than it actually had been. It is as if the design invites a certain amount of sanitization; the very presence of visitors may be working against authenticity.

A poignant case in point—and a rather rare example of an attempt to recreate a horrific reality—is the museum at the camp in Auschwitz. Housed in the original prisoners' barracks and utilizing many of the objects found on site, the display is aimed at evoking the "as if I was here" feelings. Yet the very solidity of the buildings, the clean interiors, the cut lawns outside, all produce very mixed emotions. To many visitors, it is ultimately the other visitors which render empathy impossible. And indeed, while most exhibits on the Holocaust employ some authentic materials (such as camp uniforms, for example), they rely on much more complex, multimedia approaches to the subject. The infamous simulation of riding in a boxcar, found in Los Angeles, is indeed an exception.[5]

At many architectural sites, the two frames combine, usually in the form of the guide's narrative. At the Coliseum in Rome, for example, we learn about the history of the structure itself, as well as about the Romans. Without such narrative, the building's value as a memory marker would be very low indeed. This does not mean our knowledge has to be acquired on site, of course, but it does mean that as "records of" buildings need an accompanying tale. If walking down the boulevards in Paris gives one a vague sense of immersion in history, it is not until the contextual information is available that we begin to partake in local memory.

Contrary to photographs, then, architectural structures are very symbolically dependent on the editorial memory work—as would be most artifacts. That does make them open to radical reframing practices, as when a Polish Catholic cathedral in the now Lithuanian capital Vilnius is described, on the frontal plaque, as a Lithuanian cultural monument.[6] Only a well-informed visitor to towns and villages across Eastern Europe would be able to recognize the traces of Jewish presence in buildings now functioning as storage facilities or community centers—beyond the hardly visible ornamental detail, nothing is there to suggest it.

When going to a foreign country, conscientious tourists equip themselves with many a guidebook in clear, if implicit, recognition that reading of the past calls for more than direct encounter with architectural splendors. In a sense, writers of such guides are memory interpreters par excellence, as they synthesize and translate one culture's memory into universal terms. A careful study of their efforts would be of more than passing interest to students of framing remembrance; what it is likely to reveal are different "ownership claims," for one, as buildings are placed within the varying boundaries of cultural heritage. In places where such boundaries overlap—such as Jerusalem—the potential for such claims to clash is great. But even in less turbulent locales, we can learn a considerable amount about the community from how it presents itself to visitors, on site as well as in advance.

The staking of ownership claims is not confined to architectural structures, of course. Indeed, when looking at the construction of collective memory using as its raw materials "texts" produced in the past, one of the central analytic questions is that of to whom is that memory said to belong. Or, since the material itself may carry several identification tags, as it were, it is up to the memory workers to select one that best suits their purposes.

As with many other aspects of memory work, the staking of specific ownership claims often goes unnoticed—unless such claims are being contested. For many years, for example, it seemed perfectly natural for books and films about the Holocaust to be classified under "Jewish history"; libraries, school curricula, public spaces, all reflected that separation-through-specialization scheme. And then came the efforts of theologians, cultural critics, and social scientists reflecting on the Holocaust to make its memory central to our sense of the history of Western civilization and Christianity, efforts that if only partly successful in terms of educational practices have already proved a continuous challenge to the earlier views. What also emerged, and ultimately proved most problematic, were numerous specific claims from non-Jewish groups to be remembered as victims of the Holocaust, claims potentially undermining the very idea of *Shoah*. For American curators in particular, encouraged to construct Holocaust memorials in many urban centers, these clashing visions of their respective "owners" posed serious practical as well as philosophical difficulties. Not only were they confronted with morally, intellectually—and aesthetically—challenging decisions, they also had to respond to pressure from lobbyists, the contemporary "representatives" of the different pasts.[7]

By the time such debates over ownership occur, the original "proprietors" are by definition absent from the scene. Only rarely is it possible to trace the intended path of remembrance, an identification with a particular community of memory. Contemporary advocates know this, insofar as they so frequently base their claims on appeals to honoring the original intentions. It is then most interesting to get a glimpse of the process when the authors and their texts are in fact both present, when questions about the intended memory space are not hypothetical.

In a recently published collection of stories by Canada's "ethnic" writers,[8] the editors made a rather unique allowance for the authors' own voices, with short interviews accompanying the texts themselves. Almost without exception, the idea of multicultural representation, orienting the very structure of the book, is being contested by the so neatly categorized writers. In effect, by aligning themselves with writing first, Canadian writing second, they refuse the marginalization as they see it in ethnic labelling. Should this collection be put together a hundred years from now, the editorial voice would of course prevail. Free to disagree with the frame, these writers make us sharply aware both of its existence and of its politics.

Staking memory ownership claims is often a political act. At its most basic, it bespeaks of the current definition of the community, of the membership rules as they emerge and shift. Both at a local level and nationwide, who is remembered as one of "us" rather than various "them" matters. Of special interest to us here is the important role played in this process by the intermediaries of collective memory. If words and images at times do speak for themselves, more often than not it is the subtle and not so subtle work at the level of classification that assigns them to collective owners. Once again, the strategies used become more visible for inspection when they are subject to debate—or at the very least some questioning. In my study of Poland's rather sudden appropriation of Jewish memory as its own, for example, I was able to trace many a shift in ownership patterns since these were central to the whole endeavor; editorial comments accompanying translated verses from the Talmud explicitly framed those as a part of Poland's heritage, while writings in the more contemporary Jewish philosophy would be placed under the heading "interesting culture" rather than history. Quite literally, individuals and texts were now said to belong equally to Jewish and Polish memory.

Observing such a transformation in its early stages privileged the voices of intellectuals, public-opinion makers, and editors. Once their work is done, though, once there is a fair degree of acceptance for the new rules on ownership of the past, the crucial mediating task falls to educators and popularizers of ideas. (The curriculum debates in North America would be a case in point here, as much as testifying to the fact that such stages can coincide in social practice.) With time, the redefining of "us" and "them" of remembrance is likely to result in original memory work, of course, and indeed without such fresh perspectives offered by historians or artists, the redefinitions would not be complete. Just as importantly, though, those "texts" which had been initially borrowed and reframed would retain their superior status; coming from the past, they authenticate the whole.

On November 9, 1989, crowds breached the Berlin Wall. News media the world over loudly proclaimed the day as historical. It was. But as Elie Wiesel commented with deep sadness, the date itself—November 9th—had already entered history. In 1938, the Nazi-instigated "night of the broken glass" marked the beginning of violent persecution of the Jews. In 1989, everyone seemed more than ready to forget it. Historical coincidence aside, the shift of focus that occurred was justifiably seen as symbolic of a larger shift in framing of remembrance. In the practice of memory, dates as occasions for commemoration do carry a great deal of meaning. Indeed, one of the better ways of gauging the importance of collective memory as well as of tracing its narrative structure is to look at the texture of its yearly communal cycle.[9] Dates work as a convenient shorthand for usually complex historical entities. Beyond marking certain time off for active remembrance (and here, the round anniversaries appear as the top choice), dates may also enter into the language itself as symbolic carriers of the past. In this capacity, the "date" need not be as precise as when marking a special moment; months, years, even decades or centuries may qualify as well. Local specificity imports here, not only in terms of the actual events so marked, but the very type of markers being used. In North America, references to 1930s or 1950s or 1980s, with all their multiple meanings, are fairly common. In Poland, its history of struggle with the Communist regime is neatly encapsulated in month names instead: October (1956), March (1968), December (1970), August (1980). In both contexts, though, there are days (rather than dates) that become powerful bridging devices between collective and individual memories; Americans, the ones old enough, of course, all recall their own whereabouts when they first heard of President Kennedy's assassination; Poles speak of *the* day, when remembering themselves finding out martial law had been imposed (in 1981). The lifespan of such vivid memories is of necessity limited, and they rarely cross local boundaries. (In the age of global communications, this may indeed change; one thinks of man's first steps on the moon as a case in point.) These days can, and often do, become permanently marked as dates for commemoration, thus both gaining and losing in presence. The gain is in the separate space accorded within the communal calendar; the loss is in precisely that separation from the flow of daily living.

The highly symbolic and frequently emotional charge of dates as memory markers makes them likely focal points in ideological disputes. For the United States to establish Martin Luther King's birthday as a nationally celebrated holiday was seen as a significant step towards racial equality. In Central and Eastern Europe, one of the first acts of newly elected post-Communist parliaments was often the return to old commemoration days and the cancellation of those imposed by the previous regime.[10] The debates surrounding May 1st—in theory as well as practice—signalled the difficult accommodation with the once-exploited memory tool.

These debates, together with the dispute over the "proper" celebration of King's birthday (and many similar arguments) point to an important quality of dates—their inherent "sponginess." Precisely because dates work as a memory shorthand at its most reductive capacity, their meaning can be filled in, enlarged, filled out, changed, in short constructed with much greater ease than when narratives are involved. As occasions for commemoration, dates do not define its form; here, once again, the texture of remembrance can shift, at times in quite unexpected directions. Amidst the many discussions about the legacy of 1492, for example, it became clear just how diverse the "proper meaning" of 1992 could be. What was also rather remarkable, though by no means unique, was the range of people involved in the defining and redefining process, from Native American activists to academics to government officials. Testifying to a widely shared perception of the high symbolic importance of such special memory markers, the work of intermediaries thus took on its most public turn.

To what extent the days set aside for remembrance actually function that way inevitably varies, too. Columbus Day may be simply a holiday to enjoy, while King's birthday now belongs within a larger educational effort at celebrating black history. On the 75th anniversary of the Russian Revolution (in 1992), its as-yet-unsettled legacy resulted in a confusing array of symbolic gestures, attempts to remember as well as forget. If dates cannot easily be erased altogether, transforming them as "occasions for . . . " is another matter.

If dates emerge here as especially "spongy" of memory markers—and photographs as the rather sturdy ones—the differences are of degree, rather than kind. In principle, I would argue, all traces of the past are open to continuous framing and reframing. What we need to understand better is just how open; the answers might be found by looking at what memory workers actually do with the material at hand.[11]

Among the intermediaries, one group deserves more attention than it usually receives—the translators. Their work makes it possible to claim the once foreign past as one's own—where the two are separated by language divides, as was the case with much of Polish-Jewish heritage. It may also make for a wider scope of collective memory when a community severs its linguistic links with its own past—as would be the case with further generations of immigrants to North America for whom bridges with the "old country" must be built in English.[12] More generally still, translators provide for the possibility of a crosscultural if not an international base to our sense of history, for the possibility of empathy with an altogether different view of events.

The key word here is "possible." There are no guarantees whatsoever that when an English Canadian reads, in English, a French Canadian account of Anglo-dominance, his views about Canada and his people's role would dramatically change. But, without any access to how the other side sees the matter, especially when historical grievances are concerned, there is little chance indeed for a new understanding to emerge. The fact that so few efforts are made in this direction in Canada today does not bode well for the country's future; separate, if not clashing memories are poor grounds for compromises.

If the work of translators is rarely acknowledged by students of remembrance, it is, I think, related to an implicit recognition that they do not set the priorities themselves, that translation is akin to manual labor on the construction of collective memory with blueprints and overall design decided elsewhere. Analytically, we are more interested in the engineers. Indeed, it is the presence of translation—rather than its quality—that may offer first clues as to how open to outside perspectives is a given collective memory.[13] To follow up on such clues means, though, turning one's attention to wider issues of cultural politics, be it within the marketplace or strictures of state-imposed rules. And in this way, it means joining together with a long established analytical tradition—the study of "gatekeepers."

Looking at the top levels of decision making while inquiring about the dynamics of collective memory is something I approach with considerable caution. It is all too easy to explain many social practices away by recourse to "commercialism" or "censorship." Even in places where the state clearly had control over how the past would be publicly presented, such as the Soviet Union, a student of collective memory would be well advised to investigate below the top, to ask questions about historians, writers, educators as well as the public at large. It is becoming increasingly clear that as censorship receded, beginning in the late 1980s, no magic discovery of historical truths ensued; the picture is a great deal more complex, pointing, so far, to the importance of interpretive grids over and above any of those imposed by the state, grids of collective self-definition.[14] In other words, coercion alone cannot account for the vicissitudes of the past. Where the controls had never been as tight to begin with, as would be the case in Poland, censorship carries even less explanatory power.[15] It can become a convenient rationalization for inaction, as when the void surrounding the Jew in Poland's memory is explained by state-imposed silence; the reasoning is convincing only if we ignore that in no other area was the state successful in establishing a monopoly on remembrance. It can be used as a badge of honor of sorts, as when some rather mediocre works gain acclaim solely because they were once forbidden to appear. In short, censorship itself can assume mythological qualities within the newly constructed vision of the recent past—and should be studied as such.

All this is not to deny that censors' decisions count, they do. But leaving matters at that level can be most misleading, for it leaves out the numerous stratagems people employ to write and read between the lines, their use of metaphor and humor—and the presence of eye witnesses. Our understanding of the dynamics of memory in an Orwellian universe is still much too tentative for the inquiry to close by censorship fiat.[16]

The powers of the state, where the state is powerful, are not limited to keeping the unorthodox views out of the public sphere. Indeed, it might be argued that it is in its role as a *sponsor* that the state exercises most of its control over memory work. In totalitarian regimes, the state aims to be the only sponsor, through a complex structure of cultural and scientific institutions, prominently including the media. Democratic countries differ, of course, in the scope of such state sponsorship, diffusing it among various levels of government and supplementing it with a large network of private interests. In the Western world, countries also differ sharply in terms of the overall arrangements for cultural production—and the specifics of sponsorship for memory work. Those very differences, between, let us say, nationwide, tax supported Canadian television and the American networks, make generalizations about big-business-as-gatekeeper analytically suspect. What is more, in the area of memory construction, we are likely to encounter all the different types and forms of sponsorship. In its very nature, remembrance matters at the local, regional and national levels; the work of artists is often commissioned and even the most commercial of endeavors could draw on support for higher causes. The mixture of science, journalism, education, design, and popular culture—all participants in the construction of collective memory—does not allow for generalized rules about top decision making. What it calls for is the analyst's attentiveness to the specifics, as we do want to know who is responsible for this other than that framing of remembrance.

At times, the question is of purely academic interest, in the sense that we like our inquires to be elegantly complete. But at other times, the issue of sponsorship (and control) becomes an essential one if we are to understand the public response and responsiveness to memory offerings. The fact that the Vietnam War Memorial was *not* sponsored by the U.S. government matters well beyond the veterans' community who did fund it. When a special interest group is behind proposals to commemorate its heroes, its main task often consists of hiding such patronage. The controversy over the African exhibit in Toronto would have looked very different if the exhibit did not have the official blessings. The respect enjoyed by the Catholic Church in then Communist Poland—and the wide disrespect for the regime—made me give a great deal more weight to voices originating in the former. The works of institutional history, written by people employed by the very institutions they describe, can be dismissed as hagiographic despite their intrinsic scholarly value. The television series *Holocaust* was dismissed by many a critic precisely because it was the product of a commercial network.

Sponsorship, in short, can both lend an additional authority to the work at hand and detract from it; what it actually does clearly depends on the context, cultural, social, and political. Sponsorship may also retain a fairly neutral status, again, depending on the context. Our task as students of memory then is to bring the significance of sponsors—if any—to the foreground, in order to better account for the readings the work is likely to receive. In doing that, we are in effect illuminating yet another "frame"—and another link between public and private remembrance.

A careful case by case analysis of the conditions of sponsorship—and censorship—can be most useful in yet another way. If what we are aiming to explain are the blank spaces in the public record of the past, questions about top level decision making allow us to move beyond informed cultural or political hunches. For example, when the book *Vichy and the Jews*[17] appeared in 1981, many a reviewer made a great deal of the fact that this first extensive and popular history of a morally troubling chapter in French history was written by Robert Paxton and Michael Marrus—an American and a Canadian. The French historians, together with the public, it was plausibly suggested, just did not want to delve into such a problematic era. Considering the earlier reluctance which greeted Marcel Ophuls's documentaries about that period, the explanation seemed convincing indeed. But it was not correct. French historians I questioned on the subject would point to a number of earlier works, not publicized in North America, to be sure, but important within France. And Robert Paxton[18] would point to the consistently high level of cooperation granted to him, then a junior and a foreigner, throughout the project. What he saw as the possible reason for the relatively low priority assigned to research in the area was a mundane but powerful principle of scientific work—the best scholars attracting the best students and most renown, in this case for analyses of pre-revolutionary France. *Vichy and the Jews* could not magically reset those priorities; what it did do was to move the debates into the very public stage of the media, defying any generalized ideas about self-imposed silence.

What this example also illustrates, albeit in an unusual fashion, is the important role of yet another group of memory intermediaries—the critics. In this case, the book was placed in the "important, new, controversial" frame, all the while the rather large terrain of French memory work on the Vichy period would be confined to the "insignificant" category. The strategy itself is not at all infrequent, as the label "breakthrough" works wonders for marketing purposes. Discussion of the ways of looking at the past naturally lends itself to emphasis on the new, the original. But critics do more than assess the significance of the "texts" at hand; they also, routinely, interpret them for us. And just as sponsorship alone can add weight and meaning to the work, critical insight, when respected, provides it with another influential frame. Even when not respected, the voice of critics counts for much in terms of exposure; with a tremendous number of historical books published each year, this is of special importance for the scholarly output, where only a select few enter the truly public realm. Media attention devoted to the exhibit in Toronto clearly extended the scope of controversy well beyond those directly involved. Movie reviews, in anticipation of—or follow-ing—the Oscar awards not only increase the size of potential audience for such important memory works as *Born on the Fourth of July* or *Dances with Wolves*, they also ask the viewer to think in particular ways. Television critics may be simply asking us to pay attention, not a small feat in the "zapping" zone.

Critics also, at least the good ones, provide a context for the work at hand. In this capacity, they have definite advantage over even the well-informed reader. While we can—and we often do—argue with the proposed interpretation and assessment of the "text," we are usually malequipped to disagree with the attached background. For works deal-ing with the past, the contextual information can vary a great deal, yet is inherently beyond most people's cognitive reach.

We may be offered a brief historical base line against which the work is critically scrutinized; or, other "texts" dealing with the same subject are brought forth for a comparison, or, ever more generally, the state of collective memory as such is being assessed—on all counts, the framing that is taking place is hard to reject. The most we can do is to ignore it.

The contribution from critics does at times go beyond the directing of attention and the framing of readings. At its most indepth, the critics' analysis becomes critical analysis of memory construction *tout court*.[19] Akin to the self-reflective work of writers and artists themselves, which exposes the processes of remembrance, the path taken by some critics leads us into the very center of questions about truth, narrative, memory and history. What distinguishes their voices from those coming from the academia proper is that they are heard by a much wider group. Thus while important in their own right for students of memory, the insights so expressed count for more than the useful ideas that they are. Shaping and reshaping popular thinking on the subject, especially once the intellectuals' attitudes transfer to the educational system and the mass media, ideas about memory construction become part of that very con-struction. Much work remains to be done for us to acquire a better sense of how such channelling of cultural sensibility operates in different societies, how the broadly accepted definitions of truth, authenticity, and plausibility in historical accounts help or hinder the framing strategies used by memory practitioners.[20]

An illustration from my own efforts to capture this dynamic may clarify the analytical predicament here. When the subject of Polish-Jewish relations during the Holocaust began to be seriously discussed in Poland (in the mid-1980s), it was first as a response to Claude Lanzmann's film *Shoah*, shown in parts on state run television.[21] Virtually all of the critical reviews of *Shoah* reflected on it being an unfairly selective attempt at remembrance; Lanzmann said nothing about the Poles' aid to the Jews. Historical truth thus became defined as a balance sheet of facts and figures. Perhaps more importantly, the idea of moral responsibility for the fate of Poland's Jews was directly linked to those facts and figures. As a result, the Catholic Church, for example, the prime target of Lanzmann's criticism, was exonerated from any blame by citing its record of hiding Jews during the war. (This understanding of history was not new, but it became crystallized and widely publicized.)

For Lanzmann, and indeed for most people reflecting on the Holocaust in the West, the notion of moral responsibility carried an altogether different meaning, both more diffuse and indirect. The Church was to be held responsible for its teachings, over the centuries, that allowed for widespread indifference, if not hostility towards the Jews. Much of *Shoah* spoke to this issue, with great conviction, one should add. The message was very loud and clear, and yet remained so completely outside the intellectual and emotional parameters of Poland's memory that it was not to be heard.

The role of the critics, in this case, was to explicate the already widely shared views; their voices strengthened a particular sensibility without disrupting its structure or content. It would be most interesting to examine situations where the opposite happens, where the critics set out to transform accepted ideas about remembrance, or work to question established framing strategies. What are the effects, if any, of popularizing a postmodern stance towards representation of the past?

To gauge such effects, though, it might be necessary to move beyond the relatively narrow confines of intellectual discourse in mainly print media. It is time to visit the schools. Indeed, our brief survey of memory intermediaries would be sorely incomplete without mention of educators, people directly responsible for shaping both the attitudes towards history and the contents of publicly accepted "realities of the past." Whether such responsibility translates into efficacy is an empirical question, of course; some studies indicate that schools have lost a great deal of ground to popular culture here.[22] We need to know more about that, just as we need to know more about the practices inside and outside the history classroom. Studies of textbooks, while illuminating, cannot provide us with a full picture, as any teacher might testify. Enthusiasm—or boredom—generated in school could make the difference between passive and active remembrance. The use of audiovisual aids, inviting witnesses to events to speak to the class, initiating projects in local or oral history—these are all important for how the young see the past. The degree and form of participation in communal commemorative rituals counts as well.

Educational practices can rarely be separated from the wider social and political context, though. Having gone through school in a system aiming to instill the one "correct" version of history—and having witnessed how such hegemonic strategy failed—I am perhaps extra sensitive to the possibility of cracks in the edifice of political controls. But this is not to deny the need to look at the interrelations between education and politics in general, or those between teachings about the past and their legitimating potential. Debates about the curriculum in North America are just one case in point here; the current turmoil in the schools in the once Soviet Union is another terrain well worth exploring. As students of memory construction, though, we would be well advised to treat the assumptions about the role of schools that inform such political debates as just that—assumptions. The battles fought in the educational area tell us a great deal about politics of the moment, but very little about the actual importance of victories or defeats. They naturally assign priority to what happens in schools, and even more specifically, to the contents of the courses. This emphasis may or may not be justified; much further research is called for here.

Speaking now in general terms again, I think the work of memory intermediaries deserves more attention than it has so far been granted. If "texts" generate multiple readings, and they do, focusing on how some of those readings are privileged over others is of considerable help.

## Notes

1. See also chapter 4.
2. Malgorzata Niezabitowska, *Remnants: The Last Jews of Poland* (New York: Friendly Press, 1986). (Excerpts in *National Geographic*, Sept. 1986.)

3. Especially rich in examples here is David Lowenthal, *The Past is a Foreign Country* (Cambridge: Cambridge University Press, 1985).

4. Problematizing this relationship is Ivan Karp and Steven D. Lavine, eds., *Exhibiting Cultures: The Poetics and Politics of Museum Display* (Washington, D.C.: Smithsonian Institution Press, 1991).

5. See Judith Miller, *One, by One, by One: Facing the Holocaust* (New York: Simon and Schuster, 1990).

6. Catherine Goussef, "URSS: Wilno, Vilné, Vilnius, capitale de Lituanie," in Alain Brossat, Sonia Combe, Jean-Yves Potel, Jean-Charles Szurek, eds., *A l'Est, la mémoire retrouvée* (Paris: Editions la Découverte, 1990), 494–96.

7. See also chapter 2.

8. Linda Hutcheon and Marion Richmond, eds., *Other Solitudes: Canadian Multicultural Fictions* (Toronto: Oxford University Press, 1990).

9. I am indebted to Zev Gerber for his insights on this point, especially in relation to practices in Israel. See also William M. Johnston, *Celebrations: The Cult of Anniversaries in Europe and the United States Today* (New Brunswick, N.J.: Transaction Books, 1990).

10. See Alain Brossat, Sonia Combe, Jean-Yves Potel, Jean-Charles Szurek, eds., *A l'Est, la mémoire retrouvée* (Paris: Editions la Découverte, 1990).

11. Robert Paine, "Masada: A history of a memory," (Memorial University) unpublished paper, is an illuminating case study of this process.

12. Jack Kugelmass and Jonathan Boyarin, eds. and trans., *From a Ruined Garden: The Memorial Books of Polish Jewry* (New York: Schocken Books, 1983) is an example here.

13. It is, for example, highly telling that Ronald Wright, *Stolen Continents: The New World Through Indian Eyes Since 1492* (Toronto: Penguin Books, 1992) became a national bestseller in Canada, and will be, in turn, translated into German, French and Italian. (Ronald Wright, personal communication, October 20, 1992.)

14. For further discussion, see Iwona Irwin-Zarecka, "In Search of Usable Pasts," *Society* 30, 2(January/February 1993):32–36.

15. For a rare record of the practice, see Jane Leftwich Curry, ed., *The Black Book of Polish Censorship*, translated by Jane Leftwich Curry (New York: Vintage Books, 1984).

16. Most illuminating here are studies compiled in Alain Brossat, Sonia Combe, Jean-Yves Potel, Jean-Charles Szurek, eds., *A l'Est, la mémoire retrouvée* (Paris: Editions la Découverte, 1990).

17. Michael R. Marrus and Robert O. Paxton, *Vichy France and the Jews* (New York: Basic Books, 1981).

18. Interview, April 20, 1983, in Paris.

19. See, for example, Ian Buruma, "From Hirohito to Heimat," *The New York Review* (October 26, 1989):31–32 and 40–45.

20. Charles S. Maier, *The Unmasterable Past: History, Holocaust, and German National Identity* (Cambridge, Mass.: Harvard University Press, 1988) illustrates the high analytical returns here.

21. For further discussion, see Iwona Irwin-Zarecka, "*Shoah* in Poland," in Jean M. Guiot and Joseph G. Green, eds., *From Orchestras to Apartheid*, (North York, Ontario: Captus University Publications, 1990):99–108.

22. See, for example, Henri Rousso, *The Vichy Syndrome: History and Memory in France since 1944*. Translated by Arthur Goldhammer (Cambridge, Mass.: Harvard University Press, 1991).

# Select Annotated Bibliography

The following list of sources has been compiled as an aid for students of the dynamics of collective memory. By no means exhaustive, it aims to reflect the *range* of material pertinent to the inquiry. My brief comments about the texts, in the form of mini-reviews, serve to guide the reader through the multiplicity of approaches encountered in this rapidly growing area of study. The emphasis here is on the more recent publications in English; a separate section signals some of the French works available. With a few exceptions, articles in edited volumes are not treated individually.

After some experimenting with various categorizing schemes, I have opted for a strictly alphabetical order of the listings below. If the result appears to defy any rules of intellectual order, it also reflects the riches (and the challenges) of multidisciplinary endeavor.

Anderson, Benedict. *Imagined Communities: Reflections on the Origin and Spread of Nationalism.* London and New York: Verso, 1983.

Very useful for students of collective memory, this book offers both conceptual tools and interesting empirical materials (including some from Asia). The argument stresses powers of sentiment and counters some of the extreme claims about "inventing traditions." Critical theory at its best.

Avisar, Ilan. *Screening the Holocaust: Cinema's Images of the Unimaginable.* Bloomington and Indianapolis: Indiana University Press, 1988.

Valuable for its comparative scope (North American, Western and Eastern Europe; documentary and fiction), as well as the insistence that film *can* deal with the extraordinary events in a meaningful way. Critical emphasis here is on the challenges of representation, historical truthfulness, and comprehension. Filmography.

*Between Memory and History*, edited by Marie-Noelle Bourguet, Lucette Valensi and Nathan Wachtel. *History and Anthropology*, vol. 2, part 2. October 1986.

A rare opportunity to sample French scholarship; ten of the eleven essays are case histories of reactions to the domination/suppression of collective memory. Wide range of subjects (contemporary Zaire, Jews, working class), unifying concerns with group identity. Includes a good analytical overview by Wachtel.

Boyarin, Jonathan. *Storm from Paradise: The Politics of Jewish Memory.* Minneapolis: University of Minnesota Press, 1992.

Intellectually stimulating essays, connecting the Jewish tradition and culture to questions posed by critical theory and postmodern reflection. Included is a rare case study of forgetting (on the Lower East Side in New York). Boyarin speaks directly to the experience of both being Other and "Othering."

Butler, Thomas, ed. *Memory: History, Culture and the Mind.* Oxford and New York: Basil Blackwell, 1989.

Based on Wolfson College Lectures, this collection of eight essays focuses on the themes of forgetting and healing, moving from psychology and psychoanalysis to history and anthropology. Materials include studies of Soviet Union and Yugoslavia. Interesting also for its quasi-spiritual tone of concern, placing academic analysis within a wider "Memory Movement."

Casey, Edward S. *Remembering: A Phenomenological Study.* Bloomington and Indianapolis: Indiana University Press, 1987.

A useful "reference book" on the pervasive role of memory in human experience. While the focus is on individual life-worlds, much of the terrain covered here belongs to the realm of socially shared (reminiscing, places, objects, commemoration). Ideas to work with when analyzing the complex texture of remembrance.

Connerton, Paul. *How Societies Remember.* Cambridge: Cambridge University Press, 1989.

A challenging "correction" to the prevailing emphasis on cultural texts. Connerton argues that much of tradition is transmitted through *bodily* practices and rituals, mnemonic devices responsible for "habit memory." Open to question here is his insistence that these practices lack any cognitive/interpretive component (which is said to be their key strength).

Davies, R. W. *Soviet History in the Gorbachev Revolution.* Bloomington and Indianapolis: Indiana University Press, 1989.

Accessible to nonspecialists, the book provides rich case study material. Focusing on the public debates of 1987-88, Davies looks at both the substantive changes and the profession itself; strong on historical background and current politics. A "snapshot" of an unique situation.

Davis, Fred. *Yearning for Yesterday: A Sociology of Nostalgia.* New York: The Free Press, 1979.

An early look at what has become a major cultural force, the book offers a wealth of empirically grounded insight. Combining questions about the meaning of nostalgia for the individual's identity (and life cycle) with those about the institutional and societal dynamic, Davis shows the complexity of this force. Of special interest is his balanced discussion of the media.

Dawidowicz, Lucy S. *The Holocaust and the Historians*. Cambridge, Mass.: Harvard University Press, 1981.

A sharply critical analysis of the production of social forgetting, covering the U.S., England, (West) Germany, U.S.S.R., and Poland. A prominent historian herself, Dawidowicz argues against treating the Holocaust as an "ethnic" event. Useful also as background to the more recent shifts/debates.

Dayan, Daniel, and Elihu Katz. *Media Events: The Live Broadcasting of History*. Cambridge, Mass.: Harvard University Press, 1992.

An empirically rich, comparative study of a crucial element of the global memory landscape. Very balanced in its focus on how the coverage frames the events (such as royal weddings) but also on how people creatively respond to the occasion. It shows the importance of local cultural context while uncovering patterns of new public rituals generated by television.

Dittmar, Linda, and Gene Michaud, eds. *From Hanoi to Hollywood: The Vietnam War in American Film*. New Brunswick and London: Rutgers University Press, 1990.

An excellent book. Nineteen essays offer a critical examination of over one hundred fictional and documentary films, as well as television coverage. Scholars and critics, many having served in Vietnam, focus on strategies of distortion and forgetting. Activist in tone and intent, the analysis privileges questions about coming to terms with the experience of the Vietnam era. Includes an extensive filmography.

Doneson, Judith E. *The Holocaust in American Film*. Philadelphia: The Jewish Publication Society, 1987.

An insightful analysis of how the Holocaust has become Americanized, now serving mainly as a metaphor for human suffering. Very balanced in its treatment of *The Diary of Anne Frank* and the series *Holocaust*. Doneson emphasizes the actual workings of commercial film and television, in that the study can serve as a model for others.

Eksteins, Modris. *Rites of Spring: The Great War and the Birth of the Modern Age*. Toronto: Lester & Orpen Dennys, 1989.

A bold cultural history, drawing together art, public rhetoric and private experience, this book is in part a study of how collective memory (of the war) was constructed. Rich in detail, both in terms of practices of remembrance and the wider transformations in European culture. Contains a challenging conclusion on the rise of Nazism, with issues of memory at the center.

Evans, Richard J. *In Hitler's Shadow: West German Historians and the Attempt to Escape from the Nazi Past*. New York: Pantheon Books, 1989.

Brief and balanced, the book examines key issues in the 1980s debates. Focus here is on the writings, but some social and political background is provided as well. Resource material for analysts of forgetting.

Ezrahi, Sidra DeKoven. *By Words Alone: The Holocaust in Literature*. Chicago and London: University of Chicago Press, 1980.

Valuable for its wide, comparative scope, as well as its overriding concern with the imperatives of historical reality. Included are mainly works of fiction (and poetry), from Eastern Europe, Israel, and America. Interesting reflections on language.

Fawcett, Brian. *Cambodia: A Book for People Who Find Television too Slow*. Vancouver: Talonbooks, 1986.

Provocative and often disturbing reflections, from a non-academic writer. Mixing fiction and reportage, Fawcett raises basic questions about remembering genocide in Cambodia. Another major concern is with the obliteration of cultural identity in the "global village."

Felman, Shoshana, and Dori Laub, M.D. *Testimony: Crises of Witnessing in Literature, Psychoanalysis, and History*. New York and London: Routledge, 1992.

A disturbing book. Besides interesting essays on teaching, Camus, and Lanzmann's *Shoah*, Felman offers an impassioned defense of Paul de Man's silence about his collaborating with the Nazis, a defense equating that silence to reactions on the part of Holocaust survivors. Also, only a minimal recognition is given to vast scholarship on the topic to which Felman claims to bring new insights.

Fentress, James, and Chris Wickham. *Social Memory*. Oxford and Cambridge, Mass.: Blackwell, 1992.

A major analytical statement, with focus on the uses of the past in the formation of collective identities. Insisting on moving beyond the fact/fiction dichotomy, the authors stress the role of narrative *genres* as structuring and constraining the transmission of memory. An unique empirical base, combining medieval history, studies of Sub-Saharan Africa, working class England and Sicilian mafia. Many a challenge here to oral historians.

Field, Norma. *In the Realm of a Dying Emperor: A Portrait of Japan at Century's End*. New York: Pantheon Books, 1991.

An important case history of memory, forgetting, and resistance. By chronicling three individual struggles against the official silence, Field shows just how strong Japan's reluctance is to confront its recent past. The author's own story (of mixed background and migrations) adds a lot of cultural sensitivity here.

Friedländer, Saul, ed. *Probing the Limits of Representation: Nazism and the "Final Solution."* Cambridge, Mass.: Harvard University Press, 1992.

An important book, the first to bring theoretical concerns of discourse analysis (contributions by White, LaCapra, and others) directly against the moral concerns with relativising the Holocaust. Proceedings of a conference, the book retains its debating style. Twenty essays, with focus on both historical narratives and artistic renditions (prose, poetry, film). Valuable intellectual bridging between Holocaust studies and the postmodern "mainstream."

Fussell, Paul. *The Great War and Modern Memory.* New York and London: Oxford University Press, 1975.

An imaginative and moving account of how literature and experience interpenetrate in the construction of World War I myths and images. Beyond its strengths as cultural history, the book provides illuminating examples of the interplay between individual and collective memory work. Of special interest to students of generational influence on values and ideas.

Garber, Zev, with Alan L. Berger and Richard Libowitz, eds. *Methodology in the Academic Teaching of the Holocaust.* Lanham and London: University Press of America, 1988.

The first collection to address wideranging pedagogical questions, it offers invaluable material for students of transmission of memory. Seventeen essays deal with matters of instructional content as well as audience; there is a section on the use of literature and the arts; surveys of textbook and classroom practices are also included. Interdisciplinary and interdenominational. Extensive references.

*History & Memory: Studies in Representation of the Past.* Bloomington, Indiana: Indiana University Press, 1991-.

A new journal, edited by Saul Friedländer. It brings together scholars from Europe, North America, and Israel. So far, its key emphasis has been the problematics of Holocaust memory. Included, though, are theoretically oriented studies as well as varied empirical material. Valuable resource, especially for its international scope.

Hobsbawm, Eric, and Terence Ranger, eds. *The Invention of Tradition.* Cambridge: Cambridge University Press, 1983.

A problematic classic. By documenting how governments and elites "manufacture" rituals and symbols for purposes of legitimacy, essays in this volume provide a wealth of empirical detail, yet also an analytically onesided view of memory construction. To use with caution when studying nationalism.

Irwin-Zarecka, Iwona. *Neutralizing Memory: The Jew in Contemporary Poland.* New Brunswick, N.J.: Transaction Books, 1989.

A case study in very selective remembering. While the book focuses on the "explosion" of interest in things Jewish of the early 1980s, its explanatory framework relies heavily on historical material. Of interest to students of dealing with morally troubling past, as well as those concerned with generational dynamics and oppositional memory. Also here is an extensive critique of nostalgia.

Kaes, Anton. *From Hitler to Heimat: The Return of History as Film.* Cambridge, Mass.: Harvard University Press, 1989.

An excellent analysis, with focus on self-conscious memory work, i.e., films that take both the past and remembrance as challenges. Key (West) German movies since 1970 show a pronounced shift towards questions about identity, prefiguring the historical debates of the mid-1980s. Firmly situated in their sociocultural context, the filmmakers' ideas speak to the ambiguities of Germany's engagement with the past in general.

Kammen, Michael. *Mystic Chords of Memory: The Transformation of Tradition in American Culture.* New York: Alfred A. Knopf, 1991.

A treasure trove for students of Americana, historical preservation, collecting and museums; extensive detail as well as references. Strong on the earlier periods, Kammen's treatment of the last six decades omits both movies and (most of) television; virtually nothing is said about the recent debates about "multiculturalism." The book illuminates especially well the changing ideas and practices of guardianship of memory, at the local, regional and national levels.

Karp, Ivan, and Steven D. Lavine, eds. *Exhibiting Cultures: The Poetics and Politics of Museum Display.* Washington, D.C.: Smithsonian Institution Press, 1991.

For the nonspecialist, this is a good introduction to current debates about museum practices, with emphasis on minority representation. Twenty-seven essays by professionals and scholars offer an empirically rich and varied base for questioning the relationships between the "raw materials," framing strategies and visitors' interpretation. Included is a discussion of folklore, festivals, and ethnographic exhibits, of particular interest to students of collective memory.

Karp, Ivan, Christine Mullen Kraemer, and Steven D. Lavine, eds. *Museums and Communities: The Politics of Public Culture.* Washington, D.C.: Smithsonian Institution Press, 1992.

A sequel to *Exhibiting Culture*, this volume contains mainly empirical case studies, of direct interest to students of collective memory/identity. Discussed are not only new roles for museums, but the context of tourism, historical preservation, and popular culture as well. Seventeen essays cover a wide range of ethnicities, with a special emphasis on African Americans. Altogether, a good grounding for understanding the "multiculturalism" debates.

Kruger, Barbara, and Phil Mariani, eds. *Remaking History*. Dia Art Foundation Discussion in Contemporary Culture no. 4. Seattle: Bay Press, 1989.

This collection of twelve essays by prominent advocates of "new historism" allows for a close look at the deconstructionist strategies. Some speak directly to questions about collective memory (e.g., Hoberman on Vietnam movies), others address broader concerns with representation (e.g., Treischler on AIDS discourse). Strong presence of critique of sexism, racism, and postcolonialism.

Kuchler, Susanne, and Walter Mellion, eds. *Images of Memory: On Remembering and Representation*. Washington and London: Smithsonian Institution Press, 1991.

Conceived as an inquiry into culturally and historically informed relations between memory, cognition and image production, this collection of eight essays is virtually inaccessible to people not trained in art history. Individually, too, the studies cover rather arcane subjects, making for difficult bridging with contemporary concerns.

Kugelmass, Jack, and Jonathan Boyarin, eds. and trans. *From a Ruined Garden: The Memorial Books of Polish Jewry*. New York: Schocken Books, 1983.

The unique quality of memory work presented here makes this book a valuable resource for general relection. An analytically strong introduction, plus the thematic structure of the selections together emphasize the patterns of "narrative cemeteries" constructed by survivors of communities destroyed in the Holocaust.

Langer, Lawrence L. *Holocaust Testimonies: The Ruins of Memory*. New Haven and London: Yale University Press, 1991.

A compelling, if emotionally draining book. The first analysis of interviews with survivors (most collected at Yale), it challenges us to rethink all the comforting notions about "learning from history." In stark contrast to mediated accounts, memory-as-lived defies any narrative closures. This is also a meditation on our ability to listen, comprehend, and remember.

Lincoln, Bruce. *Discourse and the Construction of Society: Comparative Studies of Myth, Ritual, and Classification*. New York and Oxford: Oxford University Press, 1989.

Though broader in scope, the book has much to offer to students of remembrance. The heuristic strategy here stresses the role of sentiment; "discourse" prominently features action. Materials under analysis include varied uses of the past. An especially interesting section on Spain during the Civil War and the "rituals of collective obscenity."

Lipsitz, George. *Time Passages: Collective Memory and American Popular Culture*. Minneapolis: University of Minnesota Press, 1990.

A close reading of select films, television programs, music and novels shows how popular culture can serve as a repository for diverse, often oppositional narratives. Interesting materials, strong anticonservative agenda; the very diffuse conceptualization of collective memory, however, lessens the book's analytical transportability.

Lowenthal, David. *The Past is a Foreign Country*. Cambridge: Cambridge University Press, 1985.

Invaluable for its analytical and empirical breadth, this is the most extensive, historically grounded examination of approaches to the past. The book shows just how varied and complex the attitudes to the past have been; focus is on social practices and ideals. The materials here are mainly British and American. Of particular interest to students of nostalgia and the commercial usages of history.

MacDonald, George F., and Stephen Alsford. *A Museum for The Global Village: Canadian Museum of Civilization*. Hull: Canadian Museum of Civilization, 1989.

An extensive insiders' report on the philosophy and practice of memory work. Valuable as material for reflecting on the current and future predicaments of museums, but also for its detailed descriptions of complex interactions between ideas, process and product. The lack of self-critical distance is compensated by the scope of presentation.

Maier, Charles S. *The Unmasterable Past: History, Holocaust, and German National Identity*. Cambridge, Mass.: Harvard University Press, 1988.

A penetrating analysis of the historians' debate, placing it in a wider context of questions about the role of collective memory and postmodern turns. Includes a highly informative discussion of the conflicts over the concept of the museum of German history, again, in a comparative perspective.

Marling, Karal Ann, and John Wetenhall. *Iwo Jima: Monuments, Memories, and the American Hero*. Cambridge, Mass.: Harvard University Press, 1991.

A fascinating, detailed account of the fate of one of the key American icons. Since the much reproduced image of the flag on Iwo Jima turns out to be historically inaccurate, this is a case study of memory construction at its most basic. Raises many questions about "proper" remembrance. It also brings the human dimension into the analytical foreground.

Marruss, Michael M. *The Holocaust in History*. Toronto: Lester & Orpen Dennys, 1987.

Arguing that it is both possible and necessary to integrate the Holocaust into the "general stream of historical consciousness," Marrus critically assesses vast scholarship in the area. This unique effort *not* to delve into reflection on remembrance raises many fundamental questions about the role of historians. Textbook format.

*Memory and Counter-Memory*, edited by Natalie Zemon Davis and Randolph Starn. Special issue of *Representations*, no. 26, Spring 1989.

A good introduction; seven essays mix empirical studies and theoretical reflection, including a translation of the key text by Pierre Nora. Editorial reflections place the growing interest in the subject in the context of current world events. A strong critique of "imperialist nostalgia" by Renato Rosaldo.

Middleton, David, and Derek Edwards, eds. *Collective Remembering*. London: Sage, 1990.

A useful introduction to the emergent bridging of psychology, social psychology, sociology, and discourse analysis. Eleven essays, with emphasis on case studies of collective action/processes; crosscultural materials. Interesting for its general tone of "discovery," exemplifying just how still powerful is the idea of memory-as-a-mental-state. Valuable references.

Miller, Judith. *One, by One, by One: Facing the Holocaust*. New York: Simon and Schuster, 1990.

An important book, for its comparative range as well as focus on collective memory (rather than historiography). Covers Germany, Austria, Holland, France, the Soviet Union; with a sharply critical chapter on the United States. Written by a *New York Times* reporter, it is rich in evocative detail, even if the brevity of chapters sacrifices some analytical depth. The first work of its kind.

*Monumental Histories*. A special issue of *Representations*, no. 35, Summer 1991.

An interesting collection of seven case studies of collective memory. Especially strong is the essay on the Vietnam Veterans Memorial by Marita Sturken and Wu Hung's history of Tiananmen Square. No analytical introduction, though.

Mosse, George L. *Fallen Soldiers: Reshaping the Memory of the World Wars*. New York and Oxford: Oxford University Press, 1990.

An important study of both the creation and the implications of the "Myth of the War Experience," with focus on Germany plus other nations defeated in 1918. Mosse looks at the public iconography, monuments, ceremonies, as well as literary narratives. Sanctification of sacrifice while domesticating death is shown in all its political force.

O'Connor, John E., and Martin A. Jackson. *American History/American Film: Interpreting the Hollywood Image.* New York: Frederick Ungar Publishing Co., 1979.

A pioneering collection of studies using films as resources for historians. Among the varied approaches present, eight essays are devoted to movies' representation of the past (especially wars and conflicts), thus offering rich case study material. Avoidance of purely textual analysis is a major strength here.

Palmer, Bryan D. *Descent into Discourse: The Reification of Language and the Writing of Social History.* Philadelphia: Temple University Press, 1990.

A good, critical entry into current debates, particularly for nonspecialists. Lucid explication of deconstructionist strategies as they apply to historical interpretation, and a strong argument for a return to materialism. Helpful to students of intellectual trends.

Rabinbach, Anson, and Jack Zipes, eds. *Germans & Jews since the Holocaust: The Changing Situation in West Germany.* New York: Holmes & Meier Publishers, 1986.

Bringing together four essays on the reaction to the series *Holocaust* with reflections on German/Jewish identity and antisemitism provides for a valuable context to the discussion. A case study in the dynamics of social forgetting.

Rousso, Henri. *The Vichy Syndrome: History and Memory in France since 1944.* Translated by Arthur Goldhammer. Cambridge, Mass.: Harvard University Press, 1991.

An ambitious and largely successful history of memory (to late 1980s). Rousso is attentive to the complexities of social practices; while focusing on public debates, he also analyzes movies, scholarship, teaching, and opinion surveys. Television, though, is only minimally treated. Some familiarity with the French scene very much enhances the reading here.

Samuel, Raphael, and Paul Thompson, eds. *The Myths We Live By.* London and New York: Routledge, 1990.

A collection of seventeen case studies (culturally very wide range of materials), unique for its oral history approach. Foregrounds the complex relations between private and public myths, the variety of uses to which the past is put as well as common narrative strategies. Of special interest to students of smaller social units. Strong introduction.

Schudson, Michael. *Watergate in American Memory: How We Remember, Forget and Reconstruct the Past.* New York: Basic Books, 1992.

An exemplary analysis, weaving together the rich empirical detail and theoretically powerful insights. Schudson argues for a balanced, free-yet-constrained view of memory construction. Of particular interest (since otherwise rare) are sections on careers, legislative reforms and language as carriers of memory. Multiple meanings of the past are brilliantly brought forth.

Skloot, Robert. *The Darkness We Carry: The Drama of the Holocaust.* Madison: The University of Wisconsin Press, 1988.

An engaging analysis of over twenty theater plays in different languages (including German), foregrounding the challenges unique to the medium. The material here offers a valuable base for reflection on the dramatic formats and strategies of remembrance.

Thelen, David, ed. *Memory and American History.* Bloomington and Indianapolis: Indiana University Press, 1990.

Originating in the special 1988 issue of the *Journal of American History*, this volume offers a good introduction to new empirical research. Thelen's strong analytical essay helps to appreciate the value of case studies which follow. Self-reflective in tone, the book also addresses questions about the role of historians in the construction of collective memory.

Young, James E. "The Biography of a Memorial Icon: Nathan Rapoport's Warsaw Ghetto Monument," in *Representations*, no. 26, Spring 1989, 69-107.

Exemplary work, part of a larger (forthcoming) study of Holocaust monuments and memorials. Young is one of the pioneers of the "history of memory." Here, he offers a rich, context-sensitive analysis, of special interest to students of shifts in meaning as impacted by time/locale.

Zelizer, Barbie. *Covering the Body: The Kennedy Assassination, the Media, and the Shaping of Collective Memory.* Chicago: University of Chicago Press, 1992.

A solid analysis of how journalists, rather than historians, became the voices of authority. Very detailed on the rhetorical strategies used over time, with a brief discussion of Stone's *JFK* as well. Missing here is any sense of the experiential base for the journalists' and the public's memories, thus of the powers of resonance. Useful references.

## French Languages Sources

Baczko, Bronislaw. *Les Imaginaires sociaux: Mémoirs et espoirs collectifs.* Paris: Payot, 1984.

An interesting collection of essays, linking reflection on memory and utopia. One of the central themes is the treatment of both by totalitarian regimes (especially Stalinism). Includes a case study of the "explosion of memory" in Poland in 1980.

Brossast, Alain, Sonia Combe, Jean-Yves Potel, Jean-Charles Szurek, eds. *A L'Est, la mémoire retrouvée*. Paris: Editions la Découverte, 1990.

A valuable collection of twenty-five case studies devoted to the vicissitudes of collective memory in the Soviet Union, Poland, East Germany, Hungary and Czechoslovakia. Includes sections on the construction of forgetting, manipulating the past, and conflicts. Much of the material is from the early stages of transformation to post-Communist societies. Wide range of phenomena covered, from the fate of monuments to commemorations to museums and archives.

Finkielkraut, Alain. *L'avenir d'une négation: Réflection sur la question du génocide*. Paris: Seuil, 1982.

An early, provocative analysis of Holocaust "revisionism," placing it squarely within the intellectual traditions on the Left. Sharpest critique is reserved for Noam Chomsky (who endorsed Faurisson's denial of the existence of gas chambers). Emphasis here is on subtle mechanisms of manipulation of language to fit ideologically derived schemes of historical interpretation.

Lapierre, Nicole. *Le silence de la mémoire: A la recherche des Juifs de Plock*. Paris: Plon, 1989.

An insightful case study of the uprooting of remembrance. Lapierre, through interviews with Jews from this small town in Poland now living around the world, reconstructs the vicissitudes of memory/identity. Also, a powerful account of the dynamics of forgetting in the town itself.

*La mémoire et l'oubli*. Special issue of *Communications*. Paris: Seuil, 1989 (no. 49).

An important collection, with focus on the mechanisms of social forgetting. Sixteen essays (with two by Americans) exemplifying the value of interdisciplinary exchange. Brief, mostly theoretical; subjects range from Freudian model to computers to amnesties. Includes a rare look at name changes (by Lapierre).

Namer, Gérard. *Batailles pour la mémoire: La commémoration en France 1944-1982*. Paris: Papyrus, 1983.

A case study of conflict with high political stakes, exemplary for its attention to public ceremonies, parades and the media coverage. The key actors here are followers of General de Gaulle and French communists, battling for acceptance of their visions of post-Revolutionary past. It is also an analysis of the production of forgetting (the 1940-45 as defeat).

Nora, Pierre, ed. *Les lieux de mémoire*, 3 volumes. Paris: Gallimard, 1982-86.

The most extensive examination to date, organized into the following themes: physical heritage, historiography and landscape (vol. 1); territory and borders, the state, museums and monuments (vol. 2); the glory and the words (vol. 3). The latter offers analyses of memories of World War I, iconography of heroic death, street names, key Paris institutions. Although all of the studies use French materials (and the collection itself is conceived as a tribute to France), there is a wealth of general insights here, a model for empirical work attending both to the sites and the construction of collective memory. Forty-nine contributions. (Four more volumes appeared in 1992-93.)

*Le temps et la mémoire aujourd'hui.* Special issue of *L'Homme et la Société.* Paris: L'Harmattan, 1988 (no. 4).

Mainly theoretical reflections, linking the study of collective memory to the constructs of time. Included are essays on the role of family histories, generations, as well as methods of field research. A broad introduction to current work in France.

Wieviorka, Annette, and Itzhok Niborski. *Les livres du souvenir: Mémoriaux juifs de Pologne.* Paris: Editions Gallimard/Julliard, 1983.

An insightful analysis of memory work, drawing primarily on the books commemorating the destroyed Jewish communities, but also on broader dynamics of Jewish tradition with its central preoccupation with remembrance. Of particular interest to students of nostalgia.

# Index